RECLAIMING THE
Public
University

Conversations on
General & Liberal Education

EDITED BY Judith Summerfield & Crystal Benedicks

PETER LANG
New York • Washington, D.C./Baltimore • Bern
Frankfurt am Main • Berlin • Brussels • Vienna • Oxford

Library of Congress Cataloging-in-Publication Data

Reclaiming the public university: conversations on general and liberal education /
edited by Judith Summerfield, Crystal Benedicks.
p. cm. — (Higher ed: questions about the purpose(s)
of colleges and universities; vol. 18)
Includes bibliographical references and index.
1. Education, Humanistic—United States.
2. Education, Higher—Aims and objectives—United States.
3. Universities and colleges—Curricula. 4. City University of New York.
I. Summerfield, Judith. II. Benedicks, Crystal.
LC1011.R387   378'.012—dc22   2007013528
ISBN 978-0-8204-8152-4
ISSN 1523-9551

Bibliographic information published by **Die Deutsche Bibliothek**.
Die Deutsche Bibliothek lists this publication in the "Deutsche
Nationalbibliografie"; detailed bibliographic data is available
on the Internet at http://dnb.ddb.de/.

Cover design by Clear Point Designs

The paper in this book meets the guidelines for permanence and durability
of the Committee on Production Guidelines for Book Longevity
of the Council of Library Resources.

© 2007 Peter Lang Publishing, Inc., New York
29 Broadway, 18th floor, New York, NY 10006
www.peterlang.com

Printed in the United States of America

To those supreme conversationalists

Phil Anderson and Jim Cherry

RECLAIMING THE
Public
University

Questions about the Purpose(s) of Colleges & Universities

Norm Denzin, Joe L. Kincheloe, Shirley R. Steinberg
General Editors

Vol. 18

PETER LANG
New York • Washington, D.C./Baltimore • Bern
Frankfurt am Main • Berlin • Brussels • Vienna • Oxford

Table OF Contents

Part III. Curriculum Renewal and Institutional Change

Part IV. Stories from the Field

Part V. Re-envisioning the Role of the Disciplines
and Doctoral Education

Part VI. Afterword

Foreword

CHANCELLOR MATTHEW GOLDSTEIN

The City University of New York

We live in a time when instant access to information often comes with a hunger for deeper understanding; when advancements sometimes race ahead of reason or when worldwide challenges cry out for imaginative solutions. In other words, we live in a time when a traditional liberal education, the pursuit of a broad base of knowledge, is more important than ever before.

The City University of New York was built on liberal learning. I concentrated in mathematics at City College and am grateful to have received a strong grounding in math and science, as well as an equally rigorous liberal education, one that emphasized the creative, progressive, and relational nature of learning. The world is a much smaller place than when I went to school, and today we have immediate access to knowledge of cultural, social, and political frameworks from around the globe. A university remains the best place to understand, probe, and debate these frameworks and their differences.

A liberal education is critical to our ability to make connections across disciplines, across concepts, across centuries, across communities. It stimulates independent thinking and a lifelong love of inquiry and knowledge. It encourages an appreciation of human endeavors and natural phenomena and an abiding devotion to the spirit of discovery and preservation.

A study of "great ideas" invites students to consider some of the fundamental issues of our time, addressing questions common to what we do and who we are. Whether in literature, history, philosophy, or economics, liberal education courses illuminate human experience over the ages. A thoughtful general education curriculum acquaints us with diverse thinkers, those who have created some of the most challenging and imaginative ideas throughout time. To read Pascal, Hegel, Wittgenstein, Chekhov, Dostoyevsky, Woolf, Ellison, and so many others is to read the world.

A liberal education should also be a hands-on pursuit, connecting students with their peers and their communities through technology, travel, and work experiences. A study of "the best that has been thought and said in the world," as Matthew Arnold put it, is heightened by an engagement with the ideas and people that comprise a student's current world.

Student surveys at the CUNY colleges indicate that many students today seek higher education in order to get a good job. They believe they are searching for a specific set of skills to serve a particular end. In truth, the skills they need to succeed in their professional lives, the ability to analyze, inquire, create, and communicate, are those a liberal education provides. To deprive ourselves of the liberal arts is to diminish our quest to have the tools to be effective problem solvers.

But how can a university best advance such an education? Are our expectations and responsibilities clear, to faculty, students, and the community? And are we appropriately focused on those questions, both individually and as an institution?

These are difficult questions, and at CUNY we are fortunate to have talented people determined to address them. As part of the University's General Education Project, scholars from across CUNY's campuses are boldly examining and re-envisioning how we educate students, led by Dr. Judith Summerfield, University Dean for Undergraduate Education. Dr. Summerfield and Dr. Crystal Benedicks, Assistant Professor of English at CUNY's Queensborough Community College, have brought together the essays in the following pages to demonstrate that learning is not a passive, casual act at CUNY; it is an active dialogue requiring frequent pauses, explanations, and interjections, and, most of all, great passion.

At CUNY, we are committed to wrestling with questions and ideas that will lead to the best educational experiences for our students and a flourishing community of engaged scholar-teachers, as this collection so richly illustrates. Together with our higher education colleagues across the country, we remain dedicated to ensuring the high-quality liberal education every student needs and deserves.

Prefatory Note

EXECUTIVE VICE CHANCELLOR AND UNIVERSITY
PROVOST SELMA BOTMAN

The City University of New York

General education, that corpus of obligatory classes required on most college campuses, is a puzzle to many students—at least while they are undergraduates. When students do not understand the value or utility of liberal learning, it may be because we academics have not made a compelling case in its favor.

Students attend college to satisfy any number of academic, professional, and social aspirations. They want to expand their knowledge, acquire specialized training for a desired profession, and earn the credentials that allow for upward mobility. And while they are prepared, and indeed often eager, to major in a field that leads to a meaningful and prosperous career, they frequently do not understand why they are required to take general education.

We need to make those reasons clear: General education may not have an express correlation to particular jobs, but it does provide students with a taste of classical literature, an introduction to significant historical and political events, an initiation into music and art, a portal to quantitative reasoning and higher order math and scientific thinking. For many students, the undergraduate general education curriculum is the only opportunity they will have to study the diversity and richness of the liberal arts and sciences.

College and university faculty across the United States value liberal education because it promotes student self-awareness and introduces undergraduates to new ideas and innovative disciplines. Undergraduates who take a broad range of courses through a liberal arts curriculum are introduced to subjects that are often unfamiliar, untraditional, and unrelated to their own direct experiences. Arts and science requirements inspire students to venture into new fields of study, investigate far-off parts of the globe, and simply expand their own worldviews. A democratic society is strengthened by those with knowledge, by those who know history and thereby comprehend current events, those who can understand the uses of probability and trend analysis as it relates to business and economy, and by those who value the arts as a way to compare and contrast human experience throughout the ages.

A liberal arts education encourages students to think, read, write, and talk about issues that may be entirely alien to them. It encourages them to extend their intellectual reach and examine (even re-examine) their own beliefs, attitudes, and opinions—to study, reflect, and change.

At The City University of New York, we are working to improve our liberal education programs, and to help students understand their worth. Through long discussions with faculty and administration, we are evaluating our curricula, assessing our pedagogies, and trying to extend general education throughout the students' entire program of study. The essays in this volume are a product of the robust conversations taking place at the University, and represent a system-wide effort to engage faculty in the most current intellectual and pedagogical debates in American higher education. I cannot think of more important work.

Acknowledgments

This volume is a coming together on the page of several years of conversations among many people, locally and nationally, all in one way or another trying to make sense of American higher education, and to contribute to its future.

To grapple with questions about liberal and general education is to take us all to our own educational experiences, to weigh and measure it all. Of the scores of faculty and administrators who are wrestling with the questions, we want to acknowledge Donald Scott, Marty Braun, Kevin Birth, Robert Whittaker, Peter Gray, Linda Stanley, Walter Brand, Nadine Posner, Paul Arcario, Jim Wilson, Francisco Soto, Ellen Belton, Amanda Carlos-Bernal, Myrna Chase, David Potash, Loretta di Lorenzo, Timothy Stevens, Jose Luis Morin, Erwin Wong, and the late Fred Purnell.

Early on, Phil Anderson, Eleanor Armour-Thomas, and Joe Kincheloe worked with us to plot the course of the project, building from local knowledge, drawing on their expertise in various quarters, and helping to build from a shared sense of both theory and practice.

Both the Chancellor, Matthew Goldstein, and Executive Vice Chancellor and Provost, Selma Botman, promote the value of a liberal education at every turn. The work here has been integrated into seminal University-wide projects to support student success and to value effective college teaching, as well as a scholarship of teaching and learning.

Cheryl Smith, wise literary critic, helped to prepare the final manuscript. A thousand thanks. Erin Martineau's astute anthropological perspective has been key to the project since she joined the team two years ago. Thanks to Sean Egan for mapping general education curricula across CUNY.

Thanks to Zhanna Kushmakova and Hector Graciano for keeping the daily work of the office running as smoothly as possible; no small feat.

Finally, we want to acknowledge those visionaries, Joe Kincheloe and Shirley Steinberg, for recognizing where work is happening that might make a difference. Thanks for taking a chance.

Part I. Prologue: The General Education Project at CUNY

The Project

Common/Uncommon Ground

JUDITH SUMMERFIELD

The City University of New York

The spectator's judgment is sure to miss the root of the matter, and to possess no truth.
—WILLIAM JAMES, "FROM A CERTAIN BLINDNESS IN HUMAN BEINGS," 1983

'Certainties' are shown to be combustible, not by being brought into contact with other 'certainties' or with doubts, but by being kindled by the presence of ideas of another order; approximations are revealed between notions normally remote from one another. Thoughts of different species take wing and play round one another, responding to each other's movements and provoking one another to fresh exertions.
—MICHAEL OAKESHOTT, "VOICE OF POETRY IN THE CONVERSATION OF MANKIND," 1962

REPRESENTATIVE STORIES

My friend's son, Michael, now a fireman in New York City, had struggled to finish college for many years. He had wanted to be a high school physical education teacher and had shuttled back and forth between the CUNY senior college, where I was teaching, and its sister community college down the road. He finally gave up and was accepted into the New York City Fire Department.

At Thanksgiving dinner last year, we had time to talk. We talked about the psychological toll of September 11 on the men and women of the fire and police departments. I knew that he had lost a number of friends and that he himself had gone for counseling. Then we began to talk of the soreness he still felt about not finishing college. He was trying to figure out what had happened, and why college had not worked for him.

He asked what I was doing now, and I told him I had begun a project on liberal education, getting faculty and administrators across the University to talk together about the purposes of a college education. He interrupted: "I think one of the problems for me was that I didn't understand what I was doing, and I got stuck in all those required courses at the beginning—that's what you mean by liberal education, don't you?—They're kind of like rites of passage that you've got to get through before you get to what you really want to do. But they don't add up. It didn't make sense to me, why we had to take those courses. And the teachers didn't seem to know, either." "Also," he said, "I don't know what a college means when it says it's a liberal arts college. You'd think that if a liberal education was really important, more than just words, that students would get it."

FACULTY ASSUMPTIONS AND BELIEFS

At the beginning of the CUNY General Education project, a group of us, faculty and administrators, sat down together to talk about our experiences as undergraduates. If we had anything in common, no matter our background or specialization or current work, it was that we had all been, at one time or another, an undergraduate. I asked that we take a moment to describe what we might call a "liberally educative experience" as an undergraduate. That was the prompt, and as with any faculty group, there were a number of questions about the assignment: Should the experience be within or outside the classroom, at the beginning or end of college, and so on? It was up to the participants, we agreed, to define their own terms.

The stories we told were, of course, journeys. Unsurprisingly, they were cast as metaphors of movement, exploration, discovery, and falling in love. They told of moving from one space in time to another, reversals, transformations, starting out in one place and ending up in another, growing up, entering new worlds, assuming new identities, of coming to know and to be known by others, of being recognized, believed in. Some told of writing the first big paper—and realizing that they could do it: They had ventured into new intellectual spaces.

Robert Whittaker told of his having been set on a particular path: His father was a dentist, and he was to be one also, until he encountered the biology "cat lab." That did it for biology and dentistry: He found his true love in Russian literature.

Fred Purnell also talked about changing his mind: He had begun in science (determined to study butterflies) and took a required philosophy course "which changed my life." The professor taught them how to investigate the big questions, how to think about the world in ways he had never imagined. Donald Scott talked of moving from a small town in Ohio to the East Coast. It was a new world, a new culture. The experience he described that has stayed with him was meeting a great, passionate lecturer, Perry Miller, the American historian, and coming to the realization that he wanted to be like him.

Karen Steele talked about going to college in the south during the Civil Rights movement, and being in a place and time where what was happening in college made sense only in the context of the outside world, and the need for social justice. That hope for a just world, she said, has never left her. Nadine Posner talked of being a philosophy major, and of wanting to explore unknown worlds, the unfamiliar, to step outside herself. I talked about taking courses with the American social historian, Robert Colodny, who asked me in an independent study I took with him in my senior year if I could read a book he was recommending in the original Portuguese. He knew fourteen languages, and approached European history from multiple perspectives, the political, economic, scientific, literary. He knew the world in ways that I wanted to, and he imagined that I could, as well.

Marlene Gottlieb and Annette Schaeffer, who had attended CUNY colleges as commuting students, talked about coming to understand the power of "taking all those disconnected required courses" belatedly, years later. The experiences did not make much sense while they were going through them. Afterwards, they realized that this had been the chance to do philosophy and history, more languages. They looked back—a bit nostalgically—on what had not been a particularly felicitous experience while they were in the middle of it. Others talked about going to college in the 1970s when there were few requirements, except for Freshman Composition, which meant you could explore various options on your own.

I have since done this impromptu experiment with a number of groups and individuals, inside and outside CUNY. I am struck each time that I initiate the conversation that no one has stopped me to challenge the premise: What are you talking about? What do you mean by a liberally educative experience? Nor do they respond with what William Labov, the sociolinguist, might call a "withering rejoinder" (Labov 1972): "*So what?* Why even have this conversation?" Even with a group of current doctoral students and with college alumni, the question opened up a dynamic conversation about "liberal education" being liberating, about new ways of knowing and thinking, of new perspectives, of gaining a critical edge, learning ways of knowing the world, and how important, now, in the globalized world, we need to know and understand each other, to embrace multiple perspectives and points of view.

The talk about ourselves, as faculty, as administrators, veered off in a number of directions: We talked about the differences of the residential and commuter campus, of the often pastoral setting of the small liberal arts college and the urban cacophony—the noise and rush of New York. We talked about CUNY students, how they are the "same" as we were, how they are different. How they are only focused on careers, as some said, how they do not have the advantages that some of us had, by living in dorms, how they have to work, often full time (48% of CUNY's students work more than 20 hours a week),[1] how they are older than we were, how they are supporting families, how they are not conventional American college students, and how at the same time they are, how so many of them do not have the fluencies they need in standard American English, how difficult it is for them, how we wish that they had the chance for the kinds of experiences that we had, how there is something vital, alive in these stories about our own "liberally educative" experiences, and that we wish our students had the chance to know what the university can give to them—and what they can give to us, and how easy it is to fall into generalities about "we and they."

Marlene Gottlieb, Professor of Spanish, talked about not talking about students' "deficiencies," their lack of preparedness, but rather figuring out how to teach to—and exploit—their strengths, their multiple languages and cultures. How to define and how to facilitate a liberal education—a liberating education—for CUNY's quarter of a million students, who commute, work, live transnationally, go back and forth between nations, cultures, and languages, who struggle to make a living, raise families, and complete a degree, who do not have the foggiest notion of what we mean by a liberal education, that was—and is—the challenge.

We agreed early on that we needed to make explicit that which we took for granted, the tacit knowledge that "we" had about the purposes of a liberal education. It was gratifying to know that we were all, somehow, members of the same club of beliefs and values, however vaguely defined, that we reaffirmed this set of beliefs at this early stage of the project and throughout the next years, that we abided by a belief system that valued this peculiarly American way of higher education, that no matter what the undergraduate degree—business, education, computer science—there is a counterpart, that of the liberal arts and sciences. How to make that part of an undergraduate education "real," to make it visible and daily, knowable and meaningful, was what we surmised we had to tackle. That would be the work of the project.

MULTIPLE PERSPECTIVES: THE VIEW FROM "CENTRAL"

My friend Michael is right: There is an enormous gap between the unspoken promises and expectations of what is called a "liberal education" and the actual day-to-day practices of undergraduate education, between what is said and what actually happens in the lives of students and faculty. This is not news—Ernest Boyer, in his landmark studies on American higher education, framed the arguments decades ago, as he described the fragmentary nature of the undergraduate experience (1987). The parts were not talking to each other, and the "disconnects" prevailed, between the professions and liberal education, among the distribution requirements, the major, and the electives. The metaphor of "disconnects," as Dale Coye points out in *Change* (1997), reaches into the fabric of American schooling, the disconnects between high school and college, between college and what our students at Queens College refer to as the "real world." What we began to do at CUNY, throughout the University, was to investigate the disconnects between the promises of a liberal education and the practices, between what we say and what we do.

When I began the General Education Project at CUNY in the spring of 2003, it was from the unique—and liminal—perspective of a Faculty Fellow at CUNY's "Central Office." I took a leave from my role as English faculty at Queens College, one of the senior colleges at CUNY, to begin a University-wide investigation of general education. In my mind, I was taking an ethnographic turn, in a decidedly novice role of anthropologist, trying to find out what I could about how General/Liberal Education worked in practice throughout the University. The starting point, given my work in narrative studies (Summerfield 1996, Summerfield and Summerfield 1986a, 1986b), would be to get to stories, faculty stories, student stories, to begin to uncover assumptions, belief systems, to find out what we were thinking, as faculty and administrators. It was critical, I thought, to bridge that gap, to get faculty and administrators talking with each other. If there was a great divide between students and faculty, there was an even greater divide between the "we and they" of faculty and administrators.

The ideal was clear—to get the colleges focused on strengthening undergraduate education; the method—how to get the colleges from their varying locations, their different, and differing perspectives, talking to each other and finding common ground, was not. Louise Mirrer, then Executive Vice Chancellor, who had brought me to the Central Office, hoped that we would look carefully and thoughtfully at what CUNY students need as college graduates to go out into the world. What do we mean by a liberal education? That was a critical question, and the starting point. Mirrer (2002) put it well, at the inaugural meeting of the Project: "We all probably share in the belief that we want a quality education for all our students, the challenge is how to go from here to there."

I had ventured forth to do this Project from the perspective of one CUNY College and out into the multiple dimensions of the entire system, through the lens of the Central Office—"Central," as CUNY's administration is called within the system.

CUNY is the largest urban, public, commuter University in the country, with seventeen undergraduate colleges spread throughout the five boroughs of New York City. My home college, Queens College, is situated within Queens County, one of the "outer boroughs." The Central Office is housed on the Upper East Side, across Manhattan from CUNY's oldest senior college, City College. CUNY's history begins with City College or CCNY, which was founded in 1847 as the "Free Academy" to "educate the whole people" of the city of New York. In its heyday in the mid-twentieth century, with its succession of Nobel Prize winners, including

Jonas Salk (1914–1995), the medical scientist who developed the polio vaccine that has been available since 1955 and has saved countless people from contracting the disease, it was known as the "poor man's Harvard." Matthew Goldstein, CUNY's current Chancellor, alumnus of CCNY, is keenly aware of the genesis of City College: He writes of the power of liberal education in the foreword to this volume. City's initial focus, which persists today, was engineering—and the sciences, and eventually architecture—but always with a commitment to the Liberal Arts.

The city's colleges grew up along with the city itself, spawning senior and community colleges within the five boroughs, each developing as a distinctive institution, with its local history and particular functions. In 1870, Hunter, a Normal college to prepare women as teachers, was opened on the Upper East Side, a few blocks from what is now the Central Office. Baruch College, originally downtown "City," and CUNY's premier business school is in lower Manhattan, as is the Borough of Manhattan Community College (BMCC), founded in the 1960s, in close proximity to Ground Zero. It is the one CUNY College to have suffered damages from the destruction of the World Trade Center. BMCC is the largest community college in the system, with 17,000 students. Hostos, in the South Bronx, with 4,500 students, is the smallest.

Within each of the other four boroughs, the Bronx, Brooklyn, Queens, Staten Island, the city's colleges, which charged no tuition until the mid 1970s, serve one of the most diverse student populations in the country. The colleges of New York were brought together in 1961 under one administrative roof, to create CUNY, The City University of New York, as a federated system.

While the Central Administration, with a Chancellor and a central Board of Trustees, now manages the entire University system—from budgets to buildings to human resources—each CUNY college, its president, administrators, and faculty, oversees what happens in the day-to-day lives of its students and faculty. What is taught —and how it is taught—happens within the college academic departments. Faculty determine curriculum and pedagogy. There is no centralized curriculum, either within the majors or within general education, but there is the promise of what Chancellor Goldstein calls an "integrated University" (2003).[2]

THE CRITICAL FIRST YEAR OF COLLEGE
AND GENERAL EDUCATION

When I left my college for Central in 2003, I brought with me several decades of teaching CUNY students—and a recent knowledge of teaching new college freshmen in their critical first year. At Queens College, a group of faculty created a space in the Freshman Year Initiative (FYI), where we could learn how best to teach first-year students. We were creating a "community of practice," with the "experts" working together to bring the new students into the various cultures of the college. In the ideal community, senior faculty were teaching first-year students alongside junior and adjunct faculty, as well as junior and senior undergraduates, who served as mentors and guides to the new students. We all learned from each other. The program is still a flourishing site for innovative teaching.[3] (See Davison and Lantz Goldhaber, this volume, and Summerfield 1999).

During the 1990s, I worked closely in FYI with Kevin Birth, a cultural anthropologist at Queens, who began to do ethnographic research with first-year students in FYI about how they see their lives as college students. His investigations—and the conversations we had—made me realize that we needed to ask different questions from those typically asked of first-year students.[4] When he asked students in the freshman program, "why do you want to go to college?" they typically talked about "getting a good job." Birth suggests that we need to see this notion of "getting" in students' discourse in at least two ways: "[F]irst, the notion of getting as related to 'acquiring something,' and second, the metaphor suggests a 'moving through space: getting ahead, getting higher, or getting somewhere' " (personal correspondence, 2001). Students are talking, he suggests, about making a change, moving from one space to another.

For many of our students, this means moving up the social ladder, and, ultimately, moving from the working class of their parents' generation to the middle class. Many of our students are, still, the first in their families to attend college. Furthermore, what college is, is not part of the cultural fabric of their lives. That still is CUNY's history, although the story is not so simple: Many of our students, who come to the city as immigrants, have parents who are more educated in their native countries than are the parents of CUNY's American-born students. In either case, coming to college is coming into a new culture. So Michael is right: There are "rites of passage," into the customs of college that are not made explicit. CUNY is, after all, a commuter college (although two Manhattan colleges are now building dormitories), where both students and faculty are on the move. While more and more of CUNY's colleges are making explicit the rites of passage through formal freshman orientations, ongoing freshman seminars, and highly organized first-semester academic communities, there are still numbers of students who, in taking a new bus to a new building in their own borough, find themselves in new and indecipherable territory. The college culture—more "free" time, less supervision, more independence—takes them by surprise; too many never move in from the "periphery" (Lave and Wenger 1991).[5]

Birth probed the issues differently: When he asked these same Queens students "What makes college-educated people different from non-college educated people?," or "What does college do for a person?" their answers focused on two notions, one of self-development, "knowing who I am," and the other, of learning to be "responsible" or "independent," of learning to manage in the world on their own. They do not, as Birth says, connect the two "in an integrated way" (personal correspondence, 2001).

They expect something to happen in college, perhaps, that will bring the two, the self and the world, together in meaningful ways.

Birth's further studies with FYI freshmen at Queens College have taken him to questions about agency, belonging, and deference in the classroom. He looks closely at the language students used in interviews about the "unremarkable activity" of "sitting," as a "common phenomenological" activity (Birth 2006). In probing the complex cultural world of CUNY, in relationship to the remarkable diversity of its students, he noted that students described themselves repeatedly as "just sitting there." Through close syntactic analysis of this most unremarkable of phrases, Birth suggests that we need to take seriously questions about notions of the self, and in particular, conceptions of the self and notions of American individualism, power, and entry into various cultures. We need to listen hard to students' language and explore the complex "common" ground in which we are all standing—or sitting.

How students' intellectual growth—or intellectual maturity—is promoted in college, or connected to a "liberal" education is not part of students' expressed expectations, but their need to know *what college is for* calls for us within higher education to recognize students' expressed—or implicit—expectations about why they are in college.[6] If liberal education is important, then we cannot rely on the hope that it somehow will be experienced by students as such. Birth's investigations of the "common phenomenological experience of sitting" served as a framework for what has come to be an exploration of another unremarkable activity: general education. No matter what specific degree or major students choose in their academic careers, the most common phenomenological curricular experience is the general part of that degree. The challenges of the General Education Project at CUNY involved coming to some agreement on what we mean by our terms, in particular, general education and liberal education, and to do so by investigating practices, words and structures, "systems and constellations of shared experiences," as Birth reminds us.

GENERAL/LIBERAL EDUCATION: OPERATIONAL DEFINITION

Early on in the Project, it became clear that we would not be able to get on with the process unless we clarified what we meant by these two key terms, and while we still, three years later, struggle with the enormity of the task of finding, exploring, or staking out common ground, we agreed that General Education was the more neutral, less value-laden term of the two,[7] and for our purposes, it represented a set of *organizational structures* that could be quantified: There exists at all seventeen undergraduate CUNY colleges a set of actual requirements that all students must take as a portion of their college degree, no matter their major program. This set of requirements, however they are organized or whatever they are named, is what we call "general" education. These requirements appear as college credits earned on a college transcript. Getting to this understanding took some doing, particularly as we were looking at the quality of the shared experience, as well as naming and counting course requirements, which, in itself, is a formidable task. What we mean by liberal education and how we define the term is less determined, as we will see.[8]

GENERAL/LIBERAL EDUCATION: INVESTIGATING SETS OF PRACTICES

To get to the realities of how we do undergraduate education at CUNY—to get the conversation going—these were the starting goals. We decided on two small working groups of "experts": one, a group of faculty; the second, a group of administrators—academic deans, and assistant or associate provosts. I wanted to hear what the talk would sound like in each of the two groups. We needed to tackle the questions about what kind of liberal education for the twenty-first century we should provide for our students, from a variety of perspectives. We had, first of all, seventeen undergraduate colleges, each with its own curriculum, its own local customs and institutional purposes. A small planning group came up with the notion of a pilot project, beginning with six of the seventeen colleges.

From the Central Office, we sent an invitation to the six college presidents, asking them for faculty and administrators on the committees who could speak to questions about general education at the respective colleges. In the letter, we framed a number of central questions around the University's mission to "strengthen undergraduate education":

> The questions [about liberal education] are very much in the public eye across the country: how do we bring students into the university and keep them not only enrolled but also engaged; how do we reconcile tensions between requirements for general education and for the professions; how do we ensure a quality education for all; how do we respect and strengthen a college's distinctiveness at the same time that we establish common goals; how do we allow for transferability from one college to another; and how do we deliver on the promises to educate students for the citizenry? (Mirrer 2002)

It was time, we said, for CUNY to enter the national debate. We would work from both ends of the spectrum, from the top administration, getting the presidents engaged, and at the same time, we would work on the ground, in the field, getting those close to the academic enterprise, the students, involved.

We were to bring to the initial questions our various identities within the institution, as faculty, administrators, but, most significantly, as scholars: We were to look at what we began to call "sets of practices," both academic practices and administrative practices. Boyer is right: The disconnects reach to the tensions within all parts of the institution itself. Faculty and administrators are largely disconnected and distrustful of each other. The administrative and academic are typically two distinct realms. At CUNY, there is a particular strain of distrust of the Central Administration: We wanted to make a clearing where we could pool our collective wisdom to work together.

We wanted for both faculty and administrators to see themselves as scholars, as researchers, and we called for them to approach their assignments as historians, anthropologists, literary and cultural critics, economists, socio-linguistics, to talk to other faculty, administrators, and students. We were to remind ourselves, again and again, to see the world through the eyes of students—to pay attention to the language we were using. We needed to "go meta," to take nothing for granted, to critically examine the words we were using or, for that matter, mis-using. What would students make of the college catalogue, the Web site, the countless letters of information they receive from various offices, who are working independently? We were to read what students read. We were to read our own texts, the mission statements, the public statements about liberal education/general education.

We also assigned ourselves articles and books to read, as we moved our conversation into the national conversation. Numbers of CUNY colleagues were already engaged in national organizations, such as AAC&U and Carnegie, and were talking with others nationally about the issues. All the colleges were, at one stage or another, wrestling with accreditation, through Middle States, and through the professional organizations, business, engineering, accounting, to balance the two parts of a college degree, the specialized and the general.

Our assignments asked us, first, to attend to the discourse and the structures of liberal/general education: how "it" was represented in the everyday practices of the academy, the daily texts of higher education, in the advertisements, catalogues, brochures, Web site, in advising guides, new freshmen handbooks, in new college faculty hiring ads. How did we represent this "it," as we came in the working group to call what we found. No wonder our students were often confused. The messages did not jive; they were often incoherent, contradictory, confusing, or incomprehensible. The messages were out of control, particularly as we had moved into the electronic age, and we realized that what the literature about higher education had been telling us for years was correct—that our own colleges had lost control of the messages and the practices. Indeed, "liberal/general education" had gotten lost, both as ideal and reality.

WHAT ARE WE TALKING ABOUT? THRASHING ABOUT IN WORDS

It was one thing to talk about our own experiences and our beliefs in something that we had elusively identified as a liberalizing event—finding our feet as undergraduates in the papers we wrote, the faculty who believed in us, the new worlds we entered. That was the easy part. Unpacking the discourse of liberal/general education at our own colleges was a feat, and we argued, sometimes heatedly, particularly in the faculty group, about what it was we were actually talking about. The differences between the two groups were marked: While the administrators talked about how the requirements we were calling general education were organized, the faculty typically did not know the requirements of their own colleges. We were hardly on the same page.

It took several months to agree that there was something to talk about—and, at the end of that first semester, we recognized that we had only just begun. To initiate anything out of Central was suspect: The groups were certain that eventually all would be revealed, that the University would mandate a universal general education curriculum. Curriculum, they kept reminding us, was in the hands of faculty, particularly through the structures of faculty governance.

At one meeting, a faculty member asked, "All right, what's broken?" Another one responded, "Nothing's necessarily broken. This kind of conversation should be ongoing—if we're talking about curriculum, it's a dynamic thing."

We agreed, though, that we needed to talk to each other if for no other reason than that our students are mobile within the system, transferring from community to senior college, and back the other way around, as well. Students started at one place and moved to another: One college had already instituted General Education requirements in the upper division, beyond the first 60 credits. Most of their graduates were, in fact, "transfer students."

The hope of an "integrated University" meant, at the least, that students would take "equivalent" courses within the system, that we could share resources, faculty, and programs. The CUNY system of seventeen undergraduate colleges is a federation of three types of college: seven *senior colleges*, which grant baccalaureate and advanced degrees; six *community colleges*, which grant associate degrees, including the A.A., A.S., and A.A.S. (Applied Associate of Science Degree), and four *comprehensive colleges*, which grant both associate and baccalaureate degrees. Each sector defines the degrees in differing—and at times contradictory—terms.

The first questions, then, had to do with the requirements, courses, activities that students "took" in common. We were to look within and across the University for common ingredients of a general education. We were looking at what we named these general degree requirements that were outside the major. We found a dizzying array of course lists and a confusion of terms within and across the seventeen campuses:

Core
Core Curriculum

General Core
Core Courses
Core Competencies
Core Requirements
Core Distribution Requirements
Core Sequence
Core Skills
Core Understandings
Core Values
Associate Degree Core
Baccalaureate Degree Core
Areas of Distribution
Distribution
Distribution Requirements
General Education
General Education Requirements
General Foundation
General Requirements
Liberal Arts
Liberal Arts Requirements
Liberal Arts and Sciences
Liberal Arts and Sciences Curricula
Liberal Arts and Sciences Core Curriculum
Liberal Arts and Sciences Requirements
Liberal Arts and Sciences Area Requirements (LASAR)
Liberal Arts and Science—General Education

We did not agree on the terminology or on what we were actually talking about. The conversations, at times, got tense. Several representatives from the community colleges insisted that we were barking up the wrong tree: They had nothing, they insisted, that all students, no matter what their degree, took in common, nothing that they called "General Education." At one point, someone said, "Oh, you mean 'the Core,' is that what you mean by a general education?" What these constellations—core, requirements, curriculum, sequences, understandings, competencies, skills, values—meant depended upon local culture, oral histories, unexamined assumptions. To change the system usually resulted in adding on new sets of requirements to existing structures—but leaving the existing structure intact. At some colleges, this constellation of requirements, whatever it was called, added up to 70 of the 120 credits for a college degree.

TWO CULTURES: THE DISCONNECTS BETWEEN
COMMUNITY AND SENIOR COLLEGES

An intense clash between two worldviews, of the community and senior colleges, surfaced almost immediately—and still persists—as we dug deeper into the differences between the two institutional structures, cultures, functions, and into our expectations of students. We agreed, though, that we had to step outside our respective territories, as we looked for a common ground of a *general* education. To do so, however, meant that we needed to recognize profound differences in the ways the two types of institutions organized the college degrees.

Although I insisted on an operational definition of general education as those college degree requirements not designated as the major (or minor) area of specialization, the project was—and still is—standing on shaky ground because the two cultures are organized in different ways. At the senior college, the bachelor's degree is defined by 120 credits, with the common expectation that the major will be declared in the upper division (after 60 credits). In practice, the General Education credits can be spread out over the four years, and, indeed, the creation of upper-division General Education requirements is now being instituted at a number of senior colleges.

At the community college, by the end of 60 credits, the student is expected to have fulfilled most, if not all, of the General Education requirements, as mandated by the State. The wrestling over what we meant by these requirements took us to an imposed common ground that virtually none in the senior colleges knew existed—but all in the community colleges lived by—the State Regulations (New York State Education Department 2003).

What most participants from the senior colleges did not know was that the general education portion of a college degree is State mandated. Every college degree, the bachelor's, associate's, and the applied associate's degree, by New York State law, has a portion of that degree designated as "liberal arts and sciences" (LAS). The LAS portion of the B.A. is two-thirds of the degree, one-half of the A.A. degree, and one-third of the A.A.S. (The percentages are modified for the B.S. and the A.S.)

CUNY mandates the credit limits of the degree: 120 for the bachelor's degree and 60 credits for the associate's degrees (including the applied associate's degree). The major course of study is determined to be either a Liberal Art or Science (i.e., English, anthropology, chemistry) or applied/vocational/professional (i.e., engineering, business, auto mechanics, nursing, education). For example, a student graduating from a senior college with a B.A. in English will have the required 120 credits, 60 for General Education, 30 for the English major, and the remaining 30 for electives. For the A.A. degree, 30 credits are designated for the LAS portion; that is, the 60-credit degree would be equally divided between the liberal arts and science portion and the specialized program. The student will most likely have a "major" in an area that is designated to be a "Liberal Arts or Sciences," with a concentration in English. For the A.A.S. degree, in say, early childhood, the portion of the degree was one-third, or 10 credits.

For the State of New York, the division between the LAS and the "vocational" is clearly defined. The senior colleges set expectations for liberal arts and sciences to be both "general" and "specialized." In fact, the accrediting agencies of specialized degrees, business and engineering, make clear how the requirements need to be balanced. For the community colleges, the balancing act is intense, particularly in the applied degrees, and for students, the stakes are high. They need to know the differences between the various degrees offered at the community colleges: The applied associate's degrees do not have the same currency as the associate's degree in transferring to the senior colleges.

Most of us in the senior colleges had never seen the State requirements, but community college colleagues live by the State "Regs," as they are increasingly pressured to squeeze into the professional degrees, particularly the A.A.S., a small number of LAS. To review and reform community college curricula in hundreds of applied programs is a mammoth task, one that is beginning in a number of the colleges. Within the Project, there is reluctant agreement that even in the applied programs, there is an LAS component—general education—that needs to be integrated into the whole college degree. The community colleges, however, are focusing more and more on defining General Education as a set of proficiencies that needs to cut across the 60 credits of the college curriculum: Writing Across the Curriculum, Math Across the Curriculum, Reading, Quantitative Reasoning, Information Literacy, Oral Communication.

The two systems organize these college degree requirements differently, and, historically, they are constituted to serve different functions. The senior colleges are firmly situated within the traditions of "liberal arts and sciences," and the community colleges are shaped, fundamentally, by applied or vocational programs. If the tensions between the professions and the liberal arts permeate the colleges, they are intensified when we try to bridge the community/senior college divide.

We agreed that the discourse and structures of CUNY needed to be scrutinized in light of the larger histories of liberal and progressive education, that these terms were vexed, complex, loaded. We agreed that we needed to know more, and that while we had tentatively accepted a functional definition, there was this something else, this elusive "it," called liberal education that we needed to unpack, historically and locally.

We began to become experts on the issues: We had to learn about our own colleges, as well as the entire system, and realized that if *we* were having difficulties sorting out what we were talking about, then how difficult was it for our students?

THE PROMISES OF A "LIBERAL" EDUCATION

What is a college education for? Not surprisingly, the promises of a liberal education are announced loud and clear in all CUNY college mission statements. Unpacking the discourse of the mission statements takes us to the center of often-heated debate in higher education: how to organize a college curriculum, and how to deliver it. At least three categories of assumptions—what we expect from our students—are obvious: the moral, epistemological, and vocational. Taken together, as they typically are in the colleges' mission statements, they represent the tensions within the institution that leave faculty stalemated, unable to change, because the curriculum, itself, rests on nothing less than history, politics, ideology, and on how we envision students.

A sampling of CUNY college mission statements takes us to the clashes of values that persist in any discussion or attempt to change a curriculum. These mission statements of several CUNY colleges, selected here from both community and senior colleges, make the case for the axiological, moral, or civic—educating the citizenry for the democracy:

> The Liberal Arts and Sciences curriculum prepares a student to be an accomplished and productive human being.

> To prepare students to become leading citizens of an increasingly global society.

> To offer a liberal arts education that gives students the preparation for enriching their lives, enhancing their understanding of the world, thinking constructively and independently, and making creative contributions to their local community and to society.

> To prepare students to become full participants in the economic and civic life of the city, the nation, and the world.

The promises take us to the tacit assumptions, those beliefs and values that shape our sense of what college is for, and how, in many cases, our students need to be—or to become. Many of the statements point to the future, to a *moral imperative*, to how "we" want "them" to be: to the way we expect our students to live their lives. These tensions between developing the self and learning how to manage in the world were echoed in the students Birth interviewed. The mission statements take us to the ontological:

> To lead enriched lives.

> To be accomplished and productive human beings.

> To become full participants in the city, nation, and world.

> To become leading citizens in an increasingly global world.

Interestingly, the mission statements not only encapsulate a history of American higher education but also those "new" challenges, articulated boldly in the "Harvard Red Book," of an increasingly "diverse" student body (Harvard 1945). At the end of World War II, the fact of "diversity" emerged out of the numbers of servicemen, through the GI Bill, entering American colleges. At this turn in history, diversity takes us into heady debates about the role of the University in an increasingly global world—and economy. Indeed, new mission statements express such awareness—and tensions:

> To provide a strong foundation for students of diverse backgrounds, preparations, and aspirations in order to further their success in their chosen vocations, their future education, and their community involvement.

> To promote an understanding of and respect for such differences as gender, age, ethnicity, culture, religion, sexual orientation, and physical ability.

Some mission statements take an epistemological turn, calling for core or common knowledge:

> To provide access to a common body of knowledge.

> To offer its exceptionally diverse student body a rigorous knowledge of the Liberal arts and sciences.

More and more, the epistemological—a focus on knowledge or "content"—is being eclipsed by the pragmatic, the practical, and by a growing list of "competencies" or "proficiencies" or "skills," particularly at the community college:

> To develop the ability to think analytically and creatively.

> To advance the use of emerging technologies.

> To provide learning experiences that ensure that students become competent in critical thinking, descriptive analysis, problem solving and interpretation, and in the communication of these skills.

The conflation of the moral, epistemological, ontological, and vocational results in a confused set of values and practices, and "immeasurable" goals, which are more and more called upon to be measured. The Collegiate Learning Assessment Test (CLA) is the first in what will certainly be a series of tests to "measure" the value of a General Education. The recent Commission on Higher Education calls for standardized tests to be developed to measure the effectiveness of a college education (Spellings 2006).

What we had to admit was the profound disconnect between the lofty ideals of the goals of a liberal education and the disorganization of the actual practices of "curriculum," what students were required to do to get a degree. The disorganization pervades the system: on the ground, students take one course after another, often not knowing why or how to connect the dots. The CUNY Gen Ed Project calls for each college to organize those practices so that they make sense to students and to faculty.

GENERAL EDUCATION: THE LARGEST "MAJOR"

Having spent many of my several decades at CUNY within a single department in one of its senior colleges, I know that most of what we do in higher education lies within the narrow confines of our own cloisters—the department or program or office where we work. Rarely do faculty and administrators talk together as colleagues who are involved in a *common* enterprise.

Boundaries are fixed, and the divisions—and distrust—run deep between the two groups. Large institutional issues take center stage, particularly at the public university, where the big conversations about resources, budgets, and decreasing state funding hold sway. How we actually do the work of the academy with our students, from scheduling courses that accommodate their frenetic lives or designing curricula that make sense to them, gets lost in the daily work of the two cultures: on the one hand, teaching and research; on the other, management of the resources.

Paradoxically, the largest common enterprise, shared by the entire university, is General Education, that set of courses, requirements, and activities that falls outside the major. Even so, general education slips between the cracks of both the administrative and the academic realm: "It" remains elusive as a project, is characteristically overseen by no one, and exists nowhere. It is not a department or a program. It does not have an office. It is an amalgam of the liberal arts and science departments, yet is neither owned nor governed by anyone. No one takes responsibility for it. No one roots for it or tries to bolster its staff, promote its faculty for tenure and promotion. No one seeks grants for it. It is by far the "largest major" at most institutions—but without a department or chair or governance structure—or a coherent administrative organization. It fails typically at both ends—the administrative and the academic (see Smith 1993).

Each semester, thousands of seats are required to *cover* the necessary general education courses to run the college, mostly in the lower division: One CUNY senior college provost counted more than 14,000 Gen Ed seats needed for the fall semester alone, more than the five largest departments put together. Decisions, for what courses are considered to be part of the Gen Ed roster, are left in the hands of the individual academic departments, which typically act in isolation from one another. The common ground lies fallow.

Looking at the General Education offerings at any college (not unlike an investigation of mission statements) is a plunge into the history of that institution and of higher education in America and the history of curriculum development as a socio-political construct. (See Philip M. Anderson, this volume.) At the beginning of the twenty-first century, the college degree is organized to provide students with a dual intellectual experience: "broad" exposure to a range of ideas, books, ways of thinking, areas of thought or knowledge, and a "deep" knowledge of a subject, through a concentration or a major.

The broad—or general education—has taken form in one of two ways:

- a "core" curriculum, promising, in its ideal form, a set of common academic experiences, or
- "areas of distribution," promising a range of experiences and choices from a menu of offerings.

The Core at CUNY's Brooklyn College, a set of ten courses (with some options), follows in the footsteps of the core curriculum at Columbia University and at the University of Chicago, but most CUNY colleges offer hybrid curricula, mostly distribution models. Some lists of "required options" have not been pruned for a decade or more. One college lists over 400 offerings in General Education, 60 of them in a foreign language but, in fact, most of these courses are offered only rarely, if at all. That department still harbors the belief, one supposes, that the language will return as a requirement, and the administration is hard pressed to shine the hard light of reality on the remaining faculty.

Until the General Education Project, General Education at most of CUNY's colleges, whether a core or areas of distribution, had not been fundamentally revised since the mid-1970s or early 1980s. Like Harvard's Core, General Education at the CUNY colleges has been a reaction against the "freeing of the curriculum" of the 1960s, when Queens College, for example, gave up its venerable core and eliminated all requirements except for Freshman Writing. In 1976, Queens introduced an "areas of distribution" model, the Liberal Arts and Science Area Requirements that came to be known as LASAR. That system, as Donald M. Scott describes in this volume, needed to be rethought, from the ground up. The Project opened up the space for the colleges to examine their largest major and to explore common ground. To examine General Education practices meant realizing that the CUNY Colleges that had not yet engaged in a revitalization of their largest major needed to do so, and as the Project turned to examining common ground, that is precisely what began to happen.

To investigate General Education as the largest major meant that we had to look at a set of practices, within both the academic and administrative realms. We had to look at how General Education was organized, who was in charge, and how Gen

Ed requirements were renewed and reviewed. We inquired into who delivered the messages of Gen Ed and who taught Gen Ed (full or part-time faculty; how the departments valued these requirements that were outside the major). Was Gen Ed a college-wide responsibility? Was teaching Gen Ed courses valued as a scholarly activity? What structures were in place for "transfer students," and who constituted the majority of graduates at most CUNY colleges?

DEGREE REQUIREMENTS OUTSIDE OF GENERAL EDUCATION

We have uncovered additional requirements that are typically outside the officially recognized general education requirements. This "hidden" college curriculum, which is often seen as "service" courses, falls into several categories. First, under the rubric of Basic Skills or Degree Requirements or College Requirements, we find a set of courses that all students must typically take: Freshman Composition, Mathematics, Foreign Languages, Physical Education, and Speech or Oral Communication. Students with appropriate New York State Regents' test scores can opt out of Foreign Languages or Mathematics, unless they need these courses as prerequisites for their majors.

Second, under the rubric of College Proficiencies, more and more colleges are adding what is being called a "horizontal curriculum." Writing, quantitative reasoning, information literacy, oral communication—these competencies are embedded within some, but not all, of the area requirements. For example, at most CUNY Colleges, a number of writing-intensive courses (usually two or three) are required for graduation, beyond the required Freshman Composition course. The set of requirements is being organized into "across the curriculum" programs: writing, math, and so on.

If these requirements are not embedded into already existing requirements, either within General Education or the major, they become additional obligations, added on to already swollen menus, with students scrambling to add/fit "W" course into their schedules at the end of their college careers.

Finally, for 85% of CUNY students at the Community Colleges, it is developmental education in the "basic skills" (reading, writing, and mathematics) that must be completed, as well, and often before students enter the "regular" curriculum. For many students, these hidden costs of a college degree, in money and time, and incomprehensibility, often result in students' leaving college.

COMING TO COMMON GROUND

At CUNY, the largest public University in the nation, we have, for the first time as an entire system, put the question of how we educate our students, *generally*, on the administrative and academic tables. The Presidents of the Colleges, in their annual reports, now report on the progress they are making in revitalizing and reorganizing General Education.

The term itself, General Education, is functioning as common fare, and while there is still discomfort in some circles about our use of that term, we have come to agree that there are organized practices that need clarification for the colleges and the University, for students, faculty, and the administration.

We have agreed that we need to distinguish between these two key terms, general education and liberal education, to come to a common language to guide our discussions and initiatives for improving Undergraduate Education. We are still struggling with the task. What we have come to, in the General Education Project, is, above all, that we have work to do, and, by engaging in the work as a common enterprise, we have a chance to effect profound change within the largest public university in the country. This collection of essays makes visible the early phase of this work.

We took important steps in these early explorations that shaped the work for the next three years: We examined our own assumptions and beliefs, trying to understand the "it," further. We looked closely at the words, what we called liberal/general education. We studied the promises we were making, through a careful examination of the college mission statements. Eventually, we began to investigate organizational structures, to see how we practiced what we preached, who was in charge of what, who was teaching what. We began to look at what we actually do.

What started as an experimental phase in January 2003 has grown to a University-wide Project that seems to have staying power: We have created an intellectual space where we can examine our work, as scholarly administrators and faculty.

In the succeeding three years, we have brought all seventeen undergraduate colleges into the Project, as well as doctoral students in the Writing Across the Curriculum, who serve as CUNY Writing Fellows.[9] The Fellows program was mandated by Board Resolution in 1999 to support the development of Writing Across the Curriculum (WAC) across the entire University. Various committees have formed, focusing on key projects: integrative learning, faculty development, disciplinary knowledge, convening University-wide projects. We have held University-wide General Education Conferences: In 2004 the First Annual General Education Conference was held at LaGuardia Community College. A University-wide seminar on Integrative Learning was organized in preparation for the conference. The 2005 Second Annual General Education Conference was held at Queensborough Community College, with Lee Shulman, President of the Carnegie Foundation, giving the keynote address.

The work for the next three years, at least, is cut out for us. Shulman left us with a provocative challenge, to "profess the Liberal Arts" (2005). His opening argument in "Professing the Liberal Arts" hits the mark:

Liberal learning, we are warned, is pursued for its own sake, and cannot be subordinated to the aims of application or vocation. I come to offer a shocking alternative view. I wish to argue that the problem with the liberal arts is not that they are endangered by the corruption of professionalism. Indeed, their problem is that they are not professional enough. If we are to preserve and sustain liberal education, we must make it more professional; *we must learn to profess the liberal arts.* (Shulman 2004, 547)

In the end, Shulman reminds us that we are talking about students' learning, and from their learning in professional settings, we can take our cues, our pedagogical strategies, what he calls "signature pedagogies." In the end, we are talking about what happens in the classroom, and the kinds of understandings and experiences that we come to as fully engaged people. We come back to the beginning of the chapter, what we heard from Michael, who took those introductory courses as "rites of passage" that he did not understand, and what my colleagues at CUNY thought of as their liberally educative moments. They had been asked into the club, but he had not. Their stories tell about being invited into the conversation, brought in from the periphery, expected to eventually learn to become expert. That is Shulman's profound contribution, that he makes it real for us, he talks about educating students to take their place within professional communities of practice. They come in as novices—we all do—and somehow along the way, we are brought into the secrets of the trade, the profession, the major, the club itself. All the "liberally educative" stories that the faculty told, in one way or another, were of being allowed in.

When we enter college, we are entering an ongoing conversation—and too often no one stops long enough to invite us in. The "great" teachers, we find out, when we begin to study them, are aware of the novices—and, with generous heart, open the doors, make the club inclusive—and perhaps make the process of learning more explicit.

That's what Shulman is talking about.

Our project at CUNY, in many ways, has just begun. This volume is a first effort to make our work visible, halting, at times, that it is. We are faculty not working in isolation, but rather working together to tend a field that has lain fallow for too long, to produce something good and sustaining for us all. At this writing, CUNY has been accepted into the Carnegie Academy of Scholarship of Teaching and Learning (CASTL) Institutional Leadership Program, where we will work with other public university systems to strengthen undergraduate education.[10] Our focus will be on Liberal/General Education, which, perhaps in the next three years, we will be able to define, organize, and improve more fully, for the entire college community. To do this work, to investigate, interrogate our own practices means more than changing the mission statement or adding a quantitative reasoning requirement. It is not enough for the college curriculum committee to pass a new set of college requirements. This work takes us all to the most common enterprise that we engage in— it is the most difficult, and, in the end, it could be the most important.

ENTERING THE CONVERSATION: CONNECTING
THE PERSONAL AND THE PUBLIC

In the end, it is what happens for the individual student, how the world of college works for him and for her. I end with a bit more about the story that was awakened for me, when I devised the "liberalizing" exercise for my colleagues, and in so doing, entertained the large question about what college is for. In doing my own assignment, I learned a lot.

The trajectory of the four courses I took with Robert Colodny might be read, now retrospectively, as the move from general education to the specialized, and also, as a journey of my own intellectual life as an undergraduate. That journey, I believe now, had to do with the need to make sense of my life in the shadow of my father's story, his escape from Russia during the Russian Civil War, and his struggle to find a safe place, after the destruction of the world and family he had known in Europe. I think now that I was also searching for intellectual and emotional space to live with certain ambiguities about my own life, about gender, religion, and class, about fitting in and where the personal could be protected, but also translated into a public sphere, where I could enter the larger—ongoing—conversation of the University.

Colodny was the instrument, and the world that he opened to me was knowledge itself. He was a European historian, and later a historian of science. He was, as I saw it then, and I see it now, a staggering intellect, a participant as well as a spectator of twentieth-century history, a veteran of the American Lincoln Brigade, and an early and outspoken critic of American involvement in Vietnam. We never, however, spoke of our lives.

The three European history classes that I attended were all jam-packed lecture halls of graduate and undergraduates—standing room only. Colodny was by then legendary, remarkable not only for his erudition and passion, but also for his delivery, his pedagogy. He was a conventional figure for the times: tweed jacket, pipe, tousled grey-streaked hair. Later, I would watch him grip the banister to descend the stairs—and learned that the injury he had suffered in the Spanish Civil War had left him partially blind and paralyzed on the left side. As he became more and more the romantic figure—after being called before the House Committee on Un-American Activities for alleged Communist activity—it was said that the injury also left him unable to attend to "normal" daily responsibilities, such as remembering to carry a wallet. His wife was said to pin a $5 bill to his inner jacket lapel, and some of us swore that we caught sight of the dollar bill when he walked. We did not, I am sure, but he became a figure of keen interest.

His lectures were anything but conventional: the world, as he represented it, was threaded together by cause and effect, moral intention and consequence, by those in power determining the untold fate and stories of the multitudes. History was the drama of the ages, and it was our responsibility as college students to enter the battlefields, the stories, and the poetry. How could the human brain comprehend that 14,000,000 Russians had lost their lives during what came to be known as the Russian Civil War, the historical moment that my father had fled the Ukraine? We needed to hear the Pushkin poem, of the voice of the mother who lost her only son, to realize that those who survived the wars were its most tragic victims.

In Colodny's class, we struggled with questions about how to represent events, about memory and loss, from that war or any other, of one disaster or another. How relevant those meta-questions, now, when we sit in our seats before any number of screens, and register the daily loss of hurricanes and droughts, and various human invasions and wars that still plague the planet. His *Struggle for Madrid*, as his lectures, were attempts to get to the "truths" of history, to listen to those who bore witness, and to struggle to listen to those who may have had alternative versions of what comes to be recorded history. "There may be errors in the account that follows," he says in his foreword to his book on Spain, "but there is little malice, and if Truth has been affronted, the witnesses may yet speak, and from the debate that ensues, the margin of error may be reduced" (Colodny 1958, 10).

It was, ultimately, his expectation of us, his students, that made me sit up straight in my seat: The notes I still have of those three courses are in a handwriting that I hardly recognize. I wrote on narrow-lined paper, front and back of the page, trying, I suppose, to take down everything Colodny uttered. I re-read now, randomly, decades later, through these faded pages, and I am struck by the power of his voice, on this first day of class of nineteenth-century European History:

Historiography without philosophy is senseless chronicle, a blind conglomeration of useless facts.

To be is to be related.

Since man makes his own history (however badly) but suffers it more than he controls it or understands it, nevertheless, he makes it.

Men make their history in terms of beliefs and values; you can't say "imperialism made war." Men make war; men may believe in war, in imperialism, nationalism.

Judgment is a moral act.

War is politics continued by means of violence.

All these notes were taken on the first day of class, when he was setting the stage for history as drama. I find, in caps in my notes, his expectations that our forty-page term paper would not be a summary. (I was a sophomore.)

DO NOT RECONSTRUCT THE NARRATIVE.

USE THE HISTORICAL IMAGINATION.

The forty-page paper that I did write for the course I called "The American Response to the Russian Revolution." I dug into American newspapers on file in the library, eyewitness accounts, journals, and later histories about how we responded here to those momentous days in March and November. I needed to understand what my father had spent much of his life also trying to understand: how history had unfolded under his young feet. He was reading in Russian and in Yiddish, and I was now reading in English, and when I came home for Christmas that year, I presented him with my findings. He thanked me for enlarging his knowledge: He was thrilled.

Colodny offered me the way to build another kind of conversation with my father, who had, until then, been my first mentor. Colodny taught me what schooling might be for—and how I could bridge the two worlds of home and the academy. This was not a deliberate part of his curriculum; in fact, one could remain anonymous in his large lecture halls, but the call for a historical imagination brought with it, as well, a moral imagination, and my early love of fiction was being called now to think about history in new ways. It was not as I had thought in high school: facts, facts, facts. I was finding ways to understand my father's stories, that I had grown up on. If all was related, then, I could connect the private and the public, the personal and the political; fact and fiction, story and history. I could bring a number of worlds together. This was a license I had not expected in college.

My last course with him was an independent study, a book a week, alternating between fiction and non-fiction: I still have the list of the books I read on the Russian Revolution, some of which I had read or skimmed during the second course: *Dr. Zhivago*, John Reed's *Ten Days That Shook the World*, John Maynard's *Russia in Flux*; some part of E. H. Carr's voluminous history of the Soviet Union, a memoir of the Russian expatriate, Ilya Ehrenberg.

I would visit Colodny's office in the Cathedral of Learning once a week, and we would talk. Mostly, I think, I'd listen. I remember coming in to find him reading: I remember the books piled everywhere, stacked in the shelves, on the floor, on the windowsill. As I noted earlier, he was said to know fourteen languages, and one day when I walked into the office, he was holding out a book and said, "Do you read Portuguese?" "Only Spanish and French," I said. "Well, then, you'll need to find this in translation."

I recovered, eventually, from the shame of being found wanting, falling below his presumed estimation of me, and realized, much later, that he had assumed, nonetheless, that I *could* have known Portuguese, that I, therefore, could have been expected to know any number of things, and that what had prevented me from envisioning myself as being fully capable of knowing any number of things was in my mind—and not his.

I have recalled that moment throughout my life, as I recall him. In the process of writing about him, I found this statement of his in a piece he wrote for the university newspaper, entitled, "Reflections on the Contemporary Problems of Liberal Education":

> A university can never be more certain that it is properly functioning than when its faculty is accused of subversion, because then some entrenched ideal is under assault and some traditional holder of power feels the tempest of new and renewing ideas. (1970)

Our Project at this most public of universities, calls for us to interrogate those entrenched ideals and practices, unsettling the certainties, the status quo, as well as the bastions of power, as we consider how to do the job of educating our students.

NOTES

1. Additional statistics about CUNY can be found at: http://www.oira.cuny.edu/.
2. For a thorough examination of CUNY's history, see Roff et al. (2000). For a sense of the heat that CUNY's Open Admissions policies have generated, and ensuing debate about access and excellence, see Marshak (1973); Lavin, Alba, and Silverstein (1981); Traub (1995), and Lavin and Hyllegard's response (1996). See also Soliday (2002) and Gill (2000). For a foray into New York City's changing demographics, see Queens College Professor of Anthropology Sanjek (1998).
3. The Freshman Year Initiative at Queens College, under the leadership of Judith Summerfield, received two back-to-back Fund for the Improvement of Post-Secondary Education (FIPSE) Grants, from 1993–2000, totaling more than $1,000,000. In 1996, FYI received a TIAA-CREF Hesburgh Award for Faculty Development. In 1998, Judith Summerfield was named "New York State Professor of the Year" by the Carnegie Foundation for the Advancement of Teaching. Currently, under the leadership of Professor Martin Braun, FYI is part of a FIPSE dissemination grant, developed by Professor Mark Carnes, Barnard College.
4. Birth's investigation was prompted, in part, by Astin's annual surveys of the American Freshman, and his desire to probe students' initial responses to a set of questions about why they think they are in college (See, for example, Astin 2003). What I represent here was part of our conversation about his research (personal correspondence, November 1, 2001). For a review of the literature on the American freshmen (and women), see http://www.gseis.ucla.edu.
5. Lave and Wenger (1991) discuss "legitimate peripheral participation," a powerful conceptual and pragmatic framework for building a "community of practice," where novices, through working closely with experts, move in from the "periphery" and develop expertise within the situated learning context.
6. There is a vast literature on why students go to college and what they get out of college, which includes Astin's national surveys and reports (1993), as well as surveys of college graduates (Light 2001), journalistic characterizations (Karabell 1998; Moffatt 1989), and even those from professors in disguise

as freshmen (Nathan 2006). For a critical look at college, schooling, and learning, there are increasingly those scholars, including Bruner, (1996), Cole (1996), Wertsch (1985), Lave and Wenger (1991), Kincheloe (2004), and Kincheloe, Steinberg, and Villaverde (1999), who critique assumptions and constructs of the "student" apart from socio-political formations of self and culture.

7   There is, of course, the philosophy of liberalism and its singular focus on individuals—on their responsibilities, on their rights—that is inextricably bound up in the historical development of liberal education. When we speak today about "liberal education" we are speaking within a long-developing conceptualization about the relationship of the state to society. I realize within myself a tension between my emotional response to the individual "awakening stories" that are shaped by liberal education and the desire to effect change at a structural, institutional level. By trying to make the University more coherent—both for individual students and for the institution as a whole—I am attempting to bridge what is evoked by "liberal" and "general."

8.   To dive into the debates about liberal and general education takes us to the history of higher education in America and the formation of the democracy, as Sean Egan and Phil Anderson explore in their essays in this volume. Further reading includes higher education histories (Veysey 1965; Lucas 2006), as well as experiments that range from a return to classical Athens at Berkeley in the 1960s (Tussman 1997) to critiques of liberalism and the University as a growing corporate enterprise (Readings 1997), as well as studies of how American colleges have not got it right (Bok 2006), and who gets left out of elite colleges (Golden 2006).

9.   One of CUNY's contributions to American higher education is in the field of rhetoric and composition, including "basic writing," which developed out of Open Admissions in the 1960s. Mina Shaughnessy's research on student writing in *Errors and Expectations* (1977), as well as a host of scholarship on teaching and learning resulted in a paradigm shift in freshman composition—a respect for the writer and serious attention to the patterns of error. See other approaches to teaching writing to CUNY's students in Ponsot and Deen (1982); Summerfield and Summerfield (1986), as well as further research on CUNY's remedial programs and testing (Sternglass 1997; Gleason 2000; Soliday 2002). See Maher (1997) for a biography of Shaughnessy. The Writing Across the Curriculum (WAC) Program at CUNY, the result of a 1999 Board of Trustees mandate that writing be enhanced in all academic departments and programs across the University coincided with a report on the University "adrift" and the elimination of remediation/open admissions at the senior colleges. The WAC Program has developed into a thriving intellectual community of practice.

10.   See the CASTL Institutional Leadership Program's description at http://www.carnegiefoundation. org/general/sub.asp?key=21&subkey=2025&topkey=21.

WORKS CITED

Astin, Alexander W. *What Matters in College? Four Critical Years Revisited.* San Francisco: Jossey-Bass, 1993.

Birth, Kevin. Personal Communication. 1 November 2001.

Birth, Kevin. "Sitting There: Discourses on the Embodiment of Agency, Belonging, and Deference in the Classroom." *Journal of Mundane Behavior*, 5.1 (2006). http://www.mundanebehavior.org/issues/v2n2/birth.htm.

Bok, Derek. *Our Underachieving Colleges: A Candid Look at How Much Students Learn and Why They Should Be Learning More.* Princeton: Princeton University Press, 2006.

Boyer, Ernest L. *College: The Undergraduate Experience in America.* New York: Harper & Row, 1987.

Bruner, Jerome. *The Culture of Education.* Cambridge: Harvard University Press, 1996.

Carnegie Academic Scholarship of Teaching and Learning (CASTL) Leadership Academy. The Carnegie Foundation for the Advancement of Teaching (2006). http://www.carnegiefoundation. org/programs/index.asp?key=21.

Cole, Michael. *Cultural Psychology: A Once and Future Discipline.* Cambridge: Belknap Press of Harvard University Press, 1996.

Colodny, Robert G. "Reflections on the Contemporary Problems of Liberal Education." *University [of Pittsburgh] Times.* 10 December 1970.

Colodny, Robert G. *The Struggle for Madrid: The Central Epic of the Spanish Conflict, 1936–37.* New York: Paine-Whitman, 1958.

Coye, Dale. "Ernest Boyer and the New American College: Connecting the Disconnects." *Change: The Magazine of Higher Learning,* May/June, 21–29 (1997).

Gill, Brian P. *Governance of the City University of New York: A System at Odds with Itself.* New York: Rand Corporation, 2000.

Gleason, Barbara. "Evaluating Writing Programs in Real Time: The Politics of Remediation." *College Composition and Communication.* 51:560–88 (2000).

Golden, Daniel. *The Price of Admission: How America's Ruling Class Buys Its Way into Elite Colleges— And Who Gets Left Outside the Gates.* New York: Crown, 2006.

Goldstein, Matthew. "Charting the Path to an Integrated University." *CUNY Matters.* June 2003. http://www1.cuny.edu/portal_ur/news/cuny_matters/june_2003/chancdesk.html.

Harvard University. *General Education in a Free Society (The Harvard Red Book).* Boston: Warren Press, 1945.

James, William. "On a Certain Blindness in Human Beings." In *Talks to Teachers on Psychology and to Students on Some of Life's Ideals.* Cambridge: Harvard University Press, 1983.

Karabell, Zachary. *What's College For? The Struggle to Define American Higher Education.* New York: Basic Books, 1998.

Kincheloe, Joe L., ed. *Multiple Intelligences Reconsidered.* New York: Peter Lang, 2004.

Kincheloe, Joe L., Shirley R. Steinberg, and Leila E. Villaverde. *Rethinking Intelligence: Confronting Psychological Assumptions about Teaching and Learning.* New York: Routledge, 1999.

Labov, William. *Language in the Inner City.* Philadelphia: University of Pennsylvania Press, 1972.

Lave, Jean, and Etienne Wenger. *Situated Learning: Legitimate Peripheral Participation.* New York: Cambridge, 1991.

Lavin, David, Richard Alba, and Richard Silberstein. *Right Versus Privilege: The Open Admissions Experiment at the City University of New York.* New York: Free Press, 1981.

Lavin, David E., and David Hyllegard. *Changing the Odds: Open Admissions and the Life Chances of the Disadvantaged.* New Haven: Yale University Press, 1996.

Light, Richard J. *Making the Most of College: Students Speak Their Minds.* Cambridge: Harvard University Press, 2001.

Lucas, Christopher. *American Higher Education: A History.* New York: Palgrave Macmillan, 2006.

Maher, Jane. *Mina P. Shaughnessy: Her Life and Work.* Urbana: NCTE, 1997.

Marshak, Robert. *Problems and Prospects of an Urban University.* New York: City College of New York, 1973.

Mirrer, Louise. Letter from Executive Vice Chancellor Louise Mirrer to CUNY College Presidents. 22 November 2002.

Moffatt, Michael. *Coming of Age in New Jersey: College and American Culture.* New Brunswick: Rutgers University Press, 1989.

Nathan, Rebekah. *My Freshman Year: What a Professor Learned by Becoming a Student*. Ithaca: Cornell University Press, 2005.

New York State Education Department. "Liberal Arts & Sciences Requirements." New York State Education Department (4 June 2003). http://www.highered.nysed.gov/ocue/liberalarts.htm.

Oakeshott, Michael. "The Voice of Poetry in the Conversation of Mankind." In *Rationalism in Politics and Other Essays*, pp. 197–247. London: Methuen, 1962.

Ponsot, Marie, and Rosemary Dean. *Beat Not the Poor Desk*. Portsmouth: Boynton Cook, 1982.

Readings, Bill. *The University in Ruins*. Cambridge: Harvard University Press, 1997.

Roff, Sandra, Anthony M. Cucchiara, and Barbara J. Dunlap. *From The Free Academy to CUNY: Illustrating Public Higher Education in New York*. New York: Fordham University Press, 2000.

Sanjek, Roger. *The Future of Us All: Race and Neighborhood Politics in New York City*. Ithaca: Cornell University Press, 1998.

Shaughnessy, Mina P. *Errors and Expectations: A Guide for the Teacher of Basic Writing*. New York: Oxford University Press, 1977.

Shulman, Lee S. *Keynote Address*. Second Annual General Education Conference. New York: Queensborough Community College, 2005.

Shulman, Lee S. *The Wisdom of Practice: Essays on Teaching, Learning, and Learning to Teach*. Edited by Suzanne M. Wilson. San Francisco: Jossey-Bass, 2004.

Smith, Virginia, "New Dimensions for General Education." In *Higher Learning in America, 1998-2000*, Arthur Levine, ed. Baltimore: Johns Hopkins University Press, 1993.

Soliday, Mary. *The Politics of Remediation: Institutional and Student Needs in Higher Education*. Pittsburgh: University of Pittsburgh Press, 2002.

Spellings, Margaret. "An Action Plan for Higher Education." Prepared Remarks at the National Press Club: U.S. Department of Education (22 September 2006). http://www.ed.gov/news/speeches/2006/09/09262006.html.

Sternglass, Marilyn S. *Time to Know Them: A Longitudinal Study of Writing and Learning at the College Level*. Mahwah, NJ: Lawrence Erlbaum Associates, 1997.

Summerfield, Judith. Fund for the Improvement of Post-secondary Education, Annual Reports on Freshman Year Initiative, 1993–2000. www.ed.gov/FIPSE/.

Summerfield, Judith. "News of the Academy: Focus on the People." *Anthropology News*, April 1999.

Summerfield, Judith. "Principles for Propagation: On Narrative and Argument." In *Argument Revisited: Argument Redefined: Negotiating Meaning in the Composition Classroom*. Thousand Oaks, CA: Sage, 1996.

Summerfield, Judith, and Geoffrey Summerfield. *Frames of Mind*. New York: Random House, 1986a.

Summerfield, Judith, and Geoffrey Summerfield. *Texts and Contexts: A Contribution to the Theory and Practice of Composition*. New York: Random House, 1986b.

Traub, James. *City on a Hill: Testing the American Dream at City College*. Reading: Addison-Wesley Publishing Company, 1994.

Tussman, Joseph. *The Beleaguered College: Essays on Educational Reform*. University of California: Institute of Governmental Studies Press 1997.

Veysey, Laurance R. R. *The Emergence of the American University*. Chicago: University of Chicago Press, 1970.

Wenger, Etienne. *Communities of Practice: Learning, Meaning, and Identity*. Cambridge: Cambridge University Press, 1998.

Wertsch, James V. *Vygotsky and the Social Formation of Mind*. Cambridge: Harvard University Press, 1985.

What Is IN This Book?

JUDITH SUMMERFIELD AND CRYSTAL BENEDICKS

The City University of New York

Our title, *Reclaiming the Public University: Conversations on General & Liberal Education*, represents the mission of our project—*to reclaim*—as well as the spirit of our intervention—*to hold a conversation*. This book brings us into the national conversations on "liberal" and "general" education, respecting the complexities of those terms and pushing at their historical and rhetorical legacies. In the late 1990s, CUNY was considered a university "adrift," having fallen, critics insisted, into disarray. Recurrent budget crises and heated public debates over what constituted acceptable student performance threatened to focus the agenda more on staying afloat than on moving the university forward. Now, under the leadership of Chancellor Matthew Goldstein, CUNY's star has risen; and it is time for all those involved in this most public of universities to attend to our shared business of teaching CUNY's quarter of a million undergraduates.

To reclaim the public university is to focus our energies on teaching all our students well, educating them for a new, increasingly complicated age. To deliver on this promise, we must interrogate the general education we provide for our students, for this is the vast, unrecognized ground we stand on. It is what students and faculty do most in common. If we can get educating our students right, generally and liberally, then we will have laid a claim to what the public university needs to be—and provide that critical balance and integration of the general and the specialized. It is what makes American higher education unique across the globe.

This is what the conversations represented in these pages are all about: We make public our debates, disagreements, and visions, our ventures into a noisy marketplace of ideas, suggestions, recollections, our hopes that what our students will "get" out of their four or five or more years at CUNY is an education that serves them well. In opening the conversation, we lay claim to the importance of our task.

Throughout this book, we use the terms "general education" and "liberal education" together, sometimes seeing them as opposites, sometimes conflating them, sometimes locating our work in the slippage between them. Some of the essays here take up the work of exploring their historical roots and cultural resonances, interrogating the relationships between them. We do not intend to come down on one side or another, but to see them as two crucial strains that matter in American higher education.

As Executive Vice Chancellor Selma Botman says in the Prefatory Note, this book is a "robust conversation." It represents participant voices, those who are actually on the ground doing the work. It represents voices speaking from locations that cut across conventional academic boundaries. It draws together CUNY itself: senior colleges and community colleges, colleges in Manhattan and colleges in the outer boroughs, professional colleges and liberal arts colleges. It includes multiple disciplines: history, English, education, Russian, French, and Spanish language and literature, nursing, physics, ESL education, anthropology, and theatre. It includes those who teach both undergraduates and graduate students. Senior deans co-write with faculty, adjuncts with tenured faculty. It includes top-level administrators and untenured faculty. It is co-edited by a University Dean who is also a full professor of English at a senior college, and an assistant professor in her first year of a tenure-track English department line at a community college.

These writings make visible how our disciplinary perspectives, our locations within the institution, and our own academic histories shape our assumptions about the nature of university culture, as well as the discourse we use to represent those assumptions. From these multiple perspectives, we create bridges across the disjunctures that often mark the academy, ways to arrive at the common ground the contributors to this book attempt to articulate.

This volume is divided into six parts: this introductory section, four thematic sections, and an afterword. Part II, "History, Politics, and Curriculum," sets the work of the book in historical perspective, reminding us that the struggle, to determine what a college education is for, has been ongoing from the beginning of American higher education. In "CUNY's Histories: Liberal Education and the Free Academy," Sean Egan turns to nineteenth-century debates about the role of colleges within a democracy. Looking back to the origins of the Free Academy (as the nascent CUNY was known in the mid-nineteenth century), Egan examines arguments for egalitarian access to higher education against charges that high literary culture is at heart anti-democratic and elitist. These debates, as he notes, were as pressing then as they are today. In "Curriculum Mapping: Climbing out of the Briar Patch," Philip M. Anderson interrogates current debates over curriculum, the role of the public university, and the idea of liberal education as contextualized in American socio-cultural history. Anderson does not map the history of institutions or ideas, but the history of curriculum. Both Egan and Anderson provide conceptual frameworks for understanding institutional structures and for unpacking assumptions embedded in curricular structures. Rather than coming down on either side of the culture wars or making arguments for what curricula ought to be, they draw attention to the need to read institutions and curricula critically, paying attention to them as historical structures that encode and enact the troubled history of American higher education.

Part III, "Curriculum Renewal and Institutional Change," turns to CUNY today, describing the uncertain processes of rethinking the institutionalization of general education at two senior colleges, a community college, and a comprehensive college. Although their stories are rich in the particularity of each college's individual mission, history, and community, they also represent the difficulties faced by colleges across America in sparking change within typically calcified structures. Two essayists in this section—Robert Whittaker at Lehman College in "General Education vs. Education Generally: Curriculum Renewal in an Urban College," and Donald M. Scott at Queens College, in "Reforming General Education at Queens College"—narrate the efforts at their senior colleges to re-envision general education. Both describe the committee work, the turf wars, the set-backs and triumphs, in which their colleges are still enmeshed.

In "The Comprehensive College as Civilized Hydra: General Education at the College of Staten Island," David Podell, Jonathan Sassi, and Jane Marcus-Delgado take up the thorny problem the College of Staten Island faced as an institution created through the merger of a senior and a community college—a situation in which embedded ideas about the roles of general education and the goals of liberal education at the senior and the community colleges are thrown into contention. Their efforts to reach a compromise stand for the efforts of community and senior colleges nationwide to reconsider their relationships to each other.

In "A Jazz Performance: Improvisations on General Education at a CUNY Community College," Linda Stanley, Anita Ferdenzi, Paul Marchese, and Margaret Reilly tell the story of their general education inquiry group. They represent the adaptability and flexibility necessary to spur change within the university setting. This essay focuses particularly on the work of general education reform at the community college, where the allocations of credits within each degree program are closely contested and where tensions run high between the liberal arts and the career programs.

In the fourth section, "Stories from the Field," the essayists speak about experiments in General Education reform in the classroom. Ann Davison and Sue Lantz

Goldhaber, in the Queens College Freshman Year Initiative, write about "Reacting to the Past" pedagogy, which uses historically based "games" to engage students in creative simulations. Davison and Lantz Goldhaber's insight in using these Barnard-originated games at Queens College, a commuter college located in the most diverse county in America, is that ESL students are brought into the grips of history at the same time that they gain fluency in academic discourse. The games locate ideas and language patterns in specific historical contexts, thus unsettling notions of literacy as ahistorical "correctness" and freeing beginning students from a debilitating sense of language-as-correctness.

Next, Robert F. Cohen and Kim Sanabria at Hostos Community College have mounted no less than a reworking of the traditionally exacerbated relationship between "remedial" and "college level" work. Their chapter, "Our Mission at Hostos: Charting a Course to Self-Empowerment," is written in the belief that it is the responsibility of a college to take as its starting point the proficiencies with which students enter, keeping in mind that many of them are rendered invisible by cultural value systems at work within higher education institutions that privilege certain types of knowledge and abilities. In their award-winning design of pedagogy that invites students into the academy starting with their very first semester, Cohen and Sanabria provide intensive, content-based scaffolding for beginning students, while refusing to represent the students as "deficient" or "remedial."

In "The Shakespeare Portal: Teaching the Canon at the Community College," Crystal Benedicks poses questions about the role of Shakespeare as a byword for high art. What kinds of assumptions about what it means to be liberally educated are implicit in curricular structures that offer canonical figures like Shakespeare as the pinnacle of literary study? In addition, what kinds of currency does Shakespeare represent for students? Through a turn to Shakespeare's history as a "popular," rather than "high art," author, she attempts to envision Shakespeare more as accessible rather than sacred.

David Potash works with the idea of the collaborative classroom in "A Shared Classroom: General Education at Baruch College," where he describes an upper level history class he designed to bring students actively into the production and dissemination of knowledge. Baruch is a business college; Potash's model class was based on the assumption that business students must be at home in oral communications of the type that is privileged at board meetings and professional presentations. Like Davison and Lantz Goldhaber, then, he invites performance studies into his classroom through the use of student presentations specifically designed to allow students to make scholarly and pedagogical choices about how to represent their chosen subjects to the classmates.

Finally, Paul Arcario and James Wilson set out in "Putting It Together: General Education at LaGuardia Community College" to first describe the articulation of general education goals at LaGuardia Community College and then to envision them in a collaborative classroom setting. For Arcario and Wilson, the goal is to create curricular and classroom practices that bring students at an urban commuter community college into a sense of connectedness with the college, the faculty and administration, and each other.

In the fifth section, "Re-envisioning the Role of the Disciplines and Doctoral Education," both Erin Martineau, Associate for Teaching, Learning, and Research at CUNY's Central Office, and Cheryl C. Smith, an assistant professor of English at Baruch College, write about the roles of individual disciplines in constructing general education. In "Disciplinary Ways of Knowing: The Value of Anthropological Thinking in General Education," Martineau questions what general education courses in anthropology teach students. For her, the big questions have to do with whether we perceive introductory anthropology courses as surveys of "fact" and anthropological information, or as introductions to historically shaped ways of thinking, to the discipline as an ongoing, often argumentative, conversation about power and knowledge. At the heart of this essay is the question of what introductory courses are imagined to do: serve as gatekeepers, or explore the unsettled questions. The answers have broad implications for general education curricula, disciplinary constructs, and the conventions of doctoral education in anthropology, where new scholars learn the parameters of their field.

In "Opening the Invisible Gateway: Some 'Common Things' About Student Writing," Smith examines the disjunctures that run across many English departments, creating disabling rifts between teaching (writing) and research (often on literature), between the "common" work of composition courses and the more exalted obligation to preserve and study literary traditions—between, in short, practice and theory. For Smith, faculty across the disciplines must make an effort to meet on common ground as colleagues equally invested in language, its multiple and academic social uses, and in teaching and research. Recognizing such common ground, she argues, will enable the development of effective teaching commons in our institutions.

The final essay—"Afterword: On Metaphors and Genres," by Crystal Benedicks, co-editor of this volume—looks back through these pages not to draw conclusions but to examine the rhetorical practices in play in a collection of essays all aimed at re-conceiving the work of the university. Her essay takes as its premise that the struggle to rethink general education is also the struggle to rethink the words used to represent it.

Together, these essays invite our readers into this ongoing conversation on the public university and General/Liberal Education. CUNY's efforts are the nation's efforts. These conversations are going on throughout the country. We need, as public universities, to reorganize the structures, engage faculty in re-envisioning why a general/liberal education for the twenty-first century matters for them and our students, and talk with each other across systems. These questions are critical at public universities across the

United States, where we are increasingly faced with students and parents asking us what college is for, why it costs so much, and why, when students want to get on with their professional careers, they are also required to take those general education courses.

At CUNY, the issues are exacerbated by the size of the university, its position in a major urban center, its attraction for immigrant students and native speakers of languages other than English, its structure of affiliated colleges that facilitates transfer, its rootedness in national history as an experiment in democratic education—its promise of access. CUNY is a crucible for the nation's most pressing questions about what college education should—or can—be. This book is meant for anyone who has a stake in the future of higher education.

Part II. History, Politics, and Curriculum

CHAPTER ONE

CUNY Histories

Liberal Education and the Free Academy

SEAN EGAN

CUNY Graduate Center

My topics for this piece are liberal education, practical education, the origins of CUNY in nineteenth-century New York City, attitudes toward higher education in the United States, egalitarianism, democracy, and the relations among these things today and a century and a half ago. All are related to my work as a Ph.D. student in English at the City University of New York Graduate Center, where I am writing a dissertation on the politics and culture of nineteenth-century New York City. As a graduate student, my inclination is to write about them in a traditional, thesis-driven scholarly form. The chosen genre for this collection, however, is the personal essay, which invites me to write about how this historical material relates to my own education and my experiences at CUNY.

This essay still has, threaded through it, a thesis about its historical subjects. Readers who prefer traditional scholarly writing might like to know what that thesis is up front, so here it is: The founding of CUNY was influenced by an egalitarian ideology of democracy and access to education that would be familiar to anyone who has heard CUNY people talk about what they love about CUNY. However, in that same time period, and partly as an out-growth of that egalitarian ideology, there existed a reaction against intellectual or literary culture because it was seen as elitist, anti-democratic, or impractical—a sentiment that will sound familiar to anyone who has ever heard or read anything about American politics today. In spite of this reaction, liberal education has done surprisingly well at CUNY from early in its history and in American higher education in general. End of thesis.

The thesis, though, is not the whole story. Behind all scholarly work is the story of an education, and behind all educations are values, priorities—our own, our family's, our neighbors', our government's. The essay offers some of the story of my education along with some of the story of liberal education in America.

Because I am studying and writing about literature in New York in the nineteenth century, I should start literarily with a quote from Walt Whitman. He is one of the primary authors I am studying, and literature scholars are always ready with a quote from their pet authors to suit any occasion.[1] This occasion is a consideration of the individual and history. Whitman considered himself as follows:

> Immense have been the preparations for me,
> Faithful and friendly the arms that have helped me. . . .
> Before I was born out of my mother generations guided me,
> My embryo has never been torpid . . . . nothing could overlay it;
> For it the nebula cohered to an orb . . . . the long slow strata piled to rest it on
> . . . . vast vegetables gave it sustenance,
> Monstrous sauroids transported it in their mouths and deposited it with care.
>
> All forces have been steadily employed to complete and delight me,
> Now I stand on this spot with my soul.
>
> —Walt Whitman, *Leaves of Grass* (1855)

Whitman's take is more cosmic and crazily egocentric than mine, but there is something to be said for thinking about the forces that have brought us to where we are in history as leading to a great opportunity. Whitman's lines bring us to the era of CUNY's founding or, to be more precise, to the era of the Free Academy's founding. Here is the flavor of the cockiness and belief in the special importance and destiny of the individual that was common in America in this period. Nothing is said directly about education, but there is some of the spirit of liberal education. Whitman shows us that he knows something about the discoveries regarding the age of the universe and the extinction of species and that he does not mind incorporating this science into his poetry. Whitman's poetry features a wide range of reference to the science and culture of his time, although he himself did not have a formal liberal education. He acquired his knowledge largely through his own wide-ranging and idiosyncratic[2] reading and interests. The spirit of self-improvement and self-development behind his intellectual curiosity also drove the political movements for greater access to education.

In my case, sauroids did not carry me in their mouths, but several serendipities have led me to where I stand thinking and writing about liberal education at CUNY. Most immediately, I am a CUNY Ph.D. student who has spent the past year working as a university fellow in CUNY Central's Office for Undergraduate Education. This experience has included time spent working on the General Education Project coordinated by that office. I have participated in the meetings of faculty and administrators from across the university, who are engaged in general education. I learned about the debates over liberal education and general education at CUNY and throughout the country. I also studied the current General Education requirements across the university.

At the same time, as part of my dissertation research, I have been studying and writing about some newspaper writers in New York City in the decades before and after the founding of the Free Academy in 1847. Specifically, I am studying the ideas that these writers had about the role of literature in a democracy. Literature in this context can be a fairly broad category that more or less includes all of the country's written intellectual or cultural production.

The connection between my administrative work and my research here was (or should have been) obvious. While I was studying intellectual culture and democratic society in New York City in the nineteenth century, I was also engaged in discussions about intellectual culture and democratic society in a public university that was founded in New York City in the nineteenth century. It only took me half the year to connect the dots. When I looked at what people said back then about liberal education and what people say today, I noticed many similarities, but, as always, the past is inconveniently different from the present. The historical comparison became more difficult (and more interesting) as I understood how ideas about education and democracy had changed.

My connection to this discussion stretches back even before I began my graduate work (which these days is starting to feel like a very long way back). Over the years that I have been studying, teaching, and working at CUNY, I have come to feel a connection to the university's students, in part because I can identify with their experiences. Like many students at CUNY, both today and throughout its history, I am an immigrant, and I am the first person in my family to go to college. Also like many other first-generation college students, I studied in a technical, professional field as an undergraduate. In my case the field was engineering. Many CUNY students follow a similar educational path. CUNY has engineering programs, as well as lots of very popular technical and career-focused programs. There are also lots of associate's degree programs that prepare students for a wide range of careers. Of course, not all the students in these programs fit the mold that I am talking about, and not all immigrant first-to-go-to-college students study in these fields. However, I have found that there is a good amount of anecdotal truth to the archetypal (and, okay, maybe stereotypical) experience that I have had. I have had many moments of recognition and bonding with students and others who have had the same experience.

There is a lot that could be said about the trend of first-generation college students studying career-focused disciplines.[3] Part of the explanation has to do with a conversation you have (or imagine having) with your parents when you are seventeen and starting college. If you tell your parents that you want to study art history, or dance, or anthropology, they will ask you "What are you going to do with that?"

(In other words, what job can you get as a result of studying those things). This question is reasonable, and generally a seventeen-year-old has no good answer because the main reason for choosing those fields is that they sounded kind of cool in the catalog. This parental question probably gets asked in families of all backgrounds, but if your parents went to college, they will generally have some faith, however vaguely defined, in the value of liberal education for its own sake. They are willing to accept, grudgingly perhaps, that a few years studying whatever you feel like is what college is all about; or at least they are more willing to accept it than a working-class family would be. I tend to think that there is a working class inclination toward career-focused or applied learning in higher education and that it is based on the reasonable observation that the key social differences between the college-educated and the non-college-educated have to do with careers and income. This practical view has an analog in CUNY's history because such views influenced its founding.

My educational career gives me an interesting perspective on liberal education because, at least by the bureaucratic definition of the term, I did not receive one. Courses in engineering are not, according to the New York State Board of Education, liberal arts and sciences courses because they are specific to a particular application or business. Liberal arts and sciences courses must take a more general approach to knowledge and provide the broad insights into humanity and the natural world that are essential to a liberal education. Such courses must account for half of the total credits for a bachelor of science degree and three-quarters of those for a bachelor of arts. For a bachelor of engineering degree (BE), which is what I have, liberal arts and sciences courses only account for one-quarter of the credits. So, as far as liberal education is concerned, those courses I took in thermodynamics might as well have been in refrigerator repair or shorthand. However, the college I attended, Cooper Union, made a valiant and in my case successful attempt to instill a liberal spirit into the education they provided. They only had one course a semester in which to deliver the liberal element of our education, but the courses in the humanities were well taught. This liberal element of my education sustained and fostered the interest I had in literature and the humanities while I was studying engineering.

After graduating from engineering school, the next educational experience I had was in the courses I took at the CUNY Graduate Center for a year or so before enrolling in the English Ph.D. program there. The courses I took were mostly in traditional humanities fields and would be considered part of the traditional liberal arts and sciences. However, graduate study is discipline-specific,[4] and ultimately its purpose is professional education, and so it does not provide an opportunity for the broad range that we usually associate with liberal education.

The liberal education I have is the result of the combined action of two fairly illiberal educational experiences, but somehow it works. I value my scientific education as an engineer for the understanding that I have gained of the work of scientific and professional fields, which has helped me in teaching writing and doing interdisciplinary curricular work. Of course, what I actually learned as an undergraduate is becoming more hazy with every year, but I maintain an avid layman's interest in science and technology. I have an uncommon perspective on the supposed division between the sciences and the humanities. I know enough about physics to roll my eyes when a literary critic refers to the Heisenberg Uncertainty Principle to make some metaphorical point about the postmodern condition (though I do not know enough physics to properly explain what the Uncertainty Principle means). I also know from personal experience that talking to scientists about the teaching of writing can be a frustrating experience.

Another quick word about my undergraduate experience will bring us back to New York City and the era of the Free Academy. My undergraduate college, Cooper Union, was founded in New York right before the Civil War. Its founder, Peter Cooper was an inventor from a humble background, who became a very successful industrialist; he is a classic example of the American dream of success through hard work and talent. He is also an early example of idealistic philanthropy. The school he founded exists today as a small and oddly specialized college offering degrees in engineering, fine arts, and architecture. It does not offer degrees in any of the traditional liberal arts and sciences disciplines. The humanities courses I referred to earlier were taught by the Faculty of Humanities and Social Sciences. There are no individual departments in the traditional disciplines. The most distinctive feature of the school is that it does not charge tuition (or, as the school's administrators prefer to put it, it grants every student a full-tuition scholarship). This policy continues Peter Cooper's vision for the institution he founded. Cooper felt that education should be as "free as air and water."[5] He shared in the egalitarian spirit of the politicians who established the Free Academy. As a prominent and civic-minded citizen, he probably knew many of those figures. (He was one of the distinguished guests invited to the Free Academy's first commencement in 1853.) What Cooper thought about the curriculum of the Free Academy and how he saw the school he founded in relation to it would be interesting subjects to investigate, but the question at hand is what the founders of the Free Academy thought about their own mission.

From early in its existence the Free Academy was concerned with providing what we would recognize as a liberal education. That interest in liberal education was specifically tied to the political idealism that inspired its founding. In other words, it was *because* the school was founded in the name of the working class or the common man that its early administrators insisted that it not be dedicated solely to professional or practical subjects. We can see this spirit in the statement of one of the early leaders involved with the Free Academy:

> Will you say to the community that at the Free Academy, they are entitled to free education for the lower and middle classes, but that those who would shine in the dress circle of society, must go to the college and the university? Will the ends of public education be

answered by declaring, if your son is to go to a counting room or a trade, you may send him to the Free Academy where, in a short period they will give him French, Spanish and German, a few colloquial phrases in each, enough to make a bargain, with book-keeping and the practical branches . . . but if you intend him for a profession, or have a fortune to leave him—if you would make him a cultivated gentleman, send him to college and teach him Greek and Latin and polite learning? (quoted in Rudy 1949, 32–33)[6]

These comments were from a speech given after the Free Academy's first year by Erastus C. Benedict, the President of the Board of Education. His observations were part of the early debate over setting the curriculum for the new institution. Within a few years that debate was settled along the lines indicated in the comments above: The Free Academy's early curriculum was established so that it filled the same role as a college. (Not just the traditional role of an academy, which was as a secondary or preparatory school.) The Free Academy's curriculum was not traditional. It combined the practical subjects like book-keeping, drafting, and engineering with what Benedict refers to as "polite learning." It also allowed students to get degrees either in the modern languages or ancient, which was a fairly cutting-edge innovation at that time.[7]

The quote above from Benedict is interesting for its idealism but also for what it says about how the Free Academy's leaders saw the liberal portion of the curriculum. You do not, for instance, get the sense that Benedict thought that the study of literature or ancient languages was very important as ends unto themselves. He refers to those subjects as merely necessary components of being a part of the upper class. Knowing a little bit about Homer and Virgil is important to being a cultivated gentleman, but that knowledge is a superficial accouterment of the upper class, like knowing which fork to use or what to wear (and notice that his first reference to this class is to "the dress circle of society"). I cannot help imagining that when Benedict said "polite learning," he said it with some degree of irony.[8] This comment captures some of the equivocal attitude that the populist Democrats who campaigned for and shaped the Free Academy had toward liberal education.

Although the Free Academy leaders did not want their students to study only practical subjects, but that did not mean that they thought less of practical subjects than liberal learning. The practical work of creating and producing tangible items was seen as worthy of greater educational grounding than it had received up to that point in time. A good example of this view appears in the first report proposing the creation of the Free Academy, which was written under the leadership of Townsend Harris. The report describes the proposed institution as acting similar to a college, but "the courses of studies to be pursued will have more especial reference to the active duties of operative life" than to the areas usually dominated by the elites such as the clergy, law, and medicine. This education would not provide a route to the upper or middle class. It would produce a working class educated in the knowledge of its own sphere. This sphere included subjects like chemistry and engineering, and it was admired by populists like Harris precisely because it was practical and thus at odds with the traditional education of the elite.

Some of that vision of a practical worker's education endures today in CUNY's large wide-ranging career-focused programs. Some of the subjects in these programs, such as book-keeping or drafting, might sound familiar to what was offered in the Free Academy, but of course the practices of those fields have changed completely. The number of students who are in medical fields (and the number of those who are women) would surprise people of the nineteenth century. Along with this technical education, CUNY still preserves the mission of providing liberal education. The challenge of meeting these dual missions is probably felt most by CUNY's community colleges whose programs range from AA and AS degrees for students transferring to four-year schools, which are essentially all liberal education, to AAS degrees to prepare for careers, which only have one-quarter of their credits available for liberal arts and sciences courses. In their efforts to balance these missions, the community colleges have contributed greatly to the work of general education at CUNY, as some of the contributions in this volume will attest.

Of course, along with career-focused programs, CUNY has excellent liberal arts and sciences programs. In fact, CUNY's academic reputation in the twentieth century was built on the quality of its liberal arts curriculum, particularly in comparison to those of selective private schools. For years City College, the best known of the colleges in the system, was referred to as "the poor man's Harvard." A great deal could be written about that comparison (for one thing the term is often used these days by critics of CUNY who contrast its past success with its alleged current failures). However, the fact that such a comparison was made for so long and is still referred to shows how different modern ideas of the City University are from early visions of the Free Academy.

The Democrats of the nineteenth century would not have envisioned a Harvard of any kind for the laboring class they championed. They would not have wanted to emulate the upper classes. Their political rhetoric extolled the laboring class for its practicality and for the concrete contributions to the nation made through its labor. These contributions are what the Townsend Harris report refers to as the "active duties of operative life." By contrast, the upper classes were critiqued for not being practical and concrete. They did not work with actual things but with ideas and papers. This critique was extended to the education of the upper classes and to book-based or abstract learning in general to the point where it was in tension with the goals of education adopted by the Free Academy.

Some forms of this populist critique are familiar. Walt Whitman is known for his heroic descriptions of working men and women, and his work contains examples of the populist suspicion of higher learning or bookishness. When Whitman lays out his poetic mission at the beginning of *Leaves of Grass*, he explains that he wants us, the readers, to become independent thinkers.

> Stop this day and night with me and you shall possess the origin of all poems,
> You shall possess the good of the earth and sun . . . . there are millions of suns left,
> You shall no longer take things at second or third hand . . . . nor look through the eyes of
> the dead . . . . nor feed on the spectres in books,
> You shall not look through my eyes either, nor take things from me,
> You shall listen to all sides and filter them from yourself.

> —Walt Whitman, *Leaves of Grass* (1855)

This is about as harsh a criticism of book learning as you can get. Books and the knowledge in them are associated with death. Of course, Whitman's point here is not to critique liberal education. He wants us to be intellectually and spiritually independent, which means having complete faith in one's own sense of what is true. With this kind of self-assuredness, it is not necessary to have one's beliefs confirmed by the contents of books. These poetic and philosophical ideas did not, in Whitman's case, translate into an opposition to education. As a loyal and partisan Democrat, he supported the educational goals of the Free Academy. Whitman's anti-bookishness in *Leaves of Grass* is about spiritual and transcendent truths and not about college courses, and it is not used to make a class critique as it was by other Jacksonians.

The combination of upper class criticism with criticism of liberal learning was common. We saw thinly veiled examples of it in the comments from Harris and Benedicts. However, it was stated more forcefully by one local political pundit named William Leggett, who probably influenced the views of the Democrats associated with the Free Academy. Leggett worked from his extreme egalitarian principles and arrived at some unconventional conclusions. Most influentially, he advocated free markets on the grounds that they operated according to popular choice and that government involvement in the economy was undemocratic because it would always benefit the elites more than the general population. He was also an important exponent of the idea that the working class contributed value to the country because its members produced and worked with tangibles. By contrast, the non-laboring classes—the lawyers, bankers, and merchants—contributed nothing because they only worked with paper and concepts. Working from those same principles, Leggett felt that the existing standards of culture and education were antithetical to democracy. He comments on the consequences of such an education as follows:

> The one leading object of modern philosophy and science is to reconcile and associate aristocratic principles with truth . . . . No student can begin to learn until he has surrendered every vestige of independence of mind, by acquiring a veneration for authority, and yielding placidly to prescription. (Leggett 1837)

The authority at issue for Leggett is the authority of great—or what he calls "distinctive"—literature and of the distinctive deeds of historical figures. Leggett felt that emphasizing such singular works and deeds led to an aristocratic view of the world—a view that the works and deeds of the common people were not worthwhile. He cautioned that, in public education,

> . . . it is necessary to guard carefully against the introduction of the distinctive literature and the individual philosophy, into our district schools. (1837)

The stakes were high because the right education would ensure that the young people of the country would learn democratic principles. He noted in the opening of "Aristocratic Education" that the republican movements on Continental Europe were led by college students, and he was dismayed that by contrast "in England and in our republican America, the colleges are the very nurseries of young aristocrats."

In opposing distinctive art, Leggett was not denying that artistic distinction existed; he just did not think it was so important. He was not concerned with America matching the cultural accomplishments of Europe, although many of his contemporaries were obsessed with the idea. A democratic American culture, he conceded, would never match the great art of the Old World, but it would succeed in a more important way: It would make art and culture available to a far larger audience than ever existed in aristocratic Europe.

Populists were not the only ones to criticize bookish and impractical education. One of the staunchest opponents of Democratic populism was Horace Greeley who made comments on education in the same vein. Greeley, the editor of the widely circulated *New York Tribune*, was known as a reformer whose paper served as a platform for radical ideas such as abolitionism and utopian socialism. He commented directly on the establishment of the Free Academy in a *Tribune* editorial on the day of the city-wide referendum in June 1847 to approve the Academy that gave a lukewarm endorsement of the proposal. As a Whig, Greeley supported education and democracy but without any of the enthusiasm about the common people seen in Jacksonians.

One of his comments on the function of education will show how different the Whig perspective on education was. Greeley, who was also a popular and sought-after lecturer, said the following in a talk to a group of college students:

> The benefits of a true education commence with the individual, but pass directly and inevitably to the community. He who is not a better brother, neighbor, friend, and citizen, because of his superior knowledge, may very well doubt whether his knowledge is really superior. . . . (1844, 137)

The idea expressed here is a familiar one. It is common enough today to include a sense of civic engagement as one of the goals of a liberal education, and we could imagine the quote above engraved on a wall or plaque somewhere on one of our university buildings. However, Greeley's emphasis on being "superior" and "better" show he was not thinking of education as a way to promote any kind of egalitarianism. The end of the sentence which is cut off above completes this picture:

> . . . may very well doubt whether his knowledge is really superior to the ignorance of the unlettered many around him.

This is not a line we would expect to see engraved anywhere at a college today or to hear in an address to our students. References to the ignorant and unlettered masses are no longer a part of our public rhetoric on education. Greeley was concerned with these masses when he criticized the populism of the Democrats. For him the college students he was addressing in this talk represented part of the solution to this political problem. College education will produce a "better" class of citizens who will provide enlightened leadership for the country. To fulfill this leadership role, these young men needed an education that would allow them to integrate their knowledge into society, and for Greeley the right education for this purpose was a practical education.

The purpose of Greeley's speech was to call for a less liberal education. Greeley thought the existing higher education that privileged young men received left them too detached from the everyday world of work to understand and relate to regular people. They should have some exposure to manual labor and to the mechanical arts and crafts and other practical matters like farming in addition to the traditional curriculum. If anything had to be cut from the curriculum, Greeley suggested cutting the required study of Greek and Latin wherever possible, and he was not convinced that everyone needed to study mathematics. Exposure to some manual labor would help students relate to the working classes, and it might provide an opportunity for them to use their education to benefit that class. It is also, Greeley felt, morally beneficial and conducive to physical health. Incorporating labor into education was central to achieving the "harmonious and healthful development of the whole human being" (1837, 119). Putting his views in our terms, Greeley envisioned liberal goals for education—the full development of the individual as a person and citizen—but rejected liberal means of achieving them.

In spite of all this critique of book learning from across the political spectrum, the Free Academy developed in its first few years into a place with a liberal curriculum. We could see movement toward this end in the comments (however begrudging) from Erastus Benedict in favor of liberal education at the Free Academy. Not long after he made those comments, the liberal element of the Free Academy's curriculum was established more formally in a report from the Executive Committee that oversaw the Free Academy (this was a committee of the city's Board of Education). That report established the programs that the school would offer. It said that the Free Academy would fulfill the dual roles of a traditional academy, which offered postprimary education intended to prepare students for college, and of a college proper, and to achieve this, "Its course of studies, therefore, should be liberal and embrace those both of the ordinary Academy and the College." The programs of study laid out in this report included the fields of mathematics, literature, and philosophy along with engineering and drawing.

It is probably not so surprising that the practice of the institution would take a more liberal approach than its political advocates might have preferred. The praise for practical workers' education and disdain for intellectual work that I have mentioned are all examples from pundits or politicians. The actual curriculum of the Free Academy, however, was designed with the institution's faculty who, naturally enough, valued the expertise and intellectual work of their disciplines.

If they were like many intellectuals in this period, the faculty probably felt that suspicion of liberal education and scholarship was rooted in an unfortunate national trait. It was a commonplace among intellectuals that the United States was obsessed with the practical and the profitable things in life and did not value learning for its own sake. The idea that America's culture is materialistic and shallow is an old one. For almost as long as people have been identifying national traits, this one has been high on the list, and it was applied particularly to Yankees (and especially to New Yorkers). Criticism of materialism appears in some of the best known writing of the time and was a staple of New England thought. Most of the beginning of Thoreau's *Walden* is dedicated to this problem. It appears in various forms in the work of Margaret Fuller and Ralph Waldo Emerson.[9] A generation before these writers, American materialism was discussed specifically as it applied to education by William Ellery Channing, a theologian and minister who was a huge influence on all those New England intellectuals. In an article on the country's developing intellectual culture, Channing considered the influence of this national trait. He was glad to see that there was some movement to expand education for the masses beyond the limits of elementary schools. However, efforts to expand the literature and the learning of the country were hindered by the tendency to value the practical and the useful. He responded to this tendency in the following fashion:

> We have said that we prize, as highly as any, useful knowledge. But by this we mean knowledge which answers and ministers to our complex and various nature; we mean that which is useful, not only to the animal man, but to the intellectual, moral, and religious man . . . . (Channing 1823, 257)

This response makes a deft rhetorical use of the populist defense of usefulness. He defends useful knowledge but expands it to include the humanities and sciences by expanding the idea of the individual. Today we would consider the "National Literature" to which Channing refers in this piece scholarly work in general: He includes scientific research as well as history and poetry. All of this work taken together represents the intellectual progress of the country, and Channing felt that however backward the United States may be in this regard, it had great potential to develop and a responsibility to do so. He further emphasizes the importance of pursuing intellectual work for its own sake, not looking for practical applications, by offering the following sage defense of intellectual inquiry:

> [A]ll truth is of a prolific nature, and has connexions not immediately perceived; and it may be, that what we call vain speculations, may, at no distant period, link themselves with some new facts or theories, and guide a profound thinker to the most important results. (Channing 1823, 258)

Channing's eloquent defense of scholarship and liberal education shares some ground with the arguments of liberal education advocates today. Those advocates also share Channing's concern about American practicality and materialism. One prominent group that promotes liberal education, the Association of American Colleges and Universities (AAC&U), devote some of their work to American perceptions and misperceptions of liberal education. Through a series of focus groups, the AAC&U has discovered that students are often indifferent to or unaware of the goals of liberal education and take a narrowly practical view of their education. In an op-ed piece in the *Chronicle of Higher Education* last year the organization's leaders discussed these findings and their concern that "some students have come to see the college degree as just a ticket to be punched on the way to their first job . . . ." (AAC&U 2006). The op-ed ends with a call for faculty and administrators in higher education to better communicate the values of liberal education. The values that the AAC&U promulgates for liberal education are probably familiar to anyone who has worked on this subject. Theirs is basically the orthodox position on liberal education. The basic definition they offer includes the following:

> Liberal education is a philosophy of education that empowers individuals with broad knowledge and transferable skills, and a strong sense of values, ethics, and civic engagement . . . By its nature, liberal education is global and pluralistic. It embraces the diversity of ideas and experiences that characterize the social, natural, and intellectual world. (AAC&U 2006)

If you allow for a wide range of interpretation for loaded terms like *empowers, skills,* and *values,* this definition is in keeping with what people at CUNY have in mind when they talk about liberal education. A wide range of interpretation is important at CUNY because the university is so decentralized. Each of its seventeen colleges creates its own curriculum and defines liberal education according to its mission and history. However, none of the colleges have goals for liberal education that are at odds with those of other colleges or the AAC&U.

Though CUNY's colleges have not had liberal education defined for them by the university's central administration, they have in recent years been directed to focus on liberal education. The central administration, in its most recent Master Plan for CUNY, made liberal education an important element in the improvement of under-graduate education.[10] That Master Plan report does provide some "overarching princi-ples" for liberal education at CUNY, but it notes that these principles have come out of the General Education Project, which included representatives from all the colleges. The first principle is the importance of providing students with a good grounding in the Liberal Arts and Sciences:

> This strong Liberal Arts and Sciences base aims to equip students with intellectual abilities necessary to negotiate an ever-changing world of information and knowledge and to act in it as engaged citizens. (CUNY Master Plan 2004–2008)

In some ways today's liberal education values, as seen in the work of CUNY and the AAC&U, clearly echo the educational goals of some of the nineteenth-century fig-ures we have looked at. The similarities are clearest in the AAC&U's advocacy campaign Liberal Education and America's Promise (LEAP). In that campaign the AAC&U focuses on the importance of liberal education in preparing citizens in a democracy, which is also a prominent element of CUNY's principles for liberal edu-cation. The AAC&U leaders, in their op-ed on the focus group results, discuss the role of education in terms that echo Greeley's comments. They write that

> Today's students [see the personal benefits of college] but they do not recognize its role in preparing them as citizens, community participants, and thoughtful people. They do not expect college to enable them to better understand the wider world; they view college as a private rather than a public good. (Schneider and Humphreys 2005)

Of course, the AAC&U's idea of education is different from Greeley's. They pro-mote the basic ideas of liberal education that he opposed. Their statement and oth-ers like it on education and citizenship do not at all imply that the educated are morally superior to the "unlettered masses" with whom Greeley was concerned.

Furthermore, in spite of all the rhetoric about educational access and democracy, there is one very important difference between today's views and those of the Free Academy's leaders. The principles of the AAC&U and CUNY reflect our contempo-rary concern about equal access to education not just for the working classes but also for racial minorities. This concern was not part of the agenda of nineteenth-century Democrats. They were, at least in New York City, stridently opposed to abolitionism and other civil rights efforts. Only a few years before the founding of the Free Academy, the Democrats had worked to defeat a proposal to grant suffrage to African American men. (Greeley, despite his anti-populism, was a dedicated supporter of this failed suf-frage proposal. It was part of the reform of New York State's constitution in 1846.)

Our idea that education is important to democracy was not shared by the leading advocates for democracy in the early nineteenth century. The Democrats (or democrats) of that period did not see higher education as necessary for democracy. How could they when so few of their own constituents had access to education? They expressed their suspicion of education because they associated the educated upper classes with anti-democratic politics. They believed that greater things are possible when people are not under the rule of kings, lords, and priests[11]; and that America's position as a new country without the burdens of established churches or aristocracies had a special obligation to fulfill this potential. In his "National Literature" piece, Channing repeats the view of many when he says that America's discovery and development are part of the working out of God's plan.

These ideas about the special destiny of America are a great example of what we would today call American exceptionalism. Whether we find it tiresome, inspiring or dreadful, American exceptionalism was an essential element of the arguments for expanding liberal education in New York City and elsewhere in the country. Moreover, it continues to be part of the rhetoric surrounding CUNY today. (See as an example the 2006 *Economist* piece on CUNY titled "Rebuilding the American Dream Machine.") The American dream is all about opportunity. Collectively, it has been the opportunity to create a democratic and just society. As a student of American history, I know how slowly and imperfectly this opportunity has been seized and how illusory it has often seemed. However, because of my background as an immigrant, my education, and my experiences at CUNY, the American dream is a term I cannot put quotation marks around or be cynical about.

Individually, the opportunity we associate with the American dream has usually meant a route to financial success. It has also, as seen in the *Economist* article and much else of the discourse around CUNY, meant access to education, which can be a route to financial success but can also be more. In education there is opportunity not just for our students but also for us. As educators, we have an opportunity to provide an education that means more than a credential or a bigger paycheck. The nature of this larger opportunity and its history is what I have tried to explore here. It is an opportunity, made possible by generations of educators, public figures and students, to be part of our students' lives, to shape this important public university and play a role in the country's destiny.

For the sake of symmetry, I will close with another quote from Whitman who, in his poetic visionary mode, would not have been surprised to hear that the questions we discuss are the ones debated in an earlier age. Though he is known as a prototypical American poet, Whitman liked to adopt a universal and cosmic perspective. So when he wants to impart to his readers a sense of historical opportunity, he does so without reference to his own optimistic historic moment, so that it can apply to future readers.

There was never any more inception than there is now,
Nor any more youth or age than there is now;
And will never be any more perfection than there is now.

NOTES

1. Whitman is a very obliging writer in this regard because his poetry has many long lists of everything under the sun. Need poetic references to clam chowder, opera, or amputation? Look no further than "Song of Myself."

2. An example of his idiosyncrasy would be his serious interest in phrenology, the science (or pseudoscience, as we would call it now) of analyzing human personality by examination of the bumps on our heads.

3. For one thing, it would be interesting to know how much actual statistical truth there is to this anecdotal trend. Even though I spent a year reading lots of statistics about CUNY and higher education, I have not found anything that breaks down the educational experience of first-generation college students.

4. A great deal is said about the importance of inter-disciplinarity in graduate study and in scholarship. It is important, but nobody gets a Ph.D. in inter-disciplinarity. Even the most adventurous inter-disciplinary scholar still has a home discipline that shapes how he or she sees the world.

5. I do not have any source for that quote; in fact I have never tried to look it up. I just remember hearing it often at Cooper. Most Cooper students recite this quote if prompted. They could probably also tell whoever wants to know that Peter Cooper invented jello, which is more or less true, though that is not how he made his fortune.

6. My discussion of the early administration of the Free Academy is all taken from the first few chapters of Rudy, which draw on the Board of Education records and reports and other archival material of the period.

7. The classicists have long since lost this one across all higher education. At CUNY, the only faint ember of classical education to be found is in Brooklyn College's Core Curriculum, which features one required course on classical culture.

8. I do not imagine him making those air quotes with his fingers the way some people do. I am pretty sure no one in the nineteenth century did that. He may have meant something along the lines of "so-called polite learning." At the very least he had some distance from the term; just on the basis of the full quote above and on his involvement with the Free Academy, it is fair to say that Benedict did not take the conservative view that properly (and politely) educated gentlemen were the only men who should lead the country.

9. Readers who know their American literature may wonder why I do not refer to Emerson on the subject of education. After all, one of his well-known early lectures was titled "The American Scholar." One reason is that I wanted to focus mostly on New Yorkers. Another reason is that connecting Emerson's great, loopy, abstract writing to mundane matters like curriculum would take more space than I have room for here. For instance, in "The American Scholar" Emerson writes that colleges are at their best "when they gather from far every ray of various genius to their hospitable halls, and by the concentrated fires, set the hearts of their youth on flame." Good luck crafting an outcomes assessment for that.

10. Actually the Master Plan uses the term "General Education" in this section, but the parts of the report I am interested in have to do with liberal education as an overall educational goal. The discussions of general education are more specifically related to curriculum.

11. The last item is a widely prevalent idea and an example of the intellectual side of the era's anti-Catholic sentiment.

WORKS CITED

AAC&U (Association of American Colleges and Universities). "Liberal Education and America's Promise." http://www.aacu.org/advocacy/leap/index.cfm.

Channing, William Ellery. "Remarks on National Literature." *A Selection from the Works of William E. Channing, D. D.* Boston: American Unitarian Association, 1855. 243–280. MOA. http://name.umdl.umich.edu/AGV0180.0001.001.

CUNY Master Plan, 2004–2008. Chancellor's Office, City University of New York. www1.cuny.edu/portal_ur/content/2004/chancellor/masterfinal.pdf.

Greeley, Horace. "The Relations of Learning to Labor." In *Hints Toward Reforms.* New York: Fowler and Wells, 1850. 112–48. MOA. http://name.umdl.umich.edu/AFT8745.0001.001.

Leggett, William. "Aristocratic Education." *The Examiner*, 1 August 1837.

"Rebuilding the American Dream Machine: A Parable of Elitism in American Universities." *The Economist.* 19 January 2006. http://www.economist.com/world/na/displaystory.cfm?story_id= 5417329.

Rudy, S. Willis. *The College of the City of New York: A History, 1847–1947.* New York: The City College Press, 1949.

Schneider, Carol Geary, and Debra Humphreys. "Putting Liberal Education on the Radar Screen." *Chronicle of Higher Education.* 23 September, 2005. http://chronicle.com/weekly/v52/i05/05b02001.htm.

CHAPTER TWO

Curriculum Mapping

Climbing out of the Briar Patch

PHILIP M. ANDERSON

Queens College and the Graduate Center

CURRICULUM HISTORY

Much of the historical investigation of higher education appears to focus on the *institutional* history of colleges and universities. There are excellent books identifying the laws and policies that resulted in establishing various parts of the university systems we now inhabit. Almost everyone seems to know about land grant colleges and many know about the religious origins of most of the elite colleges of the east and the social Darwinian origins of the colleges in the west. There are also more technical histories that enumerate the influence of groups such as the Carnegie Foundation on college and university *administration*, for example, the origin of course credits in the Carnegie unit, and additions to the college missions to meet changing times (e.g., Rudolph 1962; Brubacher and Rudy 1976; Lucas 1994).

What most histories of higher education fail to do is account for significant changes within the curriculum during the turbulent and transformative years of the twentieth century. Rudolph's singular, rather high-minded, *Curriculum: A History of the American Undergraduate Course of Study since 1636* (1977), explores the larger ideals he sees driving higher education curriculum innovation and change, almost exclusively as a philosophical debate traced back in a straight line to the Massachusetts Bay Colony (see Herbst's contemporary review, 1978, for the details). One scholarly book, however, Herbert Kliebard's *The Struggle for the American Curriculum, 1893–1958* (2004), investigates the development of the school curriculum in the context of the social movements of the first half of the twentieth century. His emphasis on *curriculum* is significant and probably unique among the various histories. The book focuses on the development of the school curriculum, but almost everything in it applies to the undergraduate curriculum in colleges and universities, and our concern here is the undergraduate curriculum.

Various opinions have been put forth about the transformation of the undergraduate curriculum during this century. For example, we find Jerome Bruner bemoaning the effects of graduate programs diverting resources from the undergraduate and school curriculum in the influential *The Process of Education* (1960), his report from the Woods Hole conference on the post-Sputnik crisis in science, mathematics, and engineering. Considering that his report came in response to a space race/national defense "crisis," the argument appears a bit college-centric. Certainly, the removal (or desertion) of professors into graduate schools and programs is not the reason why the undergraduate and school curricula have changed (or suffered) over the years. Undergraduate education has grown mostly in response to political and social changes from outside the college, including the creation of graduate research programs, many of which are funded by federal dollars, and professional schools that need to meet required accreditation and desired status goals for various vocations.

SCHOOL AND COLLEGE CURRICULUM

However, much of that discussion about graduate education concerns post-WW II developments in higher education. The foundations of U.S. higher education, especially undergraduate, were established in the first half of the twentieth century as part of a larger progressive movement, and in response to the creation of the comprehensive high school and establishment of compulsory schooling. These facts, and the attendant curricular innovations, changed the expectations for the American college. Not surprisingly, increasing the pool of high school graduates transforms society's demands on the colleges. Kliebard's categorization of the changes in the school curriculum during the first half of the twentieth century (2004) is a useful framework for analyzing assumptions underlying much of the current undergraduate curriculum. Understanding what we already have before us is the first step in managing or transforming the curriculum for the future.

Kliebard argues two key points: First, social and cultural and political movements have had a direct effect on the public school curriculum, and, second, each of the successive socio-cultural movements have been layered, uncritically, over previous curriculum structures and rationales (2004). These competing "streams" are embedded in the current curriculum, and thus account for some of the central contradictions and conundrums of the American school and college curriculum. I will not attempt to discuss all the particulars and complexities of Kliebard's historical argument. Instead, I will outline the central positions he identifies and use them as heuristic devices to unpack various and sundry elements in the current undergraduate curriculum. The intent is to show a method for analyzing curriculum. One may find different evidence or draw other conclusions from the process, but the analysis is a necessary first step.

Unfortunately, the most common version of curriculum analysis has been a simple look at additions to the undergraduate curriculum since the alleged golden era when curriculum possessed a scholarly purity. In these analyses, after citing Socrates, Plato, and Aristotle, as well as a few other ancients, one is shown how the former liberal arts and sciences curriculum has been corrupted by "vocationalism" (or as a colleague of mine named it: "creeping vocationalism"). There is even a bit of that attitude in Kliebard's book, reading between the lines. However, simply juxtaposing the academic and the vocational does not get us very far. Moreover, Kliebard's categories help us understand how complicated even this distinction remains. Certainly, curriculum analysis may employ many useful categories, but those categories are never neutral. In Kliebard's case, his categories elucidate the significant transformation of U.S. schooling by social and cultural movements from the Progressive area. I would argue that this model is a richer framework for understanding the undergraduate curriculum than "liberal arts and sciences vs. vocationalism."

Strangely, no one ever seems to want to argue for the medieval trivium and quadrivium, a curriculum much closer in time and temperament to ours. What is it about the ancient curriculum that appears more contemporary than the medieval one? Is it that the ancient one is so lacking in actual detail? Is it easier to idealize some remote past than to deal with the actual and direct influences on our current situation? More importantly, why, in these complex and transformative times, would we wish to pursue an essentialist goal in any educational argument? Kliebard's paradigm returns complexity and historical grounding to the discussion.

HUMANISM

The school curriculum, Kliebard argues, has been shaped by four great historical movements from 1893 to 1958: humanism, developmentalism, social efficiency, and social meliorism. Humanism was reflected in the various curricula put forth by the Committee of Ten (Eliot 1893), reflecting the idea of a broad general education as useful for all students headed for college. The difference in the recommended high school "tracks" was whether one studied English only (the vocational kids), modern foreign language (middle management), or the classics (the leadership classes). Charles W. Eliot's humanistic emphasis is evident in his later editorship of the Harvard Classics (1910), the first "Great Books" curriculum. However, the curriculum also signaled an interest in the teaching of science, reflecting the great age of industry. Some would argue that this humanist emphasis was in response to the success (and philosophies) of the financial and industrial titans, Carnegie, Mellon, Stanford, and so on, who eventually founded colleges reflecting the new world of industry and social Darwinism. Furthermore, one could argue that the Committee of Ten's humanistic recommendations were already a response to the "threat" of science (and its first ministers, engineering, and technology), or at least an attempt to co-opt it within the curriculum. Matthew Arnold's *Culture and Anarchy* (1867), arguing for the role of schools in developing civil order through the teaching of "high culture," becomes part of the public debate. Arnold's book had a tremendous effect on the development of the American school curriculum in the second half of the nineteenth century (Applebee 1974).

DEVELOPMENTALISM

The second curricular stream, developmentalism, growing out of the new field of psychology, produced the greatest effect on the school curriculum through its emphasis on child study. Conservatives blame Dewey for this movement, but it involved a range of intellectual and cultural forces, as well as some social imperatives. Child labor laws, compulsory schooling, and school guidance counseling (and even recess), as well as the elementary school curriculum, all owe a debt to the work of developmental psychologists.

G. Stanley Hall wrote the two-volume opus *Adolescence* (1904), creating a whole new category of human development that made the junior high school, sex education, juvenile delinquents, and teen culture a set of concerns no one had ever thought about before. While psychology seemed to grow to dominance during most of the twentieth century (*The Man in the Gray Flannel Suit*, 1956, reflecting its post-WW II pop culture zenith), developmentalism appeared, on the surface, to have very little influence on thinking about higher education. That is, unless one looks beyond the formal undergraduate curriculum to the growth of counseling and social development aims in college mission statements and practices. Whether it was how to behave at a tea party in the 1950s, survive an overdose in the 1960s, or protect oneself from STDs in the years since, colleges have expended numerous resources in the developmentalist cause.

On the other hand, the developmental point of view has had very little influence, in any scholarly way, on the undergraduate curriculum. William Perry's (1999) work stands almost alone regarding the social and psychological movement of 18-year-old freshmen to 22-year-old college graduates. Nevertheless, most college officials and professors will tell you, as will the students, that their four or more years in college change them in significant ways (i.e., the 50% on average who do not drop out because college is not meeting their needs). One could argue that the difference between early undergraduate general education and "advanced study" in the major itself is developmental, simply by its sequential and hierarchical structure. Conversely, one could argue that developmental models have been less useful in recent years because so many of today's students are "non-traditional," that is over 25 years of age. All in all, one does not hear much developmental talk in colleges.

One of the key features of the modern undergraduate college is based solidly on the principles invested in the developmentalist view: remediation. As proof of that argument, I would point to how many colleges have changed the appellation "remedial" to "developmental" in recent years. The standard argument for remediation is that the student is "not ready" for "college work." This assertion is usually made on the basis of standardized test scores or by the judgment of teachers and counselors at the high school (as a preventive) and at the college (as a remediation). Freshman Composition as a subject, everyone seems to know, began at Harvard at the turn of the twentieth century to improve the writing skills of so many "under-prepared" students.

The current neo-conservative push for "value-added education" has moved some universities to install tests at the 60-credit level. There is also a movement, reflected in new government reports, to put some sort of standardized exit testing into place for college graduation (Spellings 2006). For those who do not see the implication, the public argument, made by conservatives such as William Bennett, states that there is no "proof" that students know any more when they graduate college than when they entered. When the argument has been used in similar attacks on K-12 schools, it appears to be a subterfuge primarily aimed at controlling "liberal tendencies" in teachers (e.g., Ravitch and Finn 1988). Large pieces of the "outcomes assessment" argument represent a culture war over the content of the curriculum, a debate won by the neo-conservatives so far, as evidenced by the widespread invasion of limited, content-based standardized testing in the schools.

SOCIAL EFFICIENCY/SCIENTIFIC MANAGEMENT

One would think that neo-conservatives, with their suspicions about "soft" sciences like psychology, would not be so much on the side of developmentalism. Ideologically, they are not on the side of developmentalism. Unfortunately, much of the social efficiency thinking neo-cons love, especially as expressed as social control policies, gains its authority from the testing movement associated with developmentalism. Neo-cons love testing, not for the knowledge it can provide about human thinking and behavior, but for diagnosis and prescription in school settings, that is, for social control purposes.

The recent official position of the U.S. Department of Education's Institute of Educational Sciences (http://ies.ed.gov/), stating that all educational research must be "scientific," adds the qualifier that much of that research pursued under their restricted definition would consist of program evaluation. "Do educational programs 'work'?" is a question rooted in the social efficiency model (see www.whatworks.ed.gov/). Tracking and remediation are rationalized by a social efficiency argument that it is "a waste of money" not to provide children, or adults for that matter, with an education appropriate to their abilities. Underlying this premise is the scientific management imperative that the social sciences should serve to manage and control human behavior because "innate" human abilities can be assessed by scientific testing. This assumption harkens back to the original use of the Stanford-Binet IQ test to sort WW I draftees for their suitability as officer material—rank and IQ were seen to be a perfect match (according to the U.S. Army generals in charge, of course).

Truth be told, the use of testing has always been more about social efficiency and social meliorism (see next section) than about developmental ideals of providing an individualized education for all children. Sociologist E. A. Ross's classic, *Social Control* (1901/2002), for example, laid out the agenda. The new immigrants of the late nineteenth century were not only generally deficient (look at their IQ scores and physical development versus "real" Americans), but they harbored ideological convictions, such as communism and Catholicism, dangerous to liberal (which usually means Protestant) democracy. The curriculum needed a transformation to make it a prophylactic against foreign ideologies, and the newly comprehensive and universal public schooling was transformed by patriotic zeal. American history was re-emphasized, but the new social sciences also enter into the school curriculum through a new subject called "social studies." Students received marks on their "citizenship" as well as their reading and ciphering.

Social efficiency brought "needs assessment" into curricular thinking. One way to determine what a child needed to learn was to look at his or her future as an adult (already determined in childhood by aptitude testing) and see what that adult needed to know to do his or her job properly. Social efficiency brought us industrial arts for the newly schooled working-class boys, and home economics entered to make all women better (i.e., scientifically efficient) homemakers and mothers. In the colleges, the social sciences began to dominate the new curriculum, and reconstructionist views began to break down some of the old class, gender, and race barriers to higher education. Women and minorities were still segregated, by institution (segregated colleges), by department (women mostly limited to education studies), or level (very few graduate school opportunities), but at least they had access to higher education. More importantly, though, no matter how differently they were constructed, the college's assumptions about the heart of the curriculum remained focused on the liberal arts.

Some of that impetus to embrace the liberal arts is rooted in the conservatism of the humanist position, for example, the idea that all students, no matter what major or future profession, should be liberally educated. However, most of it came from the increasing call for standardization of the curriculum from the social efficiency point of view. This change of direction is reflected in the triumph of the SAT by the early 1930s. Previous use of restricted tests based on a uniform list of readings for college admission gave way to the democratic call for scientific testing of "scholastic aptitude" as a means for identifying young people who were college material. The tests also made it possible for undergraduate curricula to be split into not only "regular" and "remedial" tracks, but also into an "honors" track for those who scored the highest on the various scientific measures.

The new acceptance of the social sciences in the colleges and universities was a reflection of this new world of democracy and possibility. The New Deal represents the total acceptance of the social science frame as a means to a better world. The university and the state become partners in social engineering, rather than recreating the old split between church and state. Social scientists, even to this day, see themselves as the social conscience of the university. The humanists are not materialists, social scientists appear to argue, and further, they are naïve individualists not committed to the betterment of society. Thus, the notion of social responsibility enters the curriculum, bringing us to our final curricular movement.

SOCIAL MELIORISM

The last of the social moments Kliebard traces is social meliorism, perhaps a reaction to the growing influence of scientific management with the social Darwinism implicit in it, and perhaps a corrective brought on during a time dominated by two world wars, a world-wide depression, and a period of cold war when the entire survival of the human race was at stake. Social meliorism manifested itself in various ways from the time of the Great Depression until Sputnik re-awoke the scientific management monster. In the decade before WW II, many colleges engaged in social experiments, such as Meiklejohn's at Wisconsin (Tussman 1997), that tossed aside the "coverage" required by standardized curriculum and focused on "deep" study of fewer topics. The anthologies that were developed in the 1920s for social efficiency purposes were put aside to return to the study of "source" documents. Students were encouraged to connect their work in school with the world outside, even if, as in Meiklejohn's case, it meant bringing the insights of classical Greece to modern social problems. (Significant to our point about external forces shaping college curriculum, Joseph Tussman, a student of Meiklejohn's, recreated a version of the experiment at Berkeley from 1965–1969.) Professors themselves, especially the social scientists, engaged in political action, sometimes working with the state authorities to build a better society (and sometimes working against state authorities to promote more just views of society).

After WW II, social meliorism was called into play for the adolescents who had become "juvenile delinquents." Apparently, they had had insufficient male supervision during the war years; see *The Blackboard Jungle* (1954) for the popular presentation of this argument. In addition, for the new generation of baby boomers growing up under the threat of nuclear annihilation, and for the million soldiers who returned home after the war, many of whom flooded the college campuses under the GI Bill, there was more at stake than getting good grades. The ex-GIs, though, were inured to standardization, and hence big lecture halls filled to the brim, and all sorts of tests to account for learning in the absence of sufficient numbers of professors worked fine. Unfortunately, this standardized model became the norm for the generation that followed, the largest cohort of college students in history until recently, as well as subsequent generations.

POST-SPUTNIK

The Sputnik "crisis" is the end of Kliebard's analysis. He proposes that the federal government's role changed significantly after 1958. The National Defense Education Act (1958) marked the first major federal investment in education. Since the Sputnik crisis, we have seen any number of "crises," all constructed as national defense-oriented. *A Nation at Risk* (1983) and *No Child Left Behind* (2001) are the bookends of the current neo-conservative movement. (In the first, Japanese technology was the enemy; in the second, American liberalism.) The NDEA of 1958 poured federal dollars into mathematics and science and engineering and foreign language.

However, the NDEA and its amendments also promoted an academic rationalist approach to the entire curriculum, with the focus on a key word in American education: excellence. (See Readings 1996 for a critique of "excellence" in current discourse concerning colleges.) Gifted and talented programs were promoted, and new scientifically developed instructional programs were employed for those who were "slowed" by the normal pace of school instruction. The subject matter knowledge of teachers was interrogated, and summer institutes taught by professors in the disciplines were offered as a remedy. Advanced Placement examinations became popular for advanced high school students.

In the end, most of the educational reforms following Sputnik showed one big influence: There was a new sense of the interdependence of schools, especially high schools and colleges. Faced with the demographic reality of the baby boom, and all the education reports, colleges began to reflect a greater congruity with the school curriculum. Most of that contact was through standardized testing, and through the modeling and promotion of the college-developed curriculum for schools.

The revolution in education actually became a real revolution in the curriculum by the mid-1960s, with new experimental curricula and even experimental colleges (e.g., Hampshire College, founded in 1970). Most of the new colleges and curricula had one goal: individualization for the learner. The rejection of standardization and requirements meant new reading lists, new learning experiences, and new ways of representing knowledge. These were heady times, filled with young professors, high salaries, higher enrollments, and seemingly unlimited futures. The curriculum became more relevant, the requirements became more elastic, and the texts became more personalized, fueled by the paperback publishing revolution, for both students and professors.

The collapse of the post-war economic growth in the early 1970s brought about a severe reduction of curriculum offerings and many of the newest and more radical faculty. The schools settled into a back-to-basics curriculum model, and the colleges planned for reductions in enrollment and program offerings. New faculty hiring was restricted, and college faculties now number half as many full-time members as they did in the late 1960s. Many fewer professors are teaching the same number of students. This phenomenon is not merely a professional problem, but a curriculum problem as well: It calls for more standardization as a means to control the part-time instructors.

The great faith of social meliorism, that anyone could be anything, along with phenomenal post-war economic growth, promoted the rise of the great public education systems we have today, none of which strays much from these four streams of curricular influence. The contradictions inherent in the system are at least recognized as a sort of chaos in the current goals of higher education. The response, throughout the neo-conservative counter revolution, has been to reduce chaos by limiting the purpose and functions of education.

NEO-CONSERVATISM

The schools have already suffered mightily during this transformation of public responsibility for education, and the colleges are certain to be next, following Margaret Spellings's report from the administration's Commission on the Future of Higher Education (2006). The commission clearly reasserts the social efficiency model for higher education. The advantage of the social efficiency model for politicians is that it takes the curriculum out of the hands of the teacher and puts it in the hands of the policy maker. Standardized testing, as a control mechanism, makes it possible for policy makers to exert even more influence on the curriculum, especially as the curriculum is manifested in the teacher.

Teachers and professors do not help themselves in this battle by taking a pre-twentieth-century stance on mental discipline grounds, arguing simultaneously for the "rigor" and necessity of their disciplines (i.e., studying "hard" or abstruse subjects makes one a "better thinker"). The current anti-intellectual climate supports the notion that one can get by on common sense and a little "essential" knowledge. Even if we are too smart to buy the commonsense ideology, professors can no longer argue for their authority just based on their intellectual achievements. The anti-intellectual ideology of neo-conservatism has constructed an argument that intellectuals cannot be trusted precisely because they are experts. This logic has real-world consequences: It accounts for all the lawyers and former governors who have been appointed to college presidencies and for the fact that a non-professional like Margaret Spellings could be named to a Cabinet post in education.

Other changes have occurred in the past decade or so. We have witnessed the end of humanistic arguments in favor of total dominance of social efficiency. The mental and academic skills argument has gone to seed in favor of an "information processing" model of human thinking, influenced by cognitive science. Social meliorism has been reduced to the use of psychotropic drugs to control behavior. Humanism has become knowledge of certain "facts," a storehouse of "cultural literacy" that can be measured by "objective" testing (Hirsch 1988). Developmentalism has become standardized testing to segregate students into the haves and have-nots, and provide "consequences" for those who do not pass the tests. (*Consequences* is a favorite neo-con word, meaning "punishment," as in its expression as "rewards and consequences.") *No Child Left Behind* has also guaranteed "consequences" for teachers in schools where students do not perform well on standardized tests: The schools are closed and the teachers dispersed. Colleges are certainly in neo-conservative sights, but it is really independent professors and deviations from the standardized curriculum they are after.

In the end, though, today's circumstances are not really much different from the past. Colleges have always had to respond to outside influences despite rumors of a golden age of faculty governance that met some ideal of Plato's Academy. The problem is that while a part of an institution may change to respond to new approaches and politics, the college itself has not been changed, nor have the "new" structures totally replaced existing ones. In many cases, the new is set beside the old, and the college ends up with parallel curricula. Many fields appear to be split into mirror halves: studio art and art history, or writing/rhetoric and literary criticism, or physical and cultural anthropology. Others appear to be combined fields, such as biochemistry, that have not supplanted the originals, biology or chemistry. Some, such as linguistics, are spread all over the college: in English, anthropology, philosophy, et al. This proclivity for balancing incompatibles is probably a trait of the academic mind, but it suggests a lack of rational (and efficient) thinking to policy makers.

CULTURE AND CURRICULUM

There may be more to this chaotic situation than a struggle among competing ideologies. An alternative view to the "cultural zeitgeist" view promoted by Kliebard involves British sociologist Raymond Williams's theories concerning evolutionary change in culture (1976). Williams has argued that there is not one "culture," but that culture, historically constructed, reveals a "dominant culture" but also exposes a "residual culture" and an "emergent culture." The residual culture maintains remnants from the past, in many cases representing elite or upper class interests (opera is normally cited as an example). Emergent culture is constructed by the avant-garde and progressive elements that move a culture into its newer forms and directions. One could view the college curriculum in that frame of reference: Remnant culture represented by classics and religious studies, a dominant liberal arts and sciences culture that looks much like the Harvard General Education report of 1945, and an emergent culture exemplified by global studies and media studies, among others.

This evolutionary model is attractive because it allows for a vision of organic growth within a university tied to a model of evolutionary growth in society. Williams's educational theories are connected with his vision of expanding growth of educational opportunities promoting democracy. I personally prefer the Williams view of the social and cultural change over Kliebard's historical description, because I want to believe that curriculum is more organic and integrated into society than simply a reactionary response to social and political mores. Even so, both views remind us that there is more than one "culture" at play in any school curriculum, beyond the tendency to think in terms of an Arnoldian "high" culture versus "pop" culture.

Finally, whatever model one chooses to analyze and use to purposefully transform the curriculum, one must recognize that the current undergraduate curriculum is not unified and not "rational." To pursue an abstract discussion of "liberal arts" and "rigorous disciplinary study" is to fiddle while Rome is burning (I know, classical allusion, but really pop culture). To argue our disciplinary prerogative under the flag of faculty governance leaves us prey to outside forces that are trying desperately to make colleges "more accountable." We know that much of the accountability movement is the latest example of scientific management and social control, and hence we tend to resist any participation in the new curriculum imperatives. As a result, online degree programs and professional programs with growing enrollments (business, computers, education) are increasingly headed by non-faculty "directors" rather than deans of the faculty and taught by part-time faculty rather than tenured members of the institution.

One can see the problem in one of two ways. The emergent culture of the institution is being shaped by hired help, while the tenure-track faculty members manage the residual and dominant culture of the college curriculum. Alternatively, the increasing power of the scientific management, social-control impulse within society is reducing the scope and range of the liberal arts and sciences and replacing them with an "accountable" one, one that can be reduced to a single standardized test or manageable outcomes assessment. Schools have been beaten over the head with standardized test scores for decades, and various forms of technical and professional accreditation are now based almost solely on testing. Exit testing for colleges, to measure the "value added," is certainly the next step in the dominance of social efficiency in society.

So, what does all this mean for the future of the undergraduate curriculum? What is the role of the faculty in maintaining and transforming the curriculum? Before you say, "Wait, our program has evolved with the times through collegial discussion and growth and transformation in our discipline," remember two things: one, in the dominant culture departments, your curriculum looks much as it did during the 1950s (look at college catalogues from that time), and two, your discipline's role and value in the college is only in relationship to the growth and change in other disciplines. In other words, the new media curriculum affects the old media curriculum. An academic discipline's status (which has real-world consequences) within the institution is calculated on its "value" to the larger mission of the college.

For example, one factor in the decline in English departments over the past twenty years (reduction of faculty by half and even absorption into "humanities" departments) results from the removal of freshman English taught as a liberal arts "skill" and its transformation into a means of learning and representing knowledge taught in disciplinary contexts. The assertion of discipline-based reading and writing, called "writing in the disciplines" in an Orwellian twist, could be seen as either further regression into disciplinary ghettos or the triumph of cognitive science's concept of schema theory. In either case, the English department becomes smaller and less central to the mission of the college.

If one looks carefully at the current undergraduate enrollments in traditional liberal arts and sciences departments (i.e., dominant culture programs), one finds that a majority of those students are preparing to be teachers. In the science areas, most of the students are in pre-med or medical profession tracks. The greatest increase in undergraduate enrollment, though, has been in business and finance majors. The other new popular majors are forensic science, and communications/media studies, both "vocational" in emphasis. The role of the university as a social class marker has been transformed into a credentialing role (which may be the same thing in the end). To talk about the "liberalizing" influence of the curriculum in neo-conservative times, or even neo-liberal times, increasingly sounds like making arguments from another century.

DISCIPLINES

Disciplines are caught in a complicated conundrum. As I have suggested above, the argument for disciplinary knowledge as a special form of knowing was originally a mental discipline argument. Though the argument has been transformed by psychological and cognitive studies focusing on "ways of knowing," the current rationale for disciplinary study is a horse-and-cart affair. Most disciplines, mainly represented by existing academic departments, make the case for their needs based on the requirements of their "professional" organization. In other words, the chemistry department makes the case for new resources, and curricular requirements, on the requirements of the American Chemical Society. Why? Because they are accredited by the ACS. Departments argue that professional accreditation is necessary to their reputation, and therefore (they argue), their survival. So much for disciplinary arguments that resist the increasing emphasis on credentialing—the disciplines have adopted the paradigm.

Most of the current majors are organized around disciplines that have barely existed for 100 years. Most of the newer disciplines reflect changes in society and culture—the social sciences became possible only after we did away with the Great Chain of Being and the Divine Right of Kings and That's the Way God Planned It. One must remember that the worldview in the sciences is ideologically in opposition to the older humanistic disciplines, as famously articulated by C. P. Snow (1959/1993). These are not merely academic distinctions—these are different worldviews.

More importantly, these divisions of knowledge are constructed in relation to one another. Given that simple truth, much of the recent debate surrounding the undergraduate curriculum concerns its increasing fragmentation (cf. Boyer Commission 1995). Interdisciplinary curriculum, a favorite topic these days, cannot be accomplished by simply bringing together two or more disciplines. In many cases, what is lauded as interdisciplinary curriculum is merely cross-disciplinary study, in which the worldview of one discipline is forced onto another discipline's worldview. These transgressive studies can be fun, such as the "rats, lice, and disease" medical approach to history, or the psychoanalysis of literary characters. More often, though, cross-disciplinary study is an attempt to assert the dominance of one worldview over another. The "scientific approaches to the arts" are the most awkward. Certainly, history and philosophy of science are routinely dismissed by any number of scientists, especially if the scholars involved are not "real scientists." In each case, the perception is that one field is trying to appropriate, and in many cases re-define, the other. No wonder interdisciplinary study has such a sorry history.

It is also clear that the emergent culture in colleges and universities, as much in response to outside economic and political pressures as progressive academic thinking, is toward the interdisciplinary model. At many community colleges and small state universities, philosophy departments have long been folded into new Humanities Departments, and the wide range of social sciences is frequently collapsed into a Social Sciences Department. Of course, we are confusing institutional structures with disciplinary structures. However, because all academic governance of any importance is built around the academic department, institutional structure begins to define disciplinary structure. In fact, the more interdisciplinary an academic department, the more limited the disciplinary curriculum of each field represented.

Much of the current argument for the value of disciplines is an argument about the future of the undergraduate curriculum because the departmental structure "protects" the integrity of the discipline. Without departmental protection, disciplines tend to disappear over time. In other words, discussion of institutional structure is not outside the discussion of the curriculum—administrative units serve to determine and maintain academic structures. Much can be learned, or asserted, from an analysis of the administrative structure of a college, as we see in the General Education Project at CUNY.

EXTRA-CURRICULUM

Much of what has been cited here so far refers to the formal curriculum. The college experience, like all school life, includes extra-curricular issues and programmatic requirements, as well as formal course requirements. Recent intrusions into the dominant curriculum in colleges have focused more on the extra-curricular and programmatic (e.g., internship programs and standardized testing) than attempting to change the curriculum itself. Conversely, many of the internships and other "experiential" models are being promoted as replacements for part of the disciplinary majors. Limiting the number of total credits (120 credits) and then adding additional requirements force departments to re-think their curricular imperatives. The current tension is that many departments simply add the new requirement as a programmatic or extra-curricular requirement without taking out any of the current course requirements. Students are asked to add the additional time without the additional course credit.

In the end, one of the most difficult topics for a "liberal" curriculum is the transformation of academic skills into an extra-curricular activity. Freshman English at Harvard, the originator of the beast, has never been a departmental or tenure-track faculty responsibility. In some ways, the new emphasis on non-faculty teaching mandated curriculum outside of the regular curriculum originated in the Expository Writing program at Harvard. Among the colleges most of us inhabit, all academic skills now appear to exist outside the curriculum (ironically, in academic or basic skills *departments*), including ESL, reading and writing, and study skills. The librarians appear to be managing the new information literacy skills through college-wide programs.

The reason I say the topic is "difficult" is that the inhabitants of those academic skills courses are poor or disenfranchised students who must not only pay for those classes, but put in the time necessary to complete 120 credits after they escape the basic skills "curriculum" to which they have been assigned. To put a fine point on the matter, these students are held outside the community until they "prove" themselves and are also asked to make greater sacrifices of time (more important than money in most cases) to complete their degrees and receive their "credential."

CURRICULUM-IN-ACTION

If we take the time, and we treat the topic seriously, the final step in the curriculum mapping process involves looking at the local culture or, in some circles, the curriculum-in-action. After all the other analysis is done, one may understand the historical, the political, the institutional, the professional, the disciplinary, and even the spiritual elements in the undergraduate curriculum, but all of that still does not tell you how the curriculum is enacted. The actualization of the undergraduate curriculum can be expressed in faculty attitudes toward students or in "tracking" within the curriculum through formal or informal advising.

The more obvious examples usually attend to the notion of "insider" and "outsider" within disciplinary majors and, therefore, apply to the general education courses offered by the disciplines in the undergraduate curriculum. The way the curriculum argument is situated is normally between offering disciplinary courses aimed at the "non-major" that reflect a "subject and society" consumer perspective, and courses that purport to teach how one acts and thinks as a disciplinary "expert." The latter has been known to function as a means to recruit new majors.

In most instances, overt problems show up in interdepartmental agreements and usually focus on disciplinary rigor and professional requirements. For example, where family and consumer science (formerly, home economics) majors are required to take "real" chemistry in courses offered by the chemistry department and then are failed in large numbers because they are not scientific enough (i.e., they are outsiders). This phenomenon also happens frequently in secondary education, especially in the sciences. The evidence is usually in the language. Students in education are stigmatized for their professional choice. Professors in master's programs publicly distinguish between the "graduate students" and "the teachers" in normal discourse, even though both groups of students have exactly the same course background, the same GPAs, and are taking exactly the same graduate courses. If this situation occurs in graduate study and within academic majors, one can imagine how complicated the problem is in general education. Imagine further that part-time employees of the college who have little or no contact with the department and teach large numbers of first- and second-year students: In these cases, both students and faculty are outsiders to the curriculum.

MAPPING THE BRIAR PATCH

One final caveat here: As discussed above, much of the discussion of curriculum these days appears to come from a social efficiency point of view that is centered on scientific management rationales. Curriculum mapping is not about developing an essentialist program of study, a new definition of a limited and standardized curriculum. What curriculum mapping unfolds are the structures of curriculum, attempting to discover the rationale(s), the assumptions, and curriculum-in-action within existing structures. As serious scholars, we would never begin a study in our disciplinary field by not sorting through our prior knowledge and the knowledge base in the subject. Nevertheless, we talk about the complexities of the college curriculum as if Occam's razor is all we need to cut through the briar patch.

To pick up on the briar patch allusion, it is time to stop thinking of the faculty as Brer Rabbit, out-smarting the latest traps set by college administrators or politicians playing Brer Fox. We'll show them: Every time "they" throw a new requirement at us, we will just add it on as an extra-curricular expectation and punish the students. In that scenario, we are not outsmarting the "Man" but only confusing, and maybe cheating, our students. At the least, every faculty member in the department ought to be able to explain the logic of the major and the general education requirements to the students (we know how many cannot). At the most, we ought to figure out what we are doing that connects with the rest of the college, and with the students' lives now and in their credentialed futures. Otherwise, we are just hiding in the briar patch. Of course, we like it there mostly. As Joel Chandler Harris's Brer Rabbit gloats, "I was born and bred in the briar patch." Students and their parents, who are surveying the undergraduate curriculum from the outside, probably only see the tangle of thorns.

WORKS CITED

Applebee, Arthur. *Tradition and Reform in the Teaching of English: A History*. Urbana, IL: National Council of Teachers of English, 1974.

Arnold, Matthew. *Culture and Anarchy: An Essay in Social and Political Criticism*. Cambridge: Cambridge University Press, 1867.

Boyer Commission on Educating Undergraduates in the Research University. *Reinventing Undergraduate Education: A Blueprint for America's Research Universities*, 1995. http://naples.cc.sunysb.edu/Pres/boyer.nsf/webform/contents.

Brubacher, John, and Willis Rudy. *Higher Education in Transition: A History of American Colleges and Universities, 1636–1976*. Somerset, NJ: Transaction Publishers, 1997.

Bruner, Jerome. *The Process of Education*. Cambridge: Harvard University Press, Cambridge, MA, 1960.

Eliot, Charles W. *Report of the Committee of Ten*. National Education Association, 1893.

Hall, G. Stanley. *Adolescence: Its Psychology and Its Relations to Physiology, Anthropology, Sociology, Sex, Crime, Religion and Education*. Brighton, MA: Adamant Media Corporation, 1904.

Herbst, Jürgen. "Review of Curriculum: A History of the American Undergraduate Course of Study since 1636 by Frederick Rudolph." *History of Education Quarterly*, 18.4 4 (Winter 1978): 481–483.

Hirsch, E. D. Jr. *Cultural Literacy: What Every American Needs to Know*. Updated and Expanded ed., Vintage. New York: Random House, 1988.

Kliebard, Herbert. *The Struggle for the American Curriculum*, 1893–1958. 3rd ed. New York: Routledge, 2004.

Lucas, Christopher J. *American Higher Education: A History*. New York: St. Martin's Press, 1994.

National Commission on Excellence. *A Nation at Risk*. Washington, D.C.: U.S. Department of Education, 1983.

National Defense Education Act of 1958. Public Law 85–864. Vol. 72. United States Statutes at Large, pp. 1580–1605. Washington, DC: US Government Printing Office, 1959.

No Child Left Behind Act of 2001. Public Law 107–110. Vol. 115. United States Statutes at Large, pp. 1425–2094. Washington, DC: US Government Printing Office, 2002.

Perry, William. *Forms of Ethical and Intellectual Development in the College Years: A Scheme*, 1968. San Francisco: Jossey-Bass, 1999.

Ravitch, Diane, and Chester E. Finn, Jr. *What Do Our 17-Year-Olds Know? A Report on the First National Assessment of History and Literature*. New York: Harper & Row/Perennial Library, 1988.

Readings, Bill. *The University in Ruins*. Cambridge: Harvard University Press, 1996.

Ross, Edward Alsworth. *Social Control: A Survey of the Foundations of Order*, 1901. University Press of the Pacific, 2002.

Rudolph, Frederick. *The American College and University: A History*, 1962. Athens: University Press of Georgia, 1990.

Snow, C. P. *The Two Cultures*, 1959. Cambridge: Cambridge University Press, 1993.

Spellings, Margaret. *A National Dialogue: The Secretary of Education's Commission on the Future of Higher Education*. US Department of Education, 2006. http://www.ed.gov/about/bdscomm/list/hiedfuture/ reports.html.

Tussman, Joseph. *The Beleaguered College: Essays on Educational Reform*. Berkeley, CA: University of California, Institute of Governmental Studies Press, 1977.

Williams, Raymond. *Marxism and Literature*. New ed. New York: Oxford University Press, 1978.

Part III. Curriculum Renewal and Institutional Change

CHAPTER THREE

General Education vs. Education Generally

Curriculum Renewal in an Urban College

ROBERT WHITTAKER

Lehman College

Par ma foi! il y a plus de quarante ans que je dis de la prose sans que j'en susse rien,et je vous suis le plus obligé du monde de m'avoir appris cela.[1]

—MOLIÈRE, *LE BOURGEOIS GENTILHOMME*, III, IV

This is an account of educational evolution and change in the area of General Education and college education generally. The setting is the Bronx, and the institution is Lehman College of the City University of New York. Undergraduate liberal arts education is Lehman College's mission. As CUNY's only senior college on the mainland and the only public four-year higher education institution in the Bronx, the College serves students who are most often the first in their families to continue education beyond high school. With seven thousand undergraduates—90% of whom are ethnic minorities—the College faces both a challenge and an opportunity to effect individual and social change.

How to provide an effective liberal education to students whose background has often not included high-quality schooling? This question dominates faculty concerns at Lehman. In 1997, in the course of a normal process of renewal, the college reformulated its answer to this question by designing a new curriculum for the baccalaureate. This evolution in the requirements for graduation, worked out by the Undergraduate Curriculum Committee, weathered political conflicts, mostly over curricular "turf," but it finally passed the College Senate in 2002.

DISCIPLINE IS DESTINY

This new curriculum of 2002 represents the third stage in an evolutionary process extending over the nearly 40 years of Lehman College's existence as an independent CUNY unit. The College Senate provides the forum for the "curriculum wars," where departments struggle to maintain their strength, which often depends on enrollment. Moreover, in the perception of faculty, enrollment is affected by how many courses the department "owns" in the required curriculum. What you teach determines how you survive, and a discipline well represented among graduation requirements has a decided advantage (is there curricular Darwinism?). Perhaps this scenario explains the great power of the English Department on so many campuses, or of the History Department, where student historians or English majors rank well below the number of student sociologists or psychologists?

True, there are other factors, not the least of which are demographic. Curriculum, department, and discipline strength depend on the nature of the students, their preparation and aspirations. The Bronx and Lehman College provide some instructive examples. Back in the late 1960s, when CUNY was reshaping its institutional identity in the Bronx, the University's colleges were perceived in starkly ethnic terms. Bronx Community College was African American, Lehman—the Bronx-based offspring of Manhattan's Hunter College—was White, and Hostos was to become the Bilingual Community College, which is to say Hispanic American. My own experience is instructive: I came to Lehman in 1971 to head the Russian division of the Germanic and Slavic Languages Department. We had a flourishing division teaching Russian language and literature to first- and second-generation students of East European origin. These were recent immigrant families who represented post-WW II displaced populations and refugees from Soviet satellite states.[2] Indeed, when the Bronx campus of Hunter College became independent in 1968, it received the name of a great humanitarian, Herbert Lehman, who was not only a famous administrator of UN European relief, but also New York's only Jewish governor. Responding to the changing nature of our students and their interests, my department merged into the Classical, Oriental, Germanic, and Slavic Languages Department, joining another small language department in the late 1970s to become COGS. This department lasted a generation, before joining with Romance languages to become the Languages and Literature Department, in which Spanish dominates. If only Russian or German had been required of all students for graduation . . . .

The ethnic make-up of our students had changed radically over 35 years. They have always been largely from immigrant families, but they no longer came from Europe, but rather predominantly from the Americas. What was once a largely "white" population has now become overwhelmingly "minority." This new ethnic alignment brought a cultural shift with significant implications for the college curriculum. For example, the popularity of Spanish courses increased, as did the relative size of pre-professional and professional programs. If the ideals and goals of a liberal education were accepted generally by the students of the 1970s, they are not today: Our students have little understanding of the significance and value of the liberal arts and the importance of a general education.

Such a radical shift in the student ethnic make-up and cultural background demanded curriculum change, which faculty members often see as a struggle for survival. Nightmares of drastic departmental cuts are the curse (if not the cause) of the curriculum wars. Becoming a "required" discipline seems a way to counterbalance negative changes brought by shifting demographics and—the most pervasive, if not perverse force shaping CUNY educational policy—budgetary exigencies. Survival of the fittest discipline is the law of the curriculum.

Departmental and discipline interests permeated the first great curriculum change at Lehman in the early 1980s, when the college moved from requirements inherited from Hunter to a Core Curriculum. This 1984 structure resulted from broad departmental and faculty participation in the implementation and management of a three-tiered curriculum: Basic Skills included written and oral English, foreign language and physical fitness; five Core Courses were created in the humanities, history, social sciences, natural sciences, and quantitative reasoning; and seven Distribution Areas, which represented introductory coursework in departments and the first courses in a major. Departments kept their "required" courses, and to these were added multi-disciplinary Core Courses taught by faculty from several departments, which aimed at preparing students for the required Distribution Area courses. This was the era of much remediation, and the faculty hoped that basic Core Courses would provide a firm, common foundation for subsequent study in the disciplines of the Distribution. To be sure, faculty in departments and the Senate worked to ensure their discipline's robust representation on the Distribution Area list.

Over time, though, discipline demands and distinctive departmental traits contributed to the demise of the Core Curriculum. Departments with "softer" methodologies in their disciplines easily cooperated in joint Core courses. Thus, the Humanities Core thrived, but the Science Core failed dramatically. The sciences could not overcome the heavy investment in their disciplines and were unable to create a "basic" common Core, especially the "bench" sciences. Soon the Science Core requirement was replaced by a requirement of two lab sciences. In stark contrast, the Humanities Core course thrived, taught by faculty from English, Languages, Philosophy, Art, Music, History, and Political Science. Disciplinary purity rarely was an issue, and indeed the course still survives, reincarnated in 2002 as LEH300: The Humanities.

CORING THE CURRICULUM

The Sciences Core course disappeared, more and more exemptions were issued to allow substitutions for Core Social Sciences as well, and ultimately the Core Curriculum was reduced to the Humanities Core and Historical Studies Core courses. Not only did the Core need fixing, but continuing changes in our students and new educational emphases contributed to "coring" our curriculum. The College was becoming increasingly aware of its large number of transfer students and the difficulty of providing them with the liberal education promised by our mission statement. When a student transfers to Lehman with all requirements met except the major, how much of their liberal arts degree is a Lehman degree? In addition, not only the College, but the entire University had begun to focus on students' writing abilities. In 1999 the Board of Trustees mandated that colleges create Writing Across the Curriculum programs. This awareness prompted the faculty to consider writing requirements as part of a new curriculum.

The process of creating a new curriculum emerged as a faculty initiative, if not prerogative, and was conducted by faculty in the Undergraduate Curriculum Committee of the College Senate. This may not be particularly remarkable, but it is worth noting in accounting for the type of conflicts and their resolutions. The academic administration has a presence, and a significant role, but this was not an administration initiative of Provost and Deans (unlike the 1984 Core Curriculum). For this reason the curriculum conflicts were not of the usual, vertical, management-employee type that characterize a unionized faculty and staff. Rather, the struggle over dividing the "turf" was horizontal, among departments and faculty intent on serving our students while also preserving discipline "strength."

The "new" 2002 curriculum emerged as a result of an evolutionary, rather than a revolutionary process. There was no wholesale replacement of the old requirements, no bloody, violent academic revolution. Rather, a process of careful trading and calculation took place as the old Core Courses were redesigned or removed and new pieces created to replace what no longer worked. The natural sciences retained their disciplinary integrity: Two lab sciences now joined the existing requirements in math, foreign language, and English composition. (The speech and physical fitness requirements did not survive.) The Distribution Areas compensated for departments' perceived losses and were extended (largely in the social sciences) and somewhat resorted. Finally, the two most successful of the basic Core courses—the Humanities Core and Historical Studies Core courses—were preserved: Here departments and disciplines enjoyed symbioses that profited both students and faculty. The basic, multi-disciplinary introductory courses metamorphosed into upper-division, cross-disciplinary, variable topic capstone courses and were given a new extra-disciplinary designation: LEH. The code may represent LEHman, but more significantly, it suggests that no department or discipline "owns" the courses. (True, like most course-work in the liberal arts, the humanities tend to dominate here for better or for worse.) Two new curricular "species" evolved: LEH300—The Humanities, and LEH301—The American Experience, both cross-disciplinary courses (to include at least three disciplines), open only to juniors and seniors, and consisting of multiple sections on different topics designed by the individual faculty who teach them. The "American Experience" was a serendipitous curricular response to a call by one University trustee in particular who demanded that all CUNY students be required to take U.S. history before they graduate (Arenson 2000, B1). (However, in our course, much depends on the definition of "American" in the title.) These "capstones" serve two purposes. First, they provide a culminating experience for students who have completed much, if not all of their coursework outside their majors. Ideally this 300-level course allows students to bring together what has been learned in a variety of disciplines into a coherent, meaningful whole. Second, the courses offer transfer students the same opportunity as "native" Lehman students who have benefited from the considerable number of liberal arts courses required in the lower division. The result would be a consolidating experience of liberal education shared by all Lehman students, thus helping the College fulfill its stated mission. (However, in one of the more striking legacies of earlier CUNY eras, some students transferring to Lehman from the University's community colleges see these LEH courses as "remedial," which might suggest their suspicion that their previous study in the liberal arts is considered inadequate.)

Not that the capstone courses entirely avoided any departmental or disciplinary conflict—on the contrary. One of the unexpected consequences of evolution was that faculty in the natural sciences, if not the social sciences, could not offer cross-disciplinary courses in their field in a course entitled "The Humanities." Rather, only topics that reflected "the American Experience" could include the sciences, and so a course titled "From the Double Helix to Stem Cells: The Science and Politics of Molecular Biology" could only appear as LEH301. (It could not have been included in the LEH300 series because its disciplines were natural and social science, and yet the course would normally have applications beyond just the American experience.) The participation of the sciences in the capstone courses is an obviously desirable end, however difficult to achieve. The Curriculum Committee proposed that LEH300 be changed to "Studies in the Humanities and the Sciences," and the Senate passed the recommendation, but not without considerable floor debate. Several members of the faculty argued energetically that allowing science disciplines into the course would severely dilute the teaching of humanities at the College, an area which seemed to them already under heavy "attack." This argument is, on one level, an attempt to defend certain disciplines against growing student interest in majors leading directly to careers.

In a shrewd curricular tactic that avoids inter-disciplinary strife, the Curriculum Committee proposed that students be required to take four "Writing Intensive" sections in order to graduate. Three sections must be completed before the junior year, and transfer students must take less than four, depending on what coursework they bring with them. These sections were not new courses, and therefore the requirement would not affect the balance of departmental benefits in the "new" curriculum. Rather, sections of an existing course would be taught as "Writing Intensive." (Creating a sufficient number of sections and assuring a consistent "intensiveness" is a separate problem.) The departments and faculty agreed without demur that this requirement was necessary and beneficial, and it has come into being without controversy. The requirement did produce an unexpected result: Rather than avoiding Writing Intensive sections like the plague, students generally register for them sooner and in greater number than for "regular" sections. Perhaps this dynamic occurs because they are often smaller (enrollment is capped at 22 to 25), or because the faculty members are more "intensely" attentive to the students and their work, or maybe the students are eager to meet graduate requirements, however distasteful. The new curriculum, thus designed and certified, went into effect in the fall of 2002.

"NEW" CURRICULUM FOR "OLD"

Aladdin's new lamp lacked the magic of the old. The curricular shift from "old" to "new" incurred similar liabilities. The old magic was replaced by new processes of cause and effect, thereby forcing unanticipated changes. However evolutionary and gradual, the "new" curriculum nonetheless demanded some radical changes and significant adjustments. For example, without basic Core courses, the nature of the first freshman semester suddenly changed. What had been multi-disciplinary introductory courses to curricular areas now became specific departmental courses. Several departments gained a major stake in the freshman program, comparable to what English has enjoyed for years. The Freshman Year Initiative, Lehman's award-winning program that schedules incoming students into blocks of learning communities, now has become a major curricular player affecting departmental enrollments, departmental faculty teaching schedules, and even hiring adjunct instructors. This reality raises a question that earlier had attracted little attention: Who guides curriculum selection for the nearly one thousand incoming freshmen, and how are deans, departments, and faculty members involved in programming decisions? Is the loose structure of the English Composition program, which is home to FYI, sufficient to guide this major curricular force? Highly successful in increasing retention, which has been its focus over several years, FYI now finds itself faced with disciplinary and departmental considerations. Should our students take math in their first semester, when should they begin science, and how will this affect retention? These questions may not result directly from the disappearance of the Core Curriculum, but they are sharpened by the appearance of departmental courses earlier in our students' programs.

The new requirement that our students must take LEH300 and LEH301 after reaching 60 credits (i.e., as new juniors) meant that in the fall 2002 semester, these courses were filled exclusively with transfer students. (Students matriculated before fall 2002 were not subject to the new curriculum; new transfer students were the only ones who had the 60 credits to qualify.) The faculty members teaching these sections— ten in all—were not prepared to be teaching only transfers. We had never seen so many transfer students in one place, and after recovering from the shock we began to sense the significance of this large, anomalous, poorly defined, heterogeneous population for the College and its curriculum. The fact that over two-thirds of Lehman's graduating seniors were transfer students took on new significance for both curriculum requirements and classroom practices. Two different factors converged into a cross-disciplinary crisis: What is a multi-disciplinary, upper division course, and how well are transfer students prepared for this work? The faculty teaching LEH300 and LEH301 only knew about teaching upper level major courses from teaching their major students already grounded in the discipline's methodology. What adjustments should be made, if any, when teaching upper-division students who are not majors in a course that has no clear place in a sequence of discipline-specific courses? All the students in these first sections of LEH300 and LEH301 had received their basic skills training and their introductions to various disciplines at other institutions, many of them community colleges, each of which has different curricular requirements. The instructors, faced with students who seemed underprepared, who wrote poorly or lacked reading skills, often assumed that this reality reflected poor preparation outside Lehman. A crisis of faculty burnout from frustration and a lack of confidence in transfer students' abilities suddenly loomed after the first year.

Finally, the new curriculum required some magic of its own: creating writing intensive sections. The Curriculum Committee established general guidelines, but these do not create courses.[3] The trick has been bringing the Writing Across the Curriculum (WAC) Program, which produces faculty Writing Specialists trained in the integration of increased writing into the learning process, together with the curricular process of designing sections and assigning faculty, which is a departmental prerogative. There is no curricular common ground between WAC and departments, save for the faculty who have participated in the program and its workshops. Any forced alliance (which exists on other campuses) would undermine departmental confidence in the new curriculum. The process of merging the extraordinarily successful faculty development techniques of WAC with the need for Writing Intensive sections has been undertaken slowly and carefully, owing to a WAC faculty advisory committee. One consequence has been the addition of a curricular dimension to WAC, as well as a faculty development dimension to the activities of the Curriculum Committee.

In short, the earliest stages of the new curriculum, however similar it may have been to the old, involved a number of significant adjustments.

WHAT GENERAL EDUCATION?

Late in the fall of 2002, as Lehman struggled with the first semester of its "new" curriculum, the University undertook a project to strengthen general education throughout CUNY. We were invited to participate in the General Education Forum in an initial group of six colleges. The idea of general education was not new, but it was not in what we at Lehman were involved. In other words, this was not the focus or the concept of our curricular developments. The "new" curriculum had focused on liberal education generally, not on general education as a curricular structure. Despite its familiarity, we were not altogether certain what the term meant. Sure, like good University citizens we would cooperate, but what is this general education? We were assured that the conversation would be about liberal arts, general education, principles of curriculum design. Given the immediate practical concerns of making a new curriculum work, this University-wide undertaking seemed theoretical, abstract, and liable to take much time without practicable results.

Beginning with the first semester of the Gen Ed Forum, in the spring of 2003, and continuing well into the second year, 2003–2004, a group of faculty and administrators from various CUNY campuses wrestled mightily with matters that seemed intangible, incoherent, impossible. What is general education, what is liberal education, what are the liberal arts? What should they be for an urban university? What should they be for CUNY? Surveys and analyses confirmed our chaotic state: Each college had its own conceptions, definitions, requirements, solutions. Furthermore, the colleges were at various stages of curriculum implementation and renewal. The four-year colleges saw general and liberal education in terms of individual courses; the two-year colleges defined it in terms of skills and competencies. Attempting to arrive at a consensus, we resorted to personal testimony: Some described the course structures and histories of curricular change, others liberal arts courses—the most astounding of which involved a sword and the slaughter of a pig as part of a classical culture simulation. At last we realized that the questions were important, if intractable. Thoughtful, responsible academics were devoting time and energy to examining what were tacitly agreed to be topics central to undergraduate education. The lack of consensus, let alone clarity, remained unsettling.

The process itself was transformative, however chaotic the results. We at Lehman discovered that what we had been doing—evolving new curriculums to replace the old—had been General Education all along. The efforts of the Senate and its Curriculum Committee began to acquire new definition beyond just a set of required courses. Like Monsieur Jourdain, we discovered that we have been doing Gen Ed for forty years without knowing it. Like him, we were pleasantly impressed. This naming, like a christening, brought new significance to ongoing efforts. With the new attention comes new awareness, including a better definition of what our general education program is. This realization, in turn, gave a sense of shared responsibilities with sister colleges, community and senior, in the University, as well as a connectedness with national projects.

WHAT IS GENERAL EDUCATION?

General education seems clearest as a curricular concept. It is like negative space in a painting: the space between objects or their parts or around them. General education is the coursework that is not part of a major or minor concentration, i.e., it represents the courses taken alongside the major and minor. As Judith Summerfield observes,

> Paradoxically, the largest common enterprise, shared by the entire university, is General Education, that set of courses, requirements, and activities that falls outside the major. Even so, general education slips between the cracks of both the administrative and the academic realm: "It" remains elusive as a project, is characteristically overseen by no one, and exists nowhere. It is not a department or a program. It does not have an office. It is an amalgam of the liberal arts and science departments, yet is neither owned nor governed by anyone. (Summerfield, this volume)

Practically, in terms of curriculum building, the opposite of general education is departmental education. General education survives in the curricular space granted by academic departments.

General education is perhaps confusing not only because it is a negative space, but also because it is inherently ambiguous. Do you recall the drawings of two portraits or silhouettes left and right, looking at each other? Look again and the portraits recede: you see them as sides of a vase. These drawings are studies in ambiguity.

The vase is general education. The portraits are the major and the minor; or perhaps, a dual major. The irony is that, with most majors at Lehman, the profiles of the major and the minor are finely drawn, but the vase occupies by far the greatest curricular space in the picture. A 40-credit major leaves 80 credits of "general" curricular coursework. Surely such a large portion of a student's liberal education deserves a clear, well defined structure with goals and outcomes no less explicit than those of the major and minor.

This ambiguous quality is shared by descriptions of the liberal arts and liberal education. "Liberal" means free, but are the liberal arts those studies reserved for the free, i.e., the elite and leisured who have no need for pragmatic and applied knowledge? Alternatively, are the liberal arts the means to make one free and the path of escape from mental slavery and material-obsessed oppression (see the discussion in Nussbaum 1997, 293)? As in a true ambiguity, both answers are correct. Liberal education is both knowledge for its own sake, free of necessary practical application, and the means to liberate the student. It evokes both the equivalency between truth and beauty embraced by Keats and the biblical conviction that the truth will "make you free" (John 8:32).

The question, then, should not be "what is general education?" but rather "what should general education achieve and how?" Clearly the main responsibility for achieving a liberal education rests with the vase, although the picture cannot exist without the portraits as well. Liberal arts encompass the major and minor concentrations, as departmental creatures, as well as the general, non-departmental curriculum.

The effect of joining CUNY's General Education Forum for us at Lehman, at least, has been to invert the "negative space" of the non-major and non-minor into a positive part of the liberal curriculum. This effect has been bolstered by the University's increasing emphasis on undergraduate education in general and on General Education in particular. For its part, the College has concentrated its efforts in three areas: understanding the transfer student, expanding non-departmental LEH courses, and developing faculty awareness of the structure of our general education program.

LEHMAN'S TRANSFER STUDENTS

The upper-division Gen Ed cross-disciplinary courses have provided a new focus for teaching our transfer students. As noted above, LEH300 and LEH301 concentrated our transfers in one curricular place, and many of them continue to take one of these courses in their first semester at Lehman. Despite the difficulties associated with teaching them, LEH300 and LEH301 have succeeded as a major facet of our Gen Ed curriculum. We have a cadre of faculty who regularly offer different sections on a remarkable variety of topics.[4] From an initial offering of ten sections, we have developed into a program offering over 60 sections with almost 1,700 student places. (In fact, section enrollment is high, consistently above 95% of capacity.) We have more faculty interested in teaching LEH300 and LEH301 than we can accommodate, and more students wishing to enroll than we can satisfy. There is little to suggest that teaching or taking these required courses is onerous.

Despite this success, however, the same critical questions remain as described above: What levels of reading and writing can instructors expect from our students in an upper-division general education course, and how adequate is the preparation of our transfer students? What can we tell the instructors about the students they will teach in LEH300 and LEH301?

We needed answers to basic questions: What reading and writing have our students done in courses during the last year, what types of library and Internet research have they done, how many semesters have they been at Lehman, and how did they do in previous Gen Ed courses? In the fall of 2003 we began surveying our LEH300/ LEH301 students to learn what type of reading, writing, and research they had done in previous courses. In contrast to the faculty view, students saw their own preparation as more than adequate. For example, in the fall 2005 semester, 95% of our students said they had written research papers using sources in at least one course during the previous year, and 85% said they had done so in two or more courses. Furthermore, 83% said they had read scholarly articles or primary sources. Among these students, 94% had used library resources for previous course work (two-thirds had retrieved books, journal articles, or used reserves, and half had read newspapers or used reference services); 95% had used Internet indices—electronic references, full-text databases, news services—and search engines. In short, our students' perception of their own preparation does not coincide with the faculty's impression. One means to help interpret this dichotomy would be information on past student performance, but the College has been unable to provide us with the data we need to analyze student academic records. One of the great disappointments in trying to gather useful information about our students is the inability of the College and the University to convert their enormous reserves of student academic data into a resource for improving the curriculum. Institutional Research does not seem able to tell us much about the specific course performance and academic background of our students. Our requests for information about cohorts of students taking various courses in our Gen Ed program, for information on preparation and subsequent coursework performance, indeed for information on the numbers of students at various levels who have not taken Gen Ed courses—none of these requests for data has been granted. Faced with institutional inability to provide data, we have decided to apply for research grant funds to study our students' success in a few targeted courses, and in this we have met with some funding success from CUNY. This research is now under way.

How to measure transfer student performance as compared with that of "native" Lehman students has been difficult without this information. We have done some analysis of current semester grades: An early analysis suggested that students who had been at Lehman for a semester or more received significantly better grades in LEH300 and LEH301 than students for whom this was their first semester: 9% more As, about the same percentage of Bs, and fewer Cs and below, including withdrawals. However, this lower performance may be typical of new transfer student performance throughout Lehman. In addition to questions of academic preparation, there are the larger matters of how we help these students transfer in the broader sense of learning about Lehman and its policies, procedures, and expectations.

We have tried a number of ways to assist the transfer student by easing the adjustment to a new academic environment with its different, if not more demanding expectations. An experimental program to "block" LEH300 and LEH301 sections with another course to create "Transfer Learning Communities" failed because our students were too diverse in their scheduling needs. More successful, it seems, is a pilot program to integrate Academic Support Services more closely with LEH300-LEH301 sections and instructors. The faculty members frequently are neither fully aware of the College's writing and tutorial services nor do these services work as closely as they could with classroom instructors. We have begun linking sections and writing tutors, even encouraging the instructors to make tutoring a required aspect of a course for some students.

The LEH300/LEH301 courses made faculty aware of how little we know of our transfer students and the colleges they come from, even (and especially) of our principal feeder schools in the Bronx. Few of us have been to the other CUNY two-year campuses, let alone have any acquaintance with colleagues in these colleges. The need to learn about the campuses and colleagues who "produce" our transfer students—who begin the educational process that we take over and continue—prompted us to begin a program to bring faculty of two-year and four-year campuses together and encourage sharing classroom experiences. The "Bridging the Colleges" (BTC) faculty seminar opened in the fall of 2005 with the help of a grant from the CUNY Office of Undergraduate Education. Twelve faculty members—four each from the three Bronx CUNY colleges: Bronx Community, Hostos, and Lehman—are meeting monthly to discuss common perceptions and experiences and to visit one another's classrooms. The expectation is that the BTC faculty seminars will eventually improve classroom teaching and curricular offerings on all the campuses. The ultimate goal is to assist our students in making a smooth, consistent transfer across the bridge from a two-year to a four-year institution.

THE LEH100 EXPERIMENT

Lehman's de-cored curriculum left our entering freshmen with little formal intro-duction to college life and higher education. The Core courses had performed some-thing of an introductory function in the FYI blocks, but they were now replaced by introductory discipline courses meeting Distribution Area requirements. The blocks have non-credit FYI seminars to assist students in program creation and learning about student services, but these have little academic substance. Our "discovery" of General Education and awareness of its goals and objectives led us to create a three-credit course for our entering freshmen, which would examine the nature of the liberal arts, explain the philosophy behind the General Education requirements, and introduce a number of controversial questions about higher education in general. We established this experimental course, LEH100, as a cross-disciplinary, even non-disciplinary intro-duction to a liberal arts education, to the nature and goals of the education our students are embarking upon, and to the reasoning behind the courses and programs required for graduation. The course would provide a framework for program-planning decisions and for understanding the activities and services offered by the College. Furthermore, LEH100 begins the development of information literacy by introducing the student to the resources of the library, the Internet, Blackboard (our course management sys-tem), college email and their application in an academic context. Awareness of criti-cal thinking, the use of sources and academic integrity, time management and exam preparation skills—these are among the aspects of "academic literacy" which the course brings to our entering freshmen.

Perhaps the most striking aspect of LEH100 is that it introduces students to the unwritten "contract" they entered when they matriculated. If they fulfill the contract, they will get a degree. The details of this contract are laid out in the College bulletin—all the rules and regulations and requirements for graduation. The College's side of this contract is less specifically described. The responsibility of the College to offer neces-sary courses in sufficient quantity in a timely way to allow our students to progress at maximum speed is not made clear, and the obligations of the faculty to our students are not always evident—not only to students, but even to the faculty themselves. Furthermore, this contract is often hidden, in the sense that it is rarely openly discussed.

Not surprisingly, there has been considerable resistance to such a course among faculty, judging from initial reactions of Senators. Why give three credits just to learn how to be a college student? A course that originates not within a discipline or a department, but which grants academic credit and is a requirement can draw heavy fire from faculty traditionalists and defenders of departmental prerogatives. Indeed, it is not certain that this experiment will survive to become a required Gen Ed course.

A final note: Perhaps our transfer students also would benefit from a course like this—from an LEH200 to treat questions of transition and the continuing commitment to the ideals and goals of a liberal arts education. This makes good sense, given that we live in a nation of transfer students, where transferring has become a normal part of the college experience.

FACULTY DEVELOPMENT

The matter of what to teach and how to teach it has always been a department prerogative: when courses should be taught, what the syllabus should be, how the subject matter should be presented, and in what sequence. Rarely has the conversation gone on outside departmental walls. There have been notable exceptions: the Core courses at Lehman were designed and managed by groups of faculty in the humanities, social sciences, and natural sciences. In addition, the Writing Across the Curriculum program (which began just about the time the Core Curriculum was ending) brought together faculty from various disciplines to develop teaching methods that used writing as a learning tool. Apart from these efforts, attention to undergraduate education remained within the departments. An unexpected benefit of "discovering" General Education has been to "liberate" this discussion from the confines of the department. This discussion revolves around how best to teach the Gen Ed courses, what objectives to share, and what outcomes to evaluate across the spectrum of the required curriculum.

Lehman's students are required to select courses from the College's seven Distribution Areas—eight including the natural sciences area—from mathematics, foreign language, and finally from sections of the LEH300/LEH301 courses. The tacit principle behind requiring General Education courses is that there are skills and perspectives that each of the areas, English, foreign languages, math, and LEH300/LEH301 develop, no matter which courses or sections the student chooses. However, the instructors teaching these courses had never discussed these skills or perspectives, objectives, or outcomes among themselves: Instructors of Fundamentals of Sociology did not meet with those of General Psychology, instructors of the American Political System did not meet with those of Fundamentals of Economics, and so forth. Altogether, there were over some hundred courses from which students are required to choose for their Gen Ed distribution. Perhaps (I would hope) discussions of shared objectives and outcomes take place within departments, but there had been little organized opportunity for discussing teaching across departments.

In the spring term of the second year of Lehman's new Gen Ed curriculum, 2003–2004, the Curriculum Committee invited instructors of the Gen Ed courses to meet together in workshops devoted to each of the areas. Some 80 faculty members— quite a large turn-out for a new undertaking—gathered to discuss the common principles, practices, expectations, and outcomes of their Gen Ed courses. This was more than just a syllabus swap meet. The instructors were charged "to refine both the objectives of the General Education program and the mechanisms to ensure that these objectives are integrated into specific courses." In order to achieve this goal, each area was asked to "(1) define the over-all learning objectives of the distribution area; (2) describe the mechanism that will be used to ensure that these objectives are integrated into specific courses; (3) discuss how to communicate objectives and mechanisms to students and faculty; and (4) discuss assessment of learner outcomes/ course objectives" (Lehman College Undergraduate Curriculum Committee 2004). The areas have met regularly since February 2004, and for each the College has appointed a liaison to organize the various groups' activities.[5] Most areas have completed the first three tasks, and the focus now is on the final question of assessment. The challenge of communication and sharing materials and ideas on a regular basis has been met by creating organizational sites within Blackboard for each of the areas. These sites contain the proceedings of each group, a listing of courses and instructors for each area, syllabi for the course offerings, and discussion of the tasks at hand.

Faculty development continues beyond the matrix of Distribution Area courses. The new Gen Ed curriculum requires Writing Intensive sections, but finding faculty to teach the Writing Intensive sections has been a challenge. The courses exist, but the methodology in teaching Writing Intensive sections needs to be developed. The WAC faculty development program has proven invaluable in providing suggestions, examples, even materials to assist the first instructors of these WI sections. While many of the faculty teaching Writing Intensive sections are not Writing Specialists (faculty who have completed the year-long WAC development program), they benefit from an array of workshops, best practices roundtables, and other support services. The WAC program has raised faculty development to a fine art: No other program on campus has done more to enhance the level of undergraduate instruction and course design across departments and divisions. This year the General Education workshops have evolved from the distribution-area structure to join with WAC in offering workshops devoted to topics related to the skills and perspectives of all Gen Ed courses. A December workshop included such topics as "How to Use Instructional Support (Writing Center) in the Distribution Areas," "The CPE (CUNY Proficiency Exam) and the Distribution Areas," "What Does 'Interdisciplinarity' Mean?" and "Making FYI Blocks Collaborative" to name a few. Once we had identified common skills, competencies, and perspectives in the General Education program, the next logical step was to help faculty strengthen teaching in these areas.

GEN ED BECOMES EDUCATION GENERALLY

Lehman's Gen Ed program has as its focus shared goals, methods, objectives, and outcomes across departments throughout the College's undergraduate course offerings.

Defining the vase in the ambiguous image noted above and developing an awareness of the quality of this vase sharpens the definition and affects the quality of the two profiles as well. One student's vase is another student's profile, at least in the introductory and intermediate levels. We have found that the "discovery" of our General Education curriculum is part of a process of self-discovery. The process is one of reinventing ourselves: learning to do better what we have been doing all along. The added value is an increased awareness of what we are doing and why we are doing it. This process of meta-cognition helps us share with our students an awareness of the significance of what their general education can mean. Nothing is more important in preserving and strengthening liberal education against the exclusive and limiting demands of vocationalism and careerism.

Our students come outfitted with extraordinary pressures to achieve socio-economic success. College for them and for their parents and relatives usually means a career and social advancement. Teaching the values of the liberal arts to such students is a difficult task, even at times futile. Lehman's students, like so many undergraduates today, arrive focused on professions and careers, and they think in terms of majors as practical preparation for specific jobs. Their awareness of the relationship of a major to future careers is severely limited, as one might expect of students who are the first in their family, even among family acquaintances, to enter college. The goals of a liberal education—the skills and abilities as well as the perspectives and general knowledge, acquired expressly without limitation by career or profession—seem to be pointless and a waste of time to our job-oriented students. Even so, they have remarkable drive and persistence, and they manage to succeed academically in the face of extremely difficult circumstances. The purpose, if not the promise, of a liberal education is to help our students rise above their material and social limitations. It is no small task to lead our students to experience the dimensions and the depth of a liberal education, thereby allowing them to reach the intellectual, personal freedom that is theirs to achieve. However difficult, we owe it to our students to "free" them.

The process of self-discovery is a feature I have personally experienced in working on these curriculum matters at Lehman. I came to realize that I owe my own professional career to the ideals of General Education—or what we called "well- roundedness" in the 1950s when I entered college. I had decided on a career in dentistry—my father was a dentist—and chose my freshman courses from the pre-medical sequence. I had fulfilled the foreign language requirement with high school Latin, but still I felt a "well-rounded" educated person should know a modern foreign language. I asked my freshman advisor whether French or German would be better for a dentist to know. He responded that Russian would be a good choice (Tufts had begun offering the language in response to Sputnik and needed recruits). I enjoyed the language and the instructor, and I continued with it even as I stumbled badly on the rocky road that led from organic chem to cat lab. Soon I abandoned pre-dentistry (delayed adolescent revolt?) and began looking for a new major. At some point I realized that I could make a living teaching and speaking Russian and reading fabulous works of literature. This discovery put me on a path that brought me, ultimately, to Lehman College in the Bronx. In a similar way, the success of our Gen Ed curriculum can be measured by the extent to which each of our students experiences a form of self-discovery like my own. This is perhaps relatively easy with Lehman's freshmen, who come with little awareness of just how many doors can be opened before them—how many different careers and destinies there are in their general areas of interest. We succeed in liberally educating our students when they leave the College on intellectual and academic paths they were unaware of when they entered Lehman.

In a no less startling self-discovery, not long ago I realized that I, too, had been a transfer student. The Russian language offerings at Tufts College petered out by the time I was a junior. In order to continue my new life, I transferred to Indiana University, which had an energetic Slavic program with lots of new federal money for student fellowships and travel programs. I do not remember many details of the transfer experience, except that the process cost me a number of credits and much difficulty in adapting to a very different educational environment. I was pretty much on my own in that there was little support, but in the 1960s colleges had relatively few transfer students to worry about. Today at Lehman, as at many colleges, transfers represent the majority of our students. We manage to bring them some targeted liberal arts coursework in addition to major and minor concentrations—by requiring writing intensive sections and LEH300 and LEH301. We should perhaps do a better job, however, of developing their awareness of the ideals of a liberal education, especially because our transfer students often arrive with very specific program and degree goals. As a rule, they have chosen Lehman specifically for a major or pre-professional training, and they lack a sense of the power and value of liberal arts study. The General Education curriculum needs to serve our transfer students' needs no less than those of our freshmen.

As with the individual student, so for an entire program: A powerful impetus for self-improvement is the hope to achieve important change. Self-improvement can be simply reinventing oneself. Lehman's new General Education curriculum is an improvement, achieved through a reinvention of its liberal arts program. Gen Ed may not attract the attention the major concentrations enjoy from faculty and especially from students. However, it is the heart of the College's liberal education and the general transformation that we promise our students.

NOTES

1.   "My God! I've been speaking prose for over forty years and without knowing it. I'm so very grateful to you for having told me about this."

2. For an analysis of demographic changes in the Bronx, see William Bosworth's "Detailed Analysis of Bronx Racial and Ethnic Changes," The Bronx Data Center, Lehman College, http://www. lehman.edu/deannss/bronxdatactr/discover/bxtime.htm.
3. For the definition of a Writing Intensive section, see http://www.lehman.edu/lehman/programs/ generaledu/guidelines.html. For answers to frequently asked questions about WI sections for instructors, see http://www.lehman.edu/lehman/programs/generaledu/faq.html.
4. See the listings and descriptions at http://www.lehman.edu/lehman/programs/generaledu.html.
5. The liaisons have also become the central, faculty element in a General Education Advisory Council which was created by the Curriculum Committee in the spring of 2005 as the principal oversight body for General Education policy at the College.

WORKS CITED

Arenson, Karen W. "Plan Approved to Invigorate City University." *The New York Times*, 23 May 2000, p. B-1.

Bosworth, William. "Detailed Analysis of Bronx Racial and Ethnic Changes." The Bronx Data Center, Lehman College. December 2006. http://www.lehman.edu/deannss/bronxdatactr/discover/ bxtime.htm.

Lehman College Undergraduate Curriculum Committee. "Proceedings of the General Education Workshop." 27 February 2004. http://www.lehman.edu/lehman/programs/generaledu/outcomes.html.

Nussbaum, Martha C. *Cultivating Humanity*. Cambridge: Harvard University Press, 1997.

CHAPTER FOUR

The Comprehensive College AS Civilized Hydra

General Education at the College of Staten Island

DAVID PODELL, JONATHAN D. SASSI,
AND JANE MARCUS-DELGADO

College of Staten Island

If Hercules had bravely approached the College of Staten Island (CSI) campus in search of an education, he would have encountered a many-headed entity not unlike the mythical Hydra. CSI offers associate, baccalaureate, and master's degrees; it possesses some characteristics of the community college, some of the senior college, and some that differ from both. Some of the students who enter its realm never intend to receive a baccalaureate (although many in fact do), and general education may be the totality of their college education. Other tenacious adventurers engage their general education courses in their more traditional role, as a common foundation for students pursuing baccalaureate majors.

Multifaceted CSI is known at the City University of New York as one of the university's "comprehensive" colleges because it offers both two- and four-year degrees. As the only public institution of higher education in its borough, it offers degrees at each level to comprehensively serve its community. Moreover, Staten Island's population is distinct from its counterparts in the rest of New York City—politically more conservative, demographically more homogenous, and geographically more isolated by virtue of the island's distance and limited means of transportation. Thus, the budding Hercules that ventures toward CSI presents needs and challenges that reflect a cross-section of those of its unique borough.

Every student entering the College soon discovers that one of its overriding goals is to engage students in the life of the mind, and both the administration and faculty work to support this endeavor with a multi-dimensional approach. To illustrate this effort (and to force the metaphor), it may be instructive to examine two hypothetical "adventurers" who enroll in a freshman English course this semester—Pericles and Diana. The first student, Pericles, begins college to earn an associate's degree because he senses that a college diploma will help his future employment prospects. He has successfully completed the remedial requirements in reading and writing, but he still struggles with math. He works in a cell phone store thirty hours each week, and his family's semi-attached townhouse contains many more television sets than books. He is the first member of his family to attend college, and he has no career plans yet. Sitting next to him in his freshman composition class is Diana, a baccalaureate-bound future scholar who intends to double-major in philosophy and biology. Her interests range from string and chaos theories to solving math problems for fun. She plans to go to medical school and then conduct research in bioethics. These students could not be more different—their goals, academic preparation, plans, and interests could not diverge more—but general education will ultimately provide both with the concrete tools they need to succeed on their distinct professional journeys.

CSI recognizes that the general education curriculum of a comprehensive college must meet the didactic needs of both Pericles and Diana in ways that are relevant, interdisciplinarily interconnected, complementary, and intellectually demanding. The College's many heads must work together to fulfill its dual commitments to educate the masses while simultaneously striving to continuously raise the caliber of its academic programs. Members of the institution understand that every student's future profession has its own way of thinking, performing, and acting with integrity and caring—its own "signature pedagogy" (Shulman 2005)—and that general education is designed to serve as the foundation upon which this is constructed. It is a critical part of the College's mission, as stated in the undergraduate catalog, to ". . . guide and assist its students in their intellectual, personal and ethical development both for the enrichment of their individual lives and for meaningful participation in society" (College of Staten Island 2005, 9). Furthermore, the goals of its liberal arts curriculum must fulfill the needs of every Hercules that crosses its path—no matter whether it is a Pericles or a Diana—and the community in which they live.

Similarly to every multi-cephalic actor, CSI has neither become more than the sum of its parts overnight nor has it remained unchanged since conception. This chapter addresses three distinct periods in the institution's evolution: its formation resulting from a merger of a four-year and community college; its development of a general education requirement for all undergraduates; and its current and future challenges and opportunities. It aims to illustrate the ways in which the general education curriculum has served as a unifying force—as a sort of academic glue (to mix metaphors)—that best articulates the College's mission, vision, and identity. Although one might expect a college's mission and identity to determine its general education, CSI provides an example of how the opposite is equally true: the identity of a college is in some ways born out of its general education. From all of its challenges and obstacles have emerged tremendous opportunities, and the chapter concludes with a view toward the future of this dynamic, hybrid Hydra-like being that strives to represent the very best of comprehensive public education.

HISTORICAL CONTEXT

The College of Staten (CSI) was created in 1976 from the merger of an "upper-division" college, Richmond College, which had educated juniors, seniors, and master's level students since 1965, and Staten Island Community College, which had offered associate's degrees since 1955. The merger was caused by New York City's budget crises and was less than amicable. It was Richmond College that had been facing closure; thus, the community college faculty felt they had saved the jobs of the Richmond College faculty, while the Richmond faculty believed that they had raised the level of the merged institution in which the community college faculty now worked. The then president, Edmond Volpe, described how the two cultures struggled to create a unified institution in his book *The Comprehensive College* (2001). A battle for the identity of the merged college raged for several years, with each group of faculty trying to establish pre-eminence. However, in the long run, because the merged college offered baccalaureate and graduate degrees, the senior college values necessarily prevailed. These values—embracing the importance of research, focusing on the liberal arts and sciences ahead of professional programs, a desire to promote graduate education—were also the values of newly hired faculty, who made their academic homes at CSI. This battle was not unique to CSI (Roosevelt 2006); many colleges struggled with the tension between liberal and professional education. However, in few colleges was the battle waged within almost every academic department. Ultimately, the faculty appointed after the merger (few in the 1980s, some in the 1990s, and many in the period since 2000) were indifferent to the perspective of the community college (and the hostility between community and senior college faculty); they viewed themselves as faculty of a baccalaureate-granting college, and their presence has ensured that the senior college values remained pre-eminent.

Nationally, the dual structure of CSI is not unique: Many senior colleges contain programs (sometimes called a "college of general studies"), in which less prepared students enter. Indeed, within our own university, the City University of New York (CUNY), apart from the senior and community colleges, there are four so-called "comprehensive colleges," of which CSI is one. Two of the others, John Jay and New York City College of Technology, have very specific thematic missions, in criminal justice and technology, respectively. CSI and Medgar Evers College both serve local communities, although Medgar Evers is one of several CUNY colleges in its New York City borough (Brooklyn), while CSI is the only CUNY college (and public institution of higher education) in its borough (Staten Island). Consequently, its mission is to serve the needs of all students, from those whose degree objectives range from associate's to master's, and including everyone from those with significant developmental needs in English and mathematics to honors students. Put differently, the College is a senior college that admits well prepared students directly into baccalaureate programs and, at the same time, it acts as a community college serving those seeking associate's degrees and students who wish to pursue a baccalaureate degree but lack proficiency in basic skills. The challenge to the CSI faculty has been to fulfill its mission in both the major and general education. The former is less difficult: By the time students reach their major, a selection process has occurred due to less successful students dropping out or being dismissed. The latter, which by its place in the curriculum serves all students who enter as freshmen, presents the greater challenge.

The challenge is vast, but CSI can boast success due, in large part, to its geography and history, as well as careful academic planning. Because Staten Island is so isolated from the rest of New York City, connected by one bridge and a ferry (it is, in fact, closer to New Jersey), and because as an island, it has well defined borders, CSI has a very distinct identity within the community it serves: It is Staten Island's own (and only) public college. It is, in essence, a college of the community (as opposed to a community college) and Staten Islanders' sense of ownership of the college, we think, is greater than that of residents of Brooklyn or Manhattan for Brooklyn College or Hunter College, respectively. It can also claim uniqueness and difference compared to the rest of CUNY, as well as a sense of belonging to its parent institution.

Another major aspect of the college's identity is that it perceives itself as an underdog. This notion has had a significant effect on the College's progress and helped the faculty overcome the profound difficulties inherent in the merger of the two faculties in finding a shared mission. At the time of the merger, departments were created that were populated by faculty from both the community and upper division colleges who very often had academic values and expectations that were vastly different. The community college faculty tended to have a greater appreciation for the process of developing students' skills, they valued teaching above research, and many of them were primarily concerned with students' professional development. The senior college faculty tended to have higher expectations for their students, they placed greater value on publishing, and they structured the curriculum to ensure students had a rigorous education in the liberal arts and sciences. The two groups had significantly different expectations for promotion and tenure, and of their vision of their departments. However, despite the differences between the two cultures, a shared commitment to the students, the eventual arrival of new colleagues who knew neither of the two predecessor colleges, and simply the passage of time created an atmosphere in which the College could make significant strides toward improvement.

From the time of the merger in 1976 to the late 1980s, the College was largely focused on integrating the two institutions. In that period, in which the budget continued to remain problematic, almost no new faculty were appointed. In the late 1980s, planning began for a physical merger of what had been two separate colleges and were now two campuses of the same college, into one campus. The State of New York had a large piece of property centrally located in Staten Island that it decided to allocate to the merged College of Staten Island. The location was the former site of the Willowbrook State School that had housed individuals with mental retardation, sometimes in inhumane conditions. Its celebrated closure, following a television exposé by Geraldo Rivera and a contentious lawsuit brought by parents, was a landmark in the establishment of the rights of individuals with developmental disabilities. After the residents were established in smaller group homes and the State School was closed, a plan was developed to rehabilitate some buildings, demolish others, and construct new ones to create a spacious campus in a park-like setting for CSI.

The merger of the two colleges in 1976 yielded a distribution-type general education that was adopted from the curriculum of Staten Island Community College; Richmond College, which served juniors and seniors, had no need for a curriculum for first- and second-year students. With requirements in mathematics, science, the social sciences, and the humanities, it ensured that all students had a substantial liberal arts and sciences foundation. Given the large number of students in professional programs, such as business and accounting, the faculty wished all students to leave college with a balanced curriculum (Chew and McInnis-Bowers 2004). This was reflected not only in general education, but in junior- and senior-level classes, as well. For example, for students seeking to become teachers, the faculty chose not to create majors in elementary and secondary education and, instead, required students to major in liberal arts and sciences areas while completing an education sequence. In fact, the faculty designed a unique multi-disciplinary liberal arts major, "Science, Letters, and Society" (SLS), for students preparing to teach at the elementary level. To ensure that students were steeped in the liberal arts and sciences, and recognizing that elementary-level teachers must be generalists, the SLS major was designed to include coursework beyond general education in the humanities, mathematics, the sciences, and the social sciences.

IN A NEW SETTING AND A NEW ERA,
A NEW GENERAL EDUCATION

The College moved into an unfinished campus in 1993, and the next few years were devoted to settling in, as construction of the remaining buildings and the sidewalks was completed. In 1994, a new president, Marlene Springer, was appointed, and she served until her retirement in 2007. The physical merger of the two campuses and the longevity of Dr. Springer's presidency have allowed the College to pursue a consistent agenda of improvement of academic standards and programs. Associate's degree programs that were deemed obsolete by technological or curricular standards were closed, and new baccalaureate and master's programs were added. The College identified specific academic priorities, such as polymer science and international education, that reflected the interests of the faculty. New faculty hiring, which had been modest from the mid-1980s to the mid-1990s, now grew enormously, due to vacancies caused by retirements and the allocation of new lines by the University, allowing the College to put faculty resources towards its more clearly established priorities.

It was also during this period that the College began to put a significant amount of energy into rethinking and revising its general education curriculum. One part of this effort was the renaming of general education categories. The distribution requirements adopted from Staten Island Community College included the traditional categories of mathematics, the sciences, the social sciences, and the humanities, with uninformative (and uninteresting) titles such as "Group A" and "Group B2." These titles were relabeled "Scientific Analysis," "Social Scientific Analysis," and "Textual, Aesthetic, and Linguistic Analysis" to communicate more clearly their purpose. At the same time, the faculty created several new general education requirements. A "Pluralism and Diversity" requirement, which could be met by one of a number of courses, was created to ensure that students' coursework exposed them to issues relevant to the diversity of our society.

CSI's general education curriculum had, until this time, been structured as a set of distribution requirements (which could be met by a growing list of courses) and two required freshman writing courses. A new course was introduced in the late 1990s that allowed us to consider our general education a "modified core" curriculum, although it might more accurately be called a "modified distribution" curriculum. The College introduced a required course for all students, "COR 100 United States: Issues, Ideas, and Institutions," to ensure students developed an understanding of basic ideas underlying this country. The course description is as follows:

> COR 100 is a required general education course that introduces CSI students to contemporary America's constitutional democracy, multiracial society, and market economy, using the tools of the social sciences. The course seeks historical perspective by examining three

formative periods in U.S. history: the American Revolution and debate over the Constitution, the African American freedom struggle from slavery through the civil rights movement, and the evolving relationship between government regulation and the market economy during the 20th century. The course is writing intensive and is intended to develop logical, critical thought and expression.

COR 100 was intended to be taught by faculty from a variety of disciplines, including economics, history, philosophy, political science, and sociology. The faculty created the text, which was compiled from original sources and chapters of other texts, and have revised it periodically. The first freshman writing course is a pre- or co-requisite.

COR 100 has not been without its problems. Although intended as an interdisciplinary course, COR 100 is perceived by many as a history course. Indeed, at the time of registration, students often complain that they have already taken U.S. history in high school; we try to convey that COR 100 is something different, that it is a college-level, interdisciplinary course that is not a survey but is focused on the very specific issues identified in the description. Among the full-time faculty, it is taught most often by historians and only occasionally faculty from other disciplines. Faculty in political science see it as an incursion on their own introductory course.

A reliance on part-time faculty, though regrettable in the eyes of some, has had the positive effect of giving the coordinators (a historian and a historian of education) more sway over the curriculum and the pedagogy. They and the faculty who teach COR 100—largely a steady group of adjunct faculty—have worked closely together to develop a course with great consistency across sections and with imaginative pedagogy. For example, they are currently experimenting with the "Reacting to the Past" method developed by Barnard College and in use in about 25 colleges nationwide (Carnes 2005; see also Davison and Lantz-Goldhaber, this volume). Further, they have adopted a more advanced outcomes assessment approach for COR 100 than have their counterparts overseeing any other general education requirement. The curriculum and the textbook customized for the course have been revised far more frequently than those of similar courses.

To complement COR 100, the faculty created a category called "The West and the World," designed to make students familiar with the interaction between western and non-Western societies and cultures. The course credits were taken from the social science category (the imaginatively named "Group B1") and, consequently, courses accepted in fulfillment of this requirement were social science courses. Initially they were existing courses (e.g., International Economics) but gradually courses were designed specifically for this category (e.g., The West and the World: Africa Encounters Europe).

By 2001, however, faculty were becoming dissatisfied with the West and the World requirement for several reasons. First, faculty were uncomfortable with assumptions underlying the category, i.e., the privileging of "the West" as the basis of defining that which is non-Western, the ambiguity of what is and is not "the West," and the issue of non-Western populations in what have been viewed as Western countries. Second, faculty from the humanities argued that issues inherent in this category could also be understood from the perspectives of literature, cinema, and the arts. What followed was a major reform of the category, including a renaming, to "The Contemporary World," and a more precise definition:

> Courses fulfilling this requirement are designed to provide an understanding of global and regional contexts. As COR 100 explores issues, ideas, and institutions in the United States, so this requirement will cover contemporary global issues, ideas, and institutions. The courses will emphasize the interaction of societies along political, economic, and cultural dimensions. Courses will cover the development, formation, and impact of the global context and ways in which different nations, societies, and cultures influence and are influenced by global forces. Students will use comparative and historical analytic frameworks for understanding the contemporary world.

In recognition of the level of the courses, the second freshman writing course was established as a prerequisite for all courses that fulfilled the requirement.

Writing is a central element of virtually every college's general education program, because we all recognize that students must be able to communicate effectively in writing regardless of their future major or career. CSI requires that all students take two writing classes, typically during the freshman year: ENG 111, Introduction to College Writing and ENG 151, College Writing. In addition, the College in 2005 undertook a new initiative to embed writing more deeply within the general education program, as part of the University's "Writing across the Curriculum" project. Two academic departments per year are granted a small amount of reassigned time to explore ways to make their general education courses more writing intensive. In this way, all students will eventually be guaranteed to experience a content-based writing-intensive course during their general education program, apart from the English writing courses. That course may be in the humanities, social sciences, or sciences, but an emphasis will be placed on the teaching of writing within the specific disciplinary focus. The process of developing writing within these courses is incremental, and some faculty resist this initiative (one hears the familiar response "I'm not a writing teacher"); however, others, recognizing the need for our students to learn to write within their content courses, have embraced the opportunity to learn more themselves about teaching writing and to revise their courses.

The ongoing responsibility for the general education curriculum rests with the College's General Education Committee, which came into being with the adoption of a new governance structure in May 2002. The committee includes an elected faculty representative from every academic department, an undergraduate student, the two academic divisional deans, and the chief academic officer (or designee), who serves as chair. The committee's broad representation ensures that it reaches its decisions with input from all the relevant constituencies at CSI. Moreover, the committee's standing nature provides a home for the oversight and ongoing renewal of the general education program, which might otherwise get lost in the shuffle. That is, the various academic departments take ownership of their majors, but without a standing committee, there is no one beside the chief academic officer who is in a position to give consistent attention and direction to the general education program. One might say of general education that it belongs to everyone and it belongs to no one. The committee is currently chaired by a faculty member in history (Jonathan Sassi, one of the authors of this chapter). The membership varies from those with many years of experience on the committee, who have a deep understanding of the issues related to general education, to some who are relatively new to the College and who may hitherto have given little thought to general education. The student representative has often not contributed a great deal to discussions, but has been helpful in communicating changes under discussion to the student government.

One of the General Education Committee's major accomplishments of the period 2003–2005, supported by the opening of a University-wide discussion on general education, was the redefinition of its goals at CSI. Subcommittees met to articulate the overall objectives of general education and to formulate precisely worded definitions of each of the several general education categories. This exercise was meant to serve both faculty and students. As one might expect, the discussions were lengthy and arduous. What was meant by the word "laboratory" in the "Scientific Analysis" requirement? What do we mean by the word "contemporary" in the "Contemporary Analysis" requirement? Some faculty feared that their courses would be ineligible in a redefined category, others had agendas that were ideological, and still others had beliefs about what should and should not comprise a general education. Laborious as the process seemed, it was among the more exciting academic discussions that have occurred in recent years, perhaps because after the debate and discussion had ended, agreement was reached that seemed to satisfy almost everyone.

As a result, the academic departments gained a clearer sense of what were the requirements of courses that would fulfill such categories as "Scientific Analysis" or "The Contemporary World." These insights facilitated their proposing courses designed to meet those requirements. Moreover, students and faculty members alike would have a more straightforward definition of the rationale behind general education. As demonstrated by Humphreys and Davenport (2005), general education is understood differently by students and faculty. It is hoped that, with explicit descriptions of the categories of general education, CSI's students will come to understand the aims of general education and how it prepares them for their eventual majors and for lifelong learning, rather than their viewing it merely as a series of courses that one has to "get over with." In order to better disseminate these new definitions to the college community, a handy one-page brochure was created, which was mailed to all faculty members and is widely distributed during advisement. The brochure has proven popular, but we recognize the need to more explicitly teach students about the branches of knowledge that underlie CSI's general education.

The creation of a set of well-articulated goals was the first step in developing a comprehensive plan for assessing the effectiveness of teaching and learning in the general education program. A number of general education assessment projects began at CSI over the past four years. For example, the faculty members teaching COR 100 collect data about student learning by using a scoring rubric to grade sample final exams that contain a common essay question. Also, the faculty teaching general education courses in astronomy, geology, and psychology have undertaken assessment projects that have led to changes in each class's lectures, laboratories, and/or textbooks.

CHALLENGES TODAY AND OPPORTUNITIES
FOR THE FUTURE

Looking back over its relatively short history, CSI takes pride in its well-developed program of general education. Nevertheless, there is a candid recognition that the College cannot rest satisfied with its accomplishments, but must press forward to tackle the challenges that remain ahead. At the same time, these challenges create great opportunities for growth and change—and stretch our creative and intellectual horizons. We concur with a number of recent studies (e.g., Schneider 2004) that have identified several areas that are critical for new thinking and reforms in general education and the liberal arts, and CSI has made a significant commitment to their development.

One of the most prominent contemporary issues in general education at CSI is the institution of a comprehensive program of academic outcomes assessment. We are working to develop a culture in which the learning that is going on in general education courses is regularly being measured, so that needed changes can be made to teaching on an informed basis. The General Education Committee is presently formulating a multi-year plan in which every general education requirement will be scheduled into a cycle of regularly recurring assessment. The Committee has also agreed to require that all departments, when making proposals for new or revised courses, must include articulated learning objectives for each course and an outcomes assessment strategy.

While certain academic majors have long-standing commitments to the assessment of student learning, often as the result of accreditation requirements (e.g., computer science, nursing, and teacher education), for other disciplines the cultivation of a culture of assessment will require significant faculty development. It should be noted that general education is not unique in this regard; several majors also need to move in the same direction. Still, given the number of students it enrolls, its multi-departmental nature, and its broad scope, general education presents quite a challenge for assessment. At the same time, the promises of a comprehensive program of outcomes assessment in general education are correspondingly large.

Outcomes assessment will be one important strategy in addressing one of general education's knottier problems, the existence of so-called "gateway" or "killer" courses. There exist a small number of courses, particularly in mathematics, that present serious challenges to our students, as measured by the large proportion of them who are unable to finish and earn a passing grade. We have resolved to understand better what pedagogies are effective and what interventions actually help students succeed in the gateway courses, and plan to restructure our curriculum to promote greater success. Toward this end, we recently revised our developmental sequence in mathematics and introduced summer workshops to prepare students for freshman mathematics and calculus.

One way that the College plans to make its general education courses more appealing to students is through its participation in the National Science Foundation's Science Education for New Civic Engagements and Responsibilities (SENCER) project. SENCER courses investigate a complex public policy issue, and in the process teach students the requisite science and math background that they would need truly to understand the issues at stake. CSI sent a faculty team to the national SENCER conference in summer 2006 and received a grant from NSF to revise the general education curriculum in the sciences.

Of course, no effort to sustain or reform general education will gain any traction without a real sense of responsibility for it on the part of the College's faculty, particularly its full-time faculty. Like many institutions of American higher education, CUNY relies on part-time instructors to staff a large proportion of its courses, especially lower-division general education courses. Even courses that begin amid a burst of reformist enthusiasm and fanfare can slide over time into the torpor of familiarity. At CSI, for example, COR 100 has seen its proportion of full-time instructors decline year after year, as full-timers opt out of having to teach large sections of first-semester students in favor of teaching majors or graduate students. The administration and department chairpersons will have to keep working to engage faculty with the general education program, encouraging the understanding that it is, in fact, in the faculty's own interest to be engaged. If students are not stimulated by and fail to flourish in general education, what is the likelihood that they will enter their majors with either the skills or motivation they need to succeed and graduate?

We recognize the need for the ongoing re-examination and re-thinking of general education (Schneider 2004; Stearns 2002). The challenge to the College is to engage more of the new faculty in general education. As their more senior colleagues retire, the new faculty will need to embrace the responsibility of overseeing general education and keeping it vibrant. One step toward developing that sense of responsibility has been the creation of learning communities for first-semester students, in which groups of 30 students enroll in several general education courses together. The program, so far, has been limited to the better prepared entering students, i.e., students who have no remedial needs. Faculty, particularly new full-time faculty, have responded well to the opportunity to teach this population in the learning communities and it has resulted in greater participation by full-time faculty in the teaching of freshmen. The College now plans to expand the learning communities program into the second, third, and fourth semesters, primarily as a retention strategy but, secondarily, as a way to involve full-time faculty in teaching general education. Not surprisingly, among the more senior faculty, it has been some of those originally appointed to the community college who have shown the greatest interest in general education. Our hope is that the new generation of faculty, for whom the predecessor institutions hold only vague historical value, will embrace general education and, in time, mold our Hydra to meet the challenges of the new century.

Among its many heads—most scholars claim there were nine or more—the Hydra had one that was immortal and indestructible. In a very real sense, our program in general education may represent for the College this most critical and enduring component. As this chapter describes, our administrative structure, faculty, curricula, and students have all evolved and grown during CSI's short life span. Unlike its mythical counterpart, the College has demonstrated the resiliency to adapt and thrive in a complex and rapidly changing environment. We are committed to welcoming every student into this educational lair, and to giving each of them the tools to triumph—academically, personally, and professionally, to the very peak of his or her capacity.

WORKS CITED

Carnes, M.C. "Inciting Speech." *Change*, 37.2 (2005): 6–11.

Chew, E.B., and C. McInnis-Bowers, C. "Blending Liberal Art and Business Education." *Liberal Education*, 90 (2004): 56–63.

College of Staten Island, CUNY. *College of Staten Island Undergraduate Catalog, 2005–2007*. Staten Island, NY: CSI, 2005.

Humphreys, D., and A. Davenport. "What Really Matters in College: How Students View and Value Liberal Education." *Liberal Education*, 91 (2005): 36–43.

Roosevelt, G. "The Triumph of the Market and the Decline of Liberal Education: Implications for Civic Life." *Teachers College Record*, 108 (2006): 1404–1423.

Schneider, C.G. "Practicing Liberal Education: Formative Themes in the Reinvention of Liberal Learning." *Liberal Education*, 90 (2004): 6–11.

Shulman, Lee S. "Signature Pedagogies in the Professions." *Daedalus*, 134 (2005): 52–59.

Stearns, P. "General Education Revisited, Again." *Liberal Education*, 88 (2002): 42–47.

Volpe, E. *The Comprehensive College: Heading Toward a New Direction in Higher Education*. Lincoln, NE: Writers Club Press, 2001.

CHAPTER FIVE

A Jazz Performance

Improvisations on General Education at a CUNY Community College

LINDA STANLEY, ANITA FERDENZI, PAUL MARCHESE,
AND MARGARET J. REILLY

Queensborough Community College

It reminded me of a jazz performance in which the musicians are on stage. And they know what they are doing, they rehearse, but the performance is open to change, and the other musicians have to respond quickly to that change. Somebody takes off from a basic pattern, then the others have to accommodate themselves. That's the excitement, the razor's edge of a live performance of jazz. Now, in improvising on the spot in front of an audience, you find yourself in a place you could not possibly predict. But what happens when you go to this unpredictable place is that you are frequently taken into a room that you could not possibly have found if you had gone the normal way.

—From an Interview with Toni Morrison on the Writing of her Novel, *Jazz* . . .

A BASIC CHORD PROGRESSION

The real power . . . is that a group of people can come together and create . . . improvised art and negotiate their agendas . . . and that negotiation is the art.

—Wynton Marsalis

This chapter is a recording of a very fluid jazz performance that has been playing itself out at Queensborough Community College these past three years. Our efforts to reform general education at our Borough of Queens community college have led us to this musical metaphor because we have so frequently found ourselves improvising, drawing on all our knowledge and our ability to harmonize, in order to create the kind of change we have envisioned for ourselves and Queensborough Community

College students. Jazz is typically played in smoky, windowless rooms—underground and out of the mainstream. It is remarkable to compare committee work—fluorescent lights, sober attention to Robert's Rules of Order—to what goes on when master musicians really start to hear and respond to one another. That is what I want to stress here: We—a committee including myself, a physicist, an education philosopher, and a nurse/teacher, among many others—set out to riff on what is rigid, to approach the structures of general education as potentially fluid, to sing out from the infrastructure of the college. Our work is not spontaneous—it is rigorous and planned—but it demands a willingness to shift subtly and exuberantly from one strain of music to the next, one tempo to another, as we try to negotiate calcified curricular structures, entrenched politics, and the sometimes unpredictable reactions to the notes we produce.

My perspective, as narrator, is that of an English faculty member who has watched and listened and contributed to this performance from its inception. I also speak as a member of the University-wide General Education Project, the frame for our local improvisations, where one could not predict the next note.

To further clarify the context and constraints of our jazz performance, a word about our institution. Queensborough Community College was established in 1959 on a former golf course in eastern Queens, far away from the large urban centers of the city. As a result, the college attracted a white middle class student body, the majority of whom intended to transfer to a four-year CUNY institution. Consequently, the various liberal arts departments continued on as discrete disciplines as in the traditional baccalaureate college, privileging the "shopping list" approach to general education. They felt no challenge to see themselves as integrated segments of a general education curriculum. Efforts at curricular renewal were met with resistance.

Since that time, a combination of forces has made faculty at Queensborough more receptive to the University's current General Education effort. Now, in the first decade of the twenty-first century, while still on our golf course in Bayside (with the former clubhouse as a celebrated art gallery) and still teaching students who want to transfer into both professional and liberal arts programs at four-year institutions, we now teach students whose neighborhood immigrant populations make the Borough of Queens the most diversified geographical space in the world. Our students come to us from 138 different countries, primarily Jamaica, Guyana, China, and Colombia, and also from the countries of Southeast Asia. The linguistic and cultural shifts have called upon us to find and develop new curricular configurations and new pedagogical methods to engage and support these students.

These new forces gave rise to a dynamic, ongoing conversation about general education at Queensborough, led by a president invested in the scholarship of teaching, and spurred by a University initiative to hire a new generation of faculty. What follows are solo performances from a number of participants, speaking across the curriculum from their disciplinary knowledge.

Our committee was first galvanized by what we considered a pressing need: to bridge the gap between the professions and the liberal arts. Although we still have a sizeable and currently growing liberal arts population, today's Queensborough students, like students at most community colleges, largely major in the professional fields, with standard curricular structures conceived in opposition to the liberal arts. We attempted to bring these two discrete sections of the college together.

IMPROVISATION ONE: MODULATION—GENERAL EDUCATION IN THE PROFESSIONAL AND CAREER CURRICULA

My view is that you cannot close your mind and say I don't want to listen to this or that . . . if you turn a deaf ear to everything but one style, pretty soon it's not going to work out.
—BILLY ECKSTINE

In the spring of 2003, Paul Marchese, an engineer teaching in the Physics Department and a member of our committee, expressed concern that in professional and career degree programs, students have few opportunities to contextualize their learning within the humanities. What new approaches, if any, Professor Marchese asked, could we, as a committee, set in motion that would allow the curriculum of these programs to give students a more fulfilling liberal education than the 22 General Education core credits the State of New York Education Department already requires? While this number of General Education credits may seem ample, most of them are fulfilled by science and math courses already in the technology and business curricula, with only a few remaining credits available for liberal arts and humanities courses.

The task of our committee became primarily that of answering Paul's specific questions: "How can we expose the students in the inflexibly arranged technical and career programs to all the aspects of General Education?" "What is the responsibility of the College in educating students in these programs?" "Is the College the gateway not only for new career opportunities but also for a first glimpse into the world of the educated person for many of our students who are immigrants and/or the first generation in their families to attend college?" "What then is an educated person?" "In general, how should the community college differ from a 'trade' school?" Paul describes below his improvisation toward creating a bridge between the professional and career programs and the liberal arts.

PAUL MARCHESE, PHYSICS

Most engineering schools have two curricula: the professional program and the General Education requirements. The professional program is designed to teach students what they need to know to succeed as professionals in their field. The design of these programs varies, but most have similar elements: a set of introductory block courses, more advanced courses, and a capstone experience. The introductory classes in professional programs assume no previous knowledge and have little or no connection to the other courses students are taking. In engineering school, these courses were mechanics, electricity and magnetism, and thermodynamics. As the program progresses, the material becomes more complex, sometimes bringing together elements introduced in previous courses. The programs culminate in a capstone experience designed to apply all the skills and knowledge acquired throughout the program, which in engineering school is fulfilled by the senior project.

Of course, as an engineering student at Columbia University, I also had to take courses in art and literature. Columbia sought to affirm that the colleges of professional studies were not just producing engineers, doctors, and lawyers but the next great thinkers of our time. The intent of these General Education classes is now apparent to me, but at the time these courses struck a dissonant chord in my effort to master my intended profession. I felt that the General Education part of my undergraduate education was a hastily put together series of courses with little depth or continuity, a distraction rather than an integrating force. The General Education requirements mandated by the accreditation boards, although well intentioned, seemed to me to fall far short of the liberal education non-professional students received. Years later, now physics faculty myself, I was inspired by a new CUNY General Education initiative to investigate and improve the ways we educate students for a democratic citizenry. In the spring 2003 context of the first stages of the war in Iraq, this seemed an urgent need.

After months of research, discussion and deliberation, I was ready to take the lead in the jazz quartet by seeking support for an additional humanities course in the professional and career curricula. My argument had to take into account not only the lack of space for additional courses in these curricula, which are responsible to accrediting associations, but also the fact that the addition of a required humanities course would result in one fewer technology course taught by technology faculty, which in departments with dwindling enrollments would be a threat to job security.

My modus operandi was to offer a quid pro quo: *in return for adding an additional humanities course to the career curricula, the liberal arts would add a course on computer literacy to be taught in any one of several career departments. I hoped this* quid pro quo *would address the interdepartmental fighting that had defeated a similar proposal two decades earlier.*

The educational rationale for the quid pro quo *was based on my experience as an engineering student. As a student I always wondered why we were required to take first semester physics (mechanics) only to take engineering mechanics the following year. Electrical engineering students also took classes in circuits, electricity and magnetism, and then Physics II (electricity and magnetism). At first we thought that the engineering courses were the more advanced versions of the physics courses, but taking the engineering courses without first taking the physics "prerequisites" was not allowed. While engineering students clearly learn the mechanics they will need in their profession in the engineering course, I gradually realized that the reason for taking physics is to learn how to think scientifically. Students learn the theory in physics; they learn how to build a bridge in the engineering courses.*

The science requirement in the liberal arts curriculum fulfills a similar purpose. Instructors may justify the requirement by saying, "science is everywhere in our society," or "what you learn in this class will help you understand the world around you." The fact is, most liberal arts students will never use what they learn in chemistry, biology, or physics. The reason for the introductory science class, then, is to introduce scientific ways of knowing, that there are rules governing the universe and we can learn these rules by careful observation and analysis. It is impossible to explain everything related to science in one introductory course, but we can teach students how to appreciate the value of science.

Similarly, as society becomes increasingly dependent on technology, all college graduates need to be knowledgeable about technology's many applications. The course we envisioned in our new approach would introduce liberal arts students to computers and computer applications, such as word processing and the use of spreadsheets. There would be elements of electronics and communications, as well as other technologies. The course would be a more extensive version of the computer class currently required of Liberal Arts students at QCC, and would be mandatory for all non-professional students. Also, our committee was prepared to address the argument that teaching technology to liberal arts students is problematic because technology changes so quickly. We conceived that the course would be taught in such a way that students could transfer their knowledge easily as technology changed. We would teach the students to be technology savvy, not to learn specific applications.

In the end, neither career nor liberal arts faculty in the larger Gen Ed Inquiry group conceded the need of the other's course. Despite our carefully crafted *quid pro quo* argument, we had continued to underestimate the primal need to protect one's turf. With the players unwilling or unable to negotiate, we were forced to abort the performance.

So where did this leave us? We decided that, as we were committed already to this jazz quartet, we would search for new expressions in which to find a resolution to this "musical" debate. As the musician uses conflict and resolution to create tension in such dialogues, we needed to make way for a new voice that could change the dynamic of our performance.

IMPROVISATION TWO—MODULATION:
A CORNERSTONE/CAPSTONE STRUCTURE

> Because jazz finds its very life in an endless improvisation upon traditional materials, the jazzman must lose his identity even as he finds it.
>
> —RALPH ELLISON

The failure of our committee's *quid pro quo* proposal early in the spring of 2004 should have been a disappointment. It certainly was an eye-opening exposure to the politics of academia for those of us who were neophytes in fighting the academic turf wars. Like good jazz musicians, however, we took the opportunity to veer off in a different, less discordant direction. Our defeat actually became the catalyst for new questions and a new improvisation by Marge Reilly, a member of the nursing faculty who, as part of her work as "professional" faculty in a college that puts a premium on the liberal arts, was already investigating intersections between the curricula of the professional and career programs and the liberal arts curriculum. After having conducted much research for the committee, she was about to, in Lee Shulman's phrase, "profess the liberal arts" (2004).

MARGE REILLY, NURSING

As a faculty member of the Nursing Department, I found that my perspective on General Education was orchestrated by the evolution of my profession. Returning to my roots, I reflected on Florence Nightingale, the Lady with the Lamp, who revolutionized the education of nurses in the 1800s by removing them from the role of indentured servant and sending them to "schools" where they were exposed to philosophy, ethics, and the scientific method. Albeit limited in focus, this approach was a giant leap toward a new perspective on the education of nurses and a new direction. As in jazz, this was not just the choosing of a new tune, but improvising an idea first created in the mind and inspired by passion. Our committee asked, could we do any less for our students of today?

Through the research we had done in an effort to find a model for humanities courses in career departments, we had discovered that other community colleges had built a progressive structure for delivering their General Education curriculum, including both cornerstone and capstone courses, which were developmental and theme-based in their approach. One such program was the St. Louis Community College General Education Model, which cohesively integrates General Education themes throughout all its programs (St. Louis). Our own General Education curriculum, however, primarily has followed the distribution model, which is basically a list—a menu—of courses in each discipline from which students must choose to fill the required number of credits.

The cornerstone-to-capstone approach stresses an integrated progression from entry-level (cornerstone) courses up through capstone experiences. This progression recursively builds on students' previously learned knowledge and capabilities in the process of their learning to "appreciate a variety of issues, to think independently and critically; and to learn independently" (Stearns 2002, 43). A capstone experience in the semester before graduation enables students to synthesize their General Education learning often in the context of researching and compiling a project that focuses on a larger issue or institution of society.

Those of us in professional and career programs shared with Linda, the representative on our committee from the liberal arts, that this concept of advancing from the simple to complex, from cornerstone-to-capstone was the dominant framework in each of our career programs. As research tells us that "CUNY students overwhelmingly major in the professions" and that students in these programs persist to graduation at rates higher than those of students in the liberal arts and science programs (Summerfield 2006), we all began to see this structure as potentially a highly useful scaffold for the liberal arts and sciences curriculum. We began to consider a fresh melody that would again improvise from the basic chord progression to integrate the General Education curriculum. We asked ourselves the following questions: Could themes be identified that could be integrated into General Education courses and serve as a framework to foster the progression of students' thinking? Could a structure be provided within which the soloist (in this case, the student) could venture off in various directions improvising new melodies on repeated chords (themes)? More questions evolved as to what constituted suitable methods or processes that could be used to foster this developmental approach to learning. Many questions were still unresolved; however, the process of the examination was the key. We were and still are engaging in the very thought processes we want for our students—raising critical questions, integrating our observations and research, and generally trying to change what we find unsatisfactory.

I presented these ideas to a college-wide faculty meeting in spring 2004. Using the curriculum of the Nursing Department, I was able to illustrate for my Queensborough colleagues how we start with a cornerstone, or foundation course, using a few simple constructs, and integrate major threads or melodies on a repeating pattern of chord changes. As the nursing student advances through each semester, these melodies are played again and again with ever increasing complexity as the student attempts to incorporate the intricate patterns that will influence their nursing practice.

One example is the motif of legal and ethical aspects of nursing care. At the simplest level, students would ask permission of a person to take his/her blood pressure and document it. As the students progress, this motif is addressed in more complex ways, such as the right to confidentiality when a person tests positive for a sexually transmitted disease and refuses to reveal this status to his/her life partner. At the capstone or last level, this theme would again be explored on an even more complex level such as examining the cultural factors affecting the ethical perspective on one's right to die. Students first explore these threads at the personal level and gradually move upward and outward toward a more global perspective.

Next, our committee began to examine differences in the structures of the career programs and the liberal arts and science curricula. The progression that seemed very natural and logical in the career programs was clearly not apparent in the liberal arts curriculum as organized at QCC. Our agenda was to disseminate awareness and elicit support for a progressive model of learning for the liberal arts and science curricula.

Based on the research we had done on cornerstone-to-capstone models, including the St. Louis Community College Model, we solicited input from the General Education Inquiry group as to what abilities and proficiencies faculty expected students to demonstrate in the "first fifteen" credits as well as what types of experiences might comprise a capstone experience. Supported by the data we gathered, our next task was to present our proposal at the Annual Conference of the College in the fall of 2005.

Our cornerstone/capstone model was subsequently accepted as a college priority and featured in plans for the college's future.

IMPROVISATION THREE—MODULATION: CREATING A DOUBLE-HELIX PEDAGOGY

> Jazz is a very democratic musical form. It comes out of a communal experience. We take our respective instruments and collectively create a thing of beauty.
>
> —MAX ROACH

Simultaneous with developing our concept of a cornerstone/capstone structure for the General Education curriculum, our committee had realized we needed the expertise of someone schooled in the theories of teaching and learning to provide a pedagogy for our curricular structure (Applebee 1996, 101). What, if anything, we needed to know, does educational research say about this new direction we were planning for the General Education curriculum and how it might best be presented to students? We invited Anita Ferdenzi, a member of the education faculty and a leading participant in the Queensborough Community College/Queens College Dual/Joint AA/BA Degree Program in Liberal Arts and Sciences and Childhood Education to join us and provide her expert knowledge and a further improvisation.

ANITA FERDENZI, SOCIAL SCIENCES

I have been involved in the college-wide conversation on General Education for almost ten years, ever since I helped draft a series of General Education objectives as part of my work on assessing effective teaching. Working now with the cornerstone-capstone committee to make these objectives realities for all students in all classrooms, I became aware of the larger context for my private disciplinary work: the entire college community, working together to create a meaningful liberal education for our first-generation and immigrant students by enacting a curriculum with a previously missing deep and integrated structure that would provide them with both goals and rewards for achieving those goals.

As committee chairperson, Marge Reilly shared the intricacies of her exemplary nursing program cornerstone-capstone model; I became inspired to apply this approach in my development of a progressive structure for General Education requirements through a cornerstone to capstone experience for students preparing for the teaching profession. I decided I would be most helpful to the committee by designing a model that focused on my profession's research-based curriculum and instruction.

However, upon conducting a comparative analysis of the nursing and education program requirements, I found an inverse relationship between the two programs in the contextualization of General Education skills and competencies in the liberal arts and sciences. In the nursing program, General Education skills and concepts are infused into specialized nursing courses that comprise approximately half of the curriculum. Inversely, in the education program, courses in the liberal arts and sciences comprise the bulk of the coursework in the curriculum. This structural distinction heightened my challenge to create a model with sufficient flexibility to accommodate each college program, including the liberal arts and sciences program itself, and to provide a recursive/progressive spiraling structure that would simultaneously teach and reinforce General Education skills and competencies, design methods to support challenging tasks, and empower students to take responsibility for their own learning through learning-to-learn awareness. After some thought, the committee decided that this structure would be best represented by a double helix.

The double helix has momentum, motion, and structure, and as such, illustrates the recursive nature of our spiraling curriculum as it progresses from a cornerstone to capstone experience. The general education skills and competencies appear in progressive complexity as they repeat their spiraling pattern on one rail of the helix. The second rail of the helix is connected to the first by links of program-specific coursework and serves as the individual path each student follows towards transfer and career and/or professional goals. The intersecting rails of the helix represent learning opportunities for the conscious articulation of facts and ideas designed to promote connectedness in growth. (See also John Dewey's notion of a single spiraling curriculum, 1923, 50).

The key paradigm shift exemplified in this double helix model for our community college curriculum and pedagogy is illustrated by the symbol's representation of the genetic code, the very essence of human diversity. It is a student-centered model focused on the capitalization of student strengths. Integrating these guiding principles into the design of cornerstone to capstone experiences will provide the necessary blueprint for tapping into our students' strengths and, when planning curricular formats and pedagogical strategies, for promoting each student's opportunity to meet the standards of academic success.

The notion of promoting student success by a simple paradigm shift away from a focus on student deficits to capitalizing on student strengths is an elegant concept that has both empowered and inspired my education students. Two years prior, at the end of class, my education students proposed that we afford their fellow QCC students the same opportunity I had given them: to demonstrate "how they are smart" by creating works based upon the Multiple Intelligences Projects they created in my class. The powerful experience of using their intelligence area strengths to demonstrate their understanding of a given concept was highlighted by the diversity of intelligences their peers revealed through their unique presentations of the identical concept. A powerful lesson indeed, for the present student and future teacher. These students then coordinated a campus-wide event entitled "Sense It! A Celebration of the Learning Process."

Through this intrinsically motivated project, the students authentically demonstrated several criteria for professionals as outlined by Lee Shulman in his article "Professing the Liberal Arts" (2005). The first criterion is the passion for promoting student success; the second is the understanding of their fellow students' need to demonstrate how they are smart; the third, their own learning of the Multiple Intelligences theory and sharing it with faculty and students; and the fourth, their volunteer activity in organizing and coordinating this campus-wide event in service to the greater QCC community. The students had thought liberally, worked collaboratively, and integrated knowledge from various disciplines to celebrate the diversity of intelligences and talents among the greater college community.

IMPROVISATION FOUR: MODULATION—BRIDGE TO TRANSFER AS A LABORATORY

It isn't where you came from; it's where you're going that counts.

—ELLA FITZGERALD

In the spring of 2005, the committee realized that we needed to begin piloting the cornerstone to capstone structure in order to move beyond theory, which, as Soules notes, is "less than useful if not confirmed—or at least entertained—by the practice of experts" (2006). We decided to improvise again by utilizing the Bridge to Transfer program as our curricular and pedagogical laboratory. Bridge to Transfer is designed to encourage students bound for four-year colleges to move in cohorts in a progression from learning community to learning community, semester by semester, toward the completion of an associate's degree, and eventual transfer to our neighboring senior colleges within CUNY.

Bridge to Transfer targets first-semester freshmen who register in the liberal arts and sciences transfer program and demonstrate readiness to take college-level writing and math courses. We place Bridge to Transfer students in cornerstone learning communities that combine our first-year freshman writing course with required courses in other General Education disciplines. Among some of the more academically prepared students who enter Queensborough, Bridge to Transfer students often complete their associate's degree in two years. While some intend to transfer before graduation, many former Queensborough students have realized after transferring that they are less prepared to tackle the academic demands of senior colleges than they had anticipated. We have, in fact, enthusiastically embraced statistics indicating that those CUNY transfer-bound students who do remain at the community colleges through graduation are more likely to perform better with higher GPAs and persistence to graduation at the senior institutions, often even better than the students who began their college education at the four-year colleges.

We hypothesized that an integrative capstone experience might encourage students to complete their degrees at Queensborough, and the faculty teaching in the Bridge to Transfer learning communities would be the experts testing our theory. The English department proposed a possible capstone experience that in its development would mirror our double helix pedagogy. Its recursivity, we anticipated, could be incorporated into any upper level course. A capstone experience proposed for an advanced writing course, for example, would first introduce Marjane Satrapi's *Persepolis: The Story of a Childhood* (2003), a graphic-autobiographical account of a young girl's life under the Islamic Revolution, which pushes at the boundaries of writing, explores problems of representing the self, and theorizes how to situate the self in a larger social and political context. The plan also includes the use of one or two essays that would bridge the work of *Persepolis* to what follows. These works take on a first-person persona but would explore the dialogue between the self's experience and looking at external phenomena, through the writings of Adrienne Rich, Jane Tompkins, and Gloria Anzaldua, among others.

What follows in this capstone experience is the reading of *The Sneaker Book: Anatomy of an Industry and an Icon* by Tom Vanderbilt (1998). In *The Sneaker Book*, the author looks at the $11 billion sneaker industry, its history, design, manufacturing, distribution, marketing, and advertising. Students would examine how the author uses historical documents, creates a narrative to put them into a context, and advertises his product. Accomplishing this, the writers would create their own anatomy of an idea or object (composing a handful of texts that, when brought together, form a whole). The hope is that the writers would be able to draw directly upon the kinds of work they have been asked to do in previous learning communities and to focus their interest and their methodology based upon the kind of disciplinary perspective to which they are most sympathetic (Gray 2005).

However, true to the unpredictability inherent in our jazz performance, two-thirds of the students who had been enrolled in the planned capstone course collectively decided they should fulfill a history requirement instead of an English elective, dropped the English course, added the history course, and subverted the capstone experience we had planned for them. Nevertheless, they did fulfill the spirit of the capstone by enrolling in an honors history course, and we decided that their improvisation was worthy of the most talented jazz musicians, for they had made a daring move that was yet within the constraints of the curriculum itself, within the constraints, in jazz terms, of Soules's protocol of improvisation.

Despite our initial disappointment in having our plan for a capstone aborted, we were pleased with the students' sense both of community and of what they desired from a final or "capstone" experience at Queensborough, from their very education itself. The students reinforced for us that if we engage them and give them a stage of their own on which to perform, which is precisely what we want to do in General Education, then we have to be willing, as Toni Morrison writes, to recognize that "if [the voice] is really involved in the process of telling the story and letting the other voices speak, the story that it thought it knew turns out to be entirely different from what it predicted because the characters will be evolving within the story, within the book" (1995). Or as Lee Shulman asserted at our 2nd Annual CUNY Conference on General Education at QCC in May of 2006, teaching that allows the dynamic voices of students to be heard will inevitably be a "pedagogy of uncertainty."

A bridge, in musical terms, consists of contrasts as well as new directions and is normally a middle section, with an after section as well as a before, but we have chosen the bold step of letting the bridge in our performance actually draw the performance to a close. We do so because we want to be continually reminded that this particular chord progression is one that needs to remain open to new ideas and to new voices. As in all improvisations, the main idea is to create an open-ended dialogue that continually inspires new thoughts and, correspondingly, new directions.

RECAPITULATION

So, then the voice realizes, after hearing other voices, that the narrative is not going to be at all what it predicted. The more it learns about the characters (and they are not what the voice thought), it has to go on, but it goes on with more knowledge. The voice says, "Now I know. Now I know."

—TONI MORRISON, INTERVIEW ON *JAZZ*

Our original charge from the University was to keep students not only enrolled but engaged. Our cornerstone-capstone curricular structure and accompanying double-helix pedagogy launch students on this upward spiral at the moment they enter college by building cornerstone experiences based on the knowledges and capabilities that they bring with them from both life experience and former schooling. It then propels them toward a capstone experience that enables them to capitalize in myriad ways from projects to internships on what they have learned during their time with us. Through our performance, through the performance collectively of all of our faculty, we intend for our students to launch their own performances as our partners in learning.

These jam sessions have been enlightening for us, drawing us into a rhythmic partnership characterized by syncopation and swing, stretching our thinking and causing us to reflect on approaches to teaching in our own programs. We also have been inspired to examine the connections between the components of our individual programs and the greater learning community. Our challenge for the immediate future is to find the note that resonates within our college in order to encourage accommodation and negotiation by the faculty in the humanities curriculum—and possibly the sciences and math as well—in adapting and piloting our model for the General Education curriculum. In the 2006–2007 academic year, we on this committee will disperse to three new General Education committees—one addressing the cornerstone experience, another, a 30-credit milestone assessment, and the third, the capstone experience. We also intend to continue piloting our model in Bridge to Transfer, and Anita will adapt the model to the fledgling Education Academy designed to provide education students with a cohesive group educational experience.

We know our solo tunes, but in the redemptive nature of jazz improvisation, we also know that we are each a member of a larger group and that this asserting of our individual freedoms against the constraints and opportunities of the curriculum of our institution, is precisely what affirms that the institution is possible. This new knowledge, finally, is the excitement, the razor's edge of our performance.

CODA

> You know what's the loudest noise in the world, man? The loudest noise in the world is silence.
>
> —THEOLONIUS MONK

When students' voices are not heard in the classroom, how do we know if they are engaged? Jazz historically has been the music of the unheard and dispossessed, and we need to hear the loud, uneasy silence of our students if we are to give each of them an opportunity to become our partners in learning and join the classroom performance—to take their reflections and insights into solo flight within the group and to thus acquire the power in the larger society that results from informed and confident utterance.

NOTE

The authors wish to thank James Geasor, a Queensborough honors student who began his college career as a student at Juilliard School of Music, for sharing with us his immense knowledge of jazz.

WORKS CITED

Applebee, Arthur N. *Curriculum as Conversation: Transforming Traditions of Teaching and Learning.* Chicago: University of Chicago Press, 1996.

Dewey, John. *The School and Society.* Chicago: University of Chicago Press, 1923.

Gray, Peter. "EN213 B2T Capstone." E-mail to Michael Roggow, Megan Elias, David Humphries, John Talbird, Peter Bales, Shannon Kincaid, Linda Stanley, Stephen Beltzer, Jeffrey Jankowski, Lori Anderson-Moseman, 7 December 2005.

Morrison, Toni. "Toni Morrison." Interview with Angels Carabi. *Belles Lettres* (Spring 1995): 40–43.

Satrapi, Marjane. *Persepolis: The Story of a Childhood.* Alex Awards, 2003.

Shulman, Lee S. "Professing the Liberal Arts." In *The Wisdom of Practice: Essays on Teaching, Learning, and Learning to Teach.* 545–566. San Francisco: Jossey-Bass, 2004.

Soules, Marshall. "Improvising Character: Jazz, the Actor, and Protocols of Improvisation" (6 June 2006). http://www.mala.bc.ca/~soules/shepard/character.html.

St. Louis Model. http://www.stlcc.edu/genednew/report (March 2005).

Stearns, Peter. "General Education Revisited, Again." *Liberal Education,* Winter 2002, 42–47.

Summerfield, Judith. "On Liberal Education: Claiming the Public University in the New Millennium." Book proposal, 2006.

Vanderbilt, Tom. *The Sneaker Book: Anatomy of an Industry and an Icon.* The New Press: New York, 1998.

CHAPTER SIX

Reforming General Education AT Queens College

DONALD M. SCOTT

Queens College

Colleges and universities all over the country in recent years have undertaken the difficult, if not daunting, task of reviewing and reforming general education, asking not only what courses but also what pedagogies are needed to provide very different student bodies with the education they need to understand and confront a complex and continually changing global world. For colleges and universities are stubbornly inertial institutions; while piecemeal changes—a revised major, a new program, new research initiatives—although sometimes difficult to effect, are accomplished quite often and readily, change on the scale of revamping an overall general education curriculum is a complex, long-range, deeply political process. More often than not such attempts to get a whole institution to move in a different direction fail. It is small wonder that most institutions of higher education change their general education programs in twenty-five- year to thirty-year cycles.

On April 6, 2006, at its last business meeting of the academic year, the Queens College Academic Senate adopted a general education reform proposal put forward by the Senate Undergraduate Curriculum Committee (UCC). This essay is an account of how this goal was achieved and a discussion of what remains to be done to translate the proposal into a genuine, far-reaching reform of general education at Queens College. It is written is some ways from the inside. In my role as Dean of Social Science and Professor of History, I was invited to serve as chair-coordinator of a key President's Task Force on General Education. Currently I am faculty director of the Center for Teaching and Learning, which will be a central venue for the development of the courses the new general education will require. However, I also write with the detachment of an historian and scholar. My focus is Queens College—it is my particular study for an examination of the politics, processes, and challenges facing the growing movement to reform general/liberal education.

Queens College and Brooklyn College were both founded in 1937, extending the City's four-year, liberal arts colleges beyond Manhattan's City and Hunter Colleges. Its initial general education curriculum was largely a replication of Columbia University's famed core general education curriculum possibly because Columbia University Ph.D.s provided the bulk of its faculty for the first twenty-five years. This curriculum prevailed until the late 1960s when Queens College, as did many other colleges and universities, adopted a largely requirement-less system, which in 1975 was itself replaced by a set of "Liberal Arts and Sciences Area Requirements" (LASAR). When LASAR was instituted, it was expected that the menu of courses fulfilling its requirements would be limited, consisting largely of introductory survey courses in departments and the college's few interdisciplinary programs, such as American Studies. The list of LASAR courses soon expanded well beyond introductory courses, as department after department, eager to maintain enrollments and crucial FTEs in the face of uncertain enrollment and persistent underfunding, submitted more and more courses to fulfill one LASAR requirement or another. Eventually, a growing number of faculty came to believe that this proliferation of courses counting as general education courses did not serve well either general education or our students. Accordingly, in the late 1980s a broad faculty committee reviewed the LASAR system and developed an extensive reform proposal; in the 1990s the Undergraduate Curriculum Committee conducted another systematic review. Nothing came of either effort.

Mindful of these two failed attempts, the UCC in late 2000 undertook another attempt to do something about general education at Queens College. Sensing that the earlier reform efforts had failed largely because the departments—then, as now, key to the success or failure of any general curricular program—were unwilling to risk making any basic changes, the UCC decided not to challenge LASAR but chose, instead, to stay within the LASAR framework and concentrated on sharpening the existing definitions of LASAR categories and classifications. Some faculty considered the UCC efforts to be too narrowly focused and feared that adoption of the proposals, worthy as they might be, would in the end only further embed the LASAR system in the curriculum. Some feared this revision would be taken as a more basic reform than it was and thereby might prevent for years the development of the idea that deeper reform was needed or even desirable. In any case, discussion of the UCC proposals was put aside in the spring of 2003 when President James Muyskens, following a mandate from the central administration of

CUNY, appointed a broadly based President's Task Force on General Education to look at the larger issues of the curriculum and produce a final report and set of recommendations for the reform of general education by September 2004.

The President gave the task force a challenging mandate. He charged it to think deeply and broadly about what a Queens College undergraduate education needs to be in order to equip its graduates with the intellectual abilities needed to negotiate an ever-changing world of information and knowledge, and to understand a complex, changing world and act in it as citizens of the city, nation, and world. The Task Force consisted of nine members, drawn from all academic divisions. It included both senior and non-tenured faculty, all chosen to serve, not as defenders of the interests of their particular division, but as representatives in the Burkean sense, as persons selected from each of the four academic divisions whose responsibility it was to act in the best interests of the College as a whole. Moreover, the President asked the Task Force to "suspend" consideration of issues of turf and resources as it undertook its work. Inevitably, such issues would come up—as indeed they did, with a vengeance—but neither the President nor the members of the Task Force wanted such considerations to frame its work.

From one perspective, the 2002–2003 academic year was not a particularly auspicious time for the College to undertake such a review or for the President to launch an ambitious general/liberal education review. The College was just emerging from a deeply dispiriting period of turmoil. After a stormy five-year term, the previous president had resigned in the face of declining enrollments and fiscal deficit and disorder. In six years there had been five provosts. Although the interim president Russell Hotzler had succeeded in restoring order and some much needed fiscal stability, thirteen of the fourteen top academic officers of the college remained in acting capacities. Faculty morale was especially low, particularly among veteran faculty. Similarly to many financially strapped public institutions like CUNY, which had gone through a long period without being able to appoint many, if any, new faculty, Queens College had an aging faculty, a substantial majority of whom had been appointed in the 1960s and early 1970s. Many veteran faculty thought that both the institution itself and their own situations had been in steady decline for decades. Many were disengaged from most institutional matters and disinclined to invest time or energy in curricular reform. In addition, President Muyskens, appointed from outside the CUNY system, had only taken office that July. Faculty and staff were understandably nervous, having recently experienced an outsider president who had been singularly high-handed in his mode of operating, often seeking to impose programmatic changes on the institution without any real consultation with the faculty, many of whom he held in contempt. President Muyskens seemed to be very different, respectful of faculty and their prerogatives, and open and collegial in his mode of operation. Still, faculty were concerned about what kind of presidency he would in fact conduct and were uneasy about whether he might try to impose his own ideas and changes on the college.

It was also a promising time for the College to undertake general education reform. The existing system, after all, had been in place for more than thirty years. General education reform, generally, appears to happen in generational cycles: all over the country colleges and universities are examining and reforming twenty-five-year-old liberal education programs, with institutions like the Association of American Colleges and Universities and the Carnegie Foundation, as well as private and public funding agencies such as FIPSE, are providing support for many of these efforts. Closer to home, both Queens College and CUNY more generally had seen increased attention over the past decade to undergraduate education. Under Judith Summerfield's leadership, the College had established a very successful and award-winning learning community program for incoming freshmen (FYI); it adopted and was busily implementing a Writing Across the Curriculum program, and was experimenting with a new pedagogy, entitled "Reacting to the Past." More and more faculty were concerned that the college's educational structures, particularly LASAR, were no longer capable of meeting the educational needs of what had become a very different student body that confronted a vastly changed world of knowledge and an ever-changing global society. Something more than simple revision of the existing system seemed called for. In addition, due to retirements from its aging faculty, the College was rapidly being refreshed by a significant number of new and talented younger faculty. As of 2005, more than one-third of the college's full-time faculty had been hired in the previous five years. Thus, when Queens College was invited to be among the first group of six CUNY institutions to launch a full-scale—and equally important, centrally funded—review of general education at CUNY, it presented the college an opportunity to undertake a significant curricular reform that it could not afford to miss. (It also would have been politically unwise for the College to decline to participate in the CUNY-wide general education project.) In addition, Judith Summerfield, a long-time Queens College faculty member, then serving as special assistant for undergraduate education to CUNY Vice President for Academic Affairs Louise Mirrer, was the person chosen to direct the overall CUNY general education project.

The Task Force identified two immediate tasks as it began its work in the spring of 2003. It had to forge itself into a coherent and effective working entity by finding a "common" ground and mapping out a general plan of action. It was also crucial that the Task Force establish its presence and credibility with faculty, academic staff, and students. This involved gaining the attention of the community, not always an easy matter at a commuter college. The Task Force was aware of its anomalous position within the College and the skepticism and, to some extent, uneasiness that greeted its formation. It was an "extra-ordinary" and somewhat anomalous entity: appointed by the President and Provost from faculty members recommended by the four academic deans, one of whom—following CUNY guidelines—was named as the "co-ordinator" of the Task Force. Moreover, it could easily be seen as treading on territory that was firmly within the formal purview of the Academic Senate and its Undergraduate Curriculum Committee. No axiom is more firmly held by faculty than the idea that "in matters of curriculum and pedagogy the faculty is sovereign" and that the Academic Senate and its curriculum committee constituted the formal instrument by which this sovereignty was to be exercised. To be sure, there was precedent for the establishment of ad hoc committees charged to look into specific curricular issues that were composed of faculty and academic staff who were not necessarily members of the Senate or on the UCC. However, such committees were ordinarily appointed by the Senate whose own curriculum committee had already instituted its own attempt to modify the LASAR system.

President Muyskens announced the formation of the Task Force in a letter to the College and spoke of the importance of the issue and his commitment to general education reform to the College Personnel and Budget Committee (P & B), made up of all department chairs and attended ex officio by a wide range of administrators. The Task Force met weekly for two hours and set as its goal for the semester the preparation of an initial report designed to provide a conceptual framework for the discussions that would take place the next academic year and, it was hoped, yield a final report and set of proposals to be presented to the campus community by September 2004. It also quickly announced and conducted a series of open faculty and academic staff forums, held at different times and on different days so as to attract as broad participation as possible. These forums were very open-ended, intended as a venue for the Task Force to hear from and listen to the faculty's ideas about general education and the curriculum and to solicit whatever ideas, queries, or complaints anyone wished to offer. (These sessions proved very helpful as the Task Force prepared its initial report.) The Task Force was also aware of the importance of student input. It decided against polling students or organizing focus groups among them, but the coordinator and various other members of the task force met several times with the leaders of the Student Association.

In June the Task Force delivered its initial, framing report to President Muyskens and issued it to the Queens College community at the opening of the 2003–2004 academic year. The Task Force, as a matter of practicality as much as principle, ruled out calling for a "core" general education program that is confined to a few courses that all students would take in common and agreed that whatever proposal it came up with had to give students considerable choice as to the precise general education path they might pursue. The Task Force also quickly agreed that a) liberal education and its goals rather than the major and its sometimes quite vocationally oriented goals should frame a Queens College education, and b) that general education should not be confined to the first two years but extend through the students' undergraduate career. It also insisted that general education had to confront directly the vast changes and expansion in knowledge that had occurred over the preceding quarter century, as well as the dramatic changes in our student body and in the world. Finally, the Task Force declared that a central task for general/liberal education was to counteract "the fragmentation of knowledge itself" that Vartan Gregorian named as "the fundamental problem underlying the disjointed curriculum" of contemporary undergraduate education, in which the " 'curriculum' is rarely more than a collection of courses [largely] devoid of planning, context, and coherence" or much purpose beyond attaining "the degree needed to obtain decent employment" (2004, B12). It also pointed out that deep general education reform would require some changes in campus culture, most notably fostering the idea among faculty that general education was an important part of their professional responsibility, and that the time and energy faculty devoted to the course construction and revision and faculty development that curricular reform would require had to be recognized by the College and the requisite bodies when considering tenure and promotion.

The Task Force's initial report was the opening shot in what would be a full academic year devoted to as broad a campus discussion of general education as possible. The Report was issued and widely circulated with considerable fanfare, including a letter from President Muyskens extolling the report and calling for vigorous debate of the issues it raised. The President also commissioned an article on general education from the Task Force coordinator for the Queens College Alumni magazine, which was also distributed to every faculty and academic staff member. In addition, in his remarks at the fall Faculty and Staff Assembly the President made it clear that he considered general education to be at the top of the college's agenda.

The Task Force continued to hold its weekly two-hour meetings. (The members arranged their teaching schedules in order to reserve a common time for these meetings.) In the fall semester, it conducted even more forums for faculty, organized around the framework put forth in the initial Report. The Task Force coordinator also met with each of the caucuses made up of the chairpersons of the four academic divisions. In addition, the whole Task Force addressed a forum organized by the Student Association, which then distributed and tabulated a student questionnaire. It was well aware of the importance of student opinion to any reform effort, particularly the opinions of the officers of the Student Association and the student members of the Academic Senate, who comprised 30% of its voting members. As one member of the Task Force, who had been in the Senate when it adopted the LASAR system, put it, "the students are key" to the passage of any curricular reform. They could not pass a measure themselves, but without their support (they often voted as a block) any curricular measure would most likely fail. Finally, at the beginning of the spring semester, the Task Force set up four faculty Working Groups to focus more intensely on the areas the task force had singled out for special attention. The four working groups were:

1. The Entry Experience
2. Suffusing Critical Abilities across the Curriculum
3. Areas of Knowledge
4. An Integrative Capstone Experience.

More than sixty faculty and academic staff volunteered for the Working Groups. The groups met intensively for eight weeks, sometimes breaking into subgroups, and submitted written recommendations to the Task Force. Armed with these reports, its own deliberations, and email, letters, and conversations with individual faculty members, the Task Force, after intense debate over a range of possible recommendations, issued its final report, *Toward a Reorganization of General Education at Queens College*, on schedule, to the college community in September 2004.

The Task Force considered it essential that the nature and goals of a liberal education be clearly, cogently, and persuasively articulated at the outset, not because there was much that was startlingly new about such a statement, but because it thought it was important that the deliberations begin with a common acknowledgment and understanding of what liberal education entails. It defined a liberal education as one that

> expands the mind and heart, opening windows and presenting opportunities never before imagined. More than a mere accumulation of credits and subjects . . . more than preparation for a vocation, a liberal education as John Dewey argued, is an education for living, one that makes the individual an active learner who makes life connections across subject areas so as to extend their understanding of themselves and the world. (President's Task Force on General Education 2004, 8)

The goal of a Queens College liberal education "thus is to equip its graduates with the intellectual abilities to negotiate an ever-changing world of information and to understand a complex ever-changing world and act in it as citizens of the city, nation and world" (8).

The Task Force saw this education as comprised of a set of critical abilities that should permeate the curriculum. This, it argued, included attaining an understanding of the nature, operation, and claims of different areas of knowledge and creativity as well as the ability to:

> 1) understand and use effectively written, verbal, and visual communication, 2) obtain and evaluate information, including numerical and statistical data, derived from multiple sources, including the newer electronic media, 3) critically analyze hypotheses, knowledge claims, and

advocacy arguments, and 4) perceive the ethical dimensions of individual and collective behavior. (President's Task Force on General Education 2004, 8)

The devil, as they say, is in the details. How did the Task Force envision translating its general vision into concrete curricular programs and practices? The four working groups reflected the approach it adopted. The "entry experience" was concerned above all with the problem of how to orient and induct Queens College students into an educational venture that was—or purported to be and, it was believed, should be—very different from their secondary school education. This difference it felt, lay, first, in its character as liberal education and, second, in the in-depth pursuit of a particular field represented by "the major." (The LASAR deployment of introductory departmental survey courses were often both taught and experienced by students as an extension of high school education, rather than something quite different.) However, what seemed to be largely foreign to the vast majority of students was the idea of liberal education itself. The working group considered various ways of introducing students to the "college experience," of preparing them "to be college students." The Task Force proposed a specific, required introductory course, "Understanding Higher Education" as an "orienting intellectual experience for new students." The course, only briefly and somewhat ambiguously, if not to say confusingly, sketched out in *Toward a Reorganization*, was intended to "engage students— many and perhaps most of whom are the first in their family to attend college—in serious, reflective examination of their own education and [thereby] develop an understanding of the nature and purposes of their liberal education at Queens College" (2004, 12).

Few refrains have been more insistent in the many recent discussions, reports, and calls for reform of higher education than for colleges and universities to foster in their students the capacity for "critical thinking." The Task Force strongly endorsed this goal but did not consider "critical thinking" to be a discrete, isolated ability to be taught in a few foundational or introductory courses. Instead, it argued that the acquisition and deepening of critical abilities should take place within substantive contexts, integral to the pursuit of the specific subject matter a course addresses and the knowledge practices it employs. Writing, for example, is not simply an abstract, stand-alone activity but is always writing about something—hence the call to "diffuse" critical abilities throughout the curriculum by embedding them in specific, substantive courses. The Task Force identified four such abilities as essential to critical thinking:

1. expression and persuasion—being able to communicate through writing and speaking;
2. thinking through numeracy—the understanding of and ability to engage in quantitative analysis and reasoning;

3. creating knowledge—the understanding of and ability to conduct research;
4. information literacy—the understanding of and ability to use media sources for information and communication.

It called for diffusing them throughout the curriculum (via mechanisms adapted from the Writing Across the Curriculum program) in courses, which would incorporate fostering proficiency in a particular ability as a specific goal of the course. It endorsed the WAC program and called for a similar program for numeracy, requiring that every student take a college mathematics course and three "numeracy intensive" courses. In addition, it argued that these courses should neither be clustered in the first two years nor in the last two years but spread across the student's entire undergraduate career.

The crux of *Toward a Reorganization*, as with any proposal for a new or reformed general education program, lay in its approach to the particular "areas of knowledge" in which students would be required to take the courses that together would fulfill the college's general education requirements. Under LASAR the designation of required areas of knowledge was explicitly mapped onto the divisional structure of the college, calling for Humanities 1 and 2 courses, Social Science courses, and courses in the Natural Sciences. The Task Force eschewed this approach. Instead, partly drawing upon the definitions produced by the UCC's recent examination of general education, it identified five "areas of knowledge": Language and Literature (2 courses); Arts (1 course); Culture, Society and Historical Perspective (2 courses); Scientific Inquiry and the Natural World (2 courses, one of which must be a lab course); the United States Experience (1 course); and Ethics, Morality, and Religion (1 course). Moreover, believing that general education should be addressed by explicitly designated general education courses that would be spread across the student's whole undergraduate career, it called for a two-tiered structure for the areas of knowledge requirements. Courses in the above categories were designated as Foundations courses that would ordinarily be completed within students' first two years. Although the Task Force argued that "connections among areas of knowledge are as important as the areas themselves" it did not consider interdisciplinarity per se to be the principal purpose of the Foundations courses. Rather, the intention was to enable students to experience the range of methodologies and philosophies as well the content associated with many areas of human knowledge and understanding. In addition to these Foundations courses, then, the Task Force recommended that students be required to take three "Integration and Synthesis" courses in their final two years. These courses would be topical and thematic courses that crossed disciplinary boundaries to address significant issues and problems with resonances for understanding the contemporary world. Moreover, the Task Force did not recommend including specifically topical courses on topics such as globalization, or race, class, and gender among the Areas of Knowledge requirements. Rather, the Task Force thought it preferable to address such important topics throughout the designated areas of knowledge categories. Accordingly, it recommended that area of knowledge courses:

1. be global and comparative in their reach;
2. address issues of diversity and the nature and construction of various forms of difference;
3. utilize the rich diversity of the College the Borough of Queens as a unique and valuable educational resource;
4. engage students in active inquiry;
5. involve reading and analysis of primary documents and materials.

In some ways, the Task Force's most important move was its insistence that general education courses had to be given a distinct and explicit definition and designation, and that institutionally they be located outside the departmental structure. The Task Force was convinced that however cogent it might have been at the outset, over the years the LASAR system had devolved into a vast New York delicatessen menu of wholly departmental courses, in large measure because general education at Queens had neither a distinct intellectual identity nor a specified institutional location. Accordingly, the Task Force argued that all Foundation and Integration and Synthesis courses be given explicit, non-departmental labels. Full-time equivalencies (FTEs), it suggested, might follow the instructor and be assigned to the instructor's "home" department. Departments, if they so desired, could permit particular general education courses to count toward the fulfillment of their requirements for the major. In addition, it argued that General Education needed to have a specific institutional location. It called for the establishment of something like an "Office of General Education," which would be responsible for oversight of general education. It suggested that the newly created Center for Teaching and Learning serve as an important venue for the development of the courses the new general education program would need as it became operational. It further suggested the establishment of a general education subcommittee of the UCC, similar to the subcommittee on WAC courses, as the mechanism for examining and approving general education courses.

The Task Force's final report was again widely distributed and presented to the College with considerable fanfare. It was widely considered to be the document that would (or should) frame the debate over general education that, it was hoped, would end up with a genuine reform of general education. At the fall Faculty and Staff Assembly, President Muyskens introduced the members of the Task Force and the UCC and then devoted all his remarks to general education. He called for vigorous debate and made clear his expectation that after thorough discussion the College would adopt a significant new general education program. This was an important move on his part because it clearly signaled the importance he attached to general education reform and the work of the two committees, without in any way seeming to usurp the faculty's role in curricular matters. The UCC and the Task Force conducted a series of joint forums on the ideas and proposals contained in the Task Force's final report and the Task Force coordinator again visited the four divisional caucuses and met with several departments to answer questions about it and its proposals.

The response to the report was uneven, as might be expected. Most of the people, such as the members of the working groups, who had been actively involved in fashioning the report or who had followed its work closely were largely positive in their response and were particularly appreciative of the final report's comprehensive vision and its attempt to clearly articulate a general education program that represented a real departure from the LASAR system. Others, as expected, responded mainly if not solely to those parts of the report that either by commission or omission seemed to have a direct impact on their areas of interest. Overall, however, it still remained the case that, as much as the Task Force, the President, and others had tried over the preceding three semesters to direct the faculty's attention to general education reform, most faculty had not yet really engaged the issue. For many, general education remained a matter of indifference, but others held back from joining the issue because they realized that it was too early in the game to give much attention to education reform. The time for real engagement, they reasoned, was when the UCC put specific action proposals before the Academic Senate. That was when issues of turf and resources would certainly emerge.

With the issuance of *Toward a Reorganization* the general education reform effort moved into a new phase and onto new, tricky terrain. The Task Force had completed its assigned task and dissolved itself. Its members, as individuals, would continue to play an active role in advocating reform, but as an entity the Task Force itself had no further role to play. The center of the reform effort shifted to the college community at large which now had to be brought more fully into the discussion. Most importantly, the responsibility for moving any reform forward now lay with the Undergraduate Curriculum Committee of the Academic Senate. It was responsible for preparing and presenting any reform measures to the Senate for final action. However, when the Task Force passed the reform baton to the UCC, the relationship between the two was an ambiguous and somewhat uneasy one. From the moment the President first announced the formation of the Task Force, he made it clear that the Task Force had a specific role to play and that it was not intended to intrude upon the responsibilities and authority of the UCC and the Senate, a sentiment he and the Task Force itself repeated on various occasions. The coordinator of the Task

Force and the chair of the UCC worked hard to keep the channels of communication open.

Necessarily, however, the Task Force had conducted its work independently, outside the formal governance structure. For three semesters the Task Force had been front and center, the initiator of the campus discussion and the public face of general education reform at Queens. When general education reform was addressed, it was in reference to the work of the Task Force. It was not at all clear as the baton was passed what the stance of the UCC toward the Task Force and its Report would or should be. Had the Task Force de facto intruded upon and usurped the UCC's role? Would or should the UCC's task be largely one of translation, of taking the Report and transforming it into formal action proposals? Alternatively, should it take a more independent and active role in which it fashioned its own proposals, informed perhaps by the ideas and suggestions contained in *Toward a Reorganization*, but not confined or constrained by it? Conversely, what should be the relationship of the Task Force to the UCC as it took up its specified responsibility in the reform process? (The ambiguities of the situation were reflected in the confusion as to whether people should address their responses to the report and suggestions for what should finally be proposed to the Task Force or to the UCC.)

The UCC, like the Task Force before it, found itself in a tricky and somewhat unprecedented position. On the one hand, it was important that it maintain its independence and properly fulfill its formal responsibility to review courses and curricular proposals, sending them back to the originating unit for revision and then presenting them with its endorsement to the Senate for approval. However, general education reform was a somewhat different matter. No regularly constituted body was its originator and sponsor. Instead it sprang from an ad hoc task force which had not presented its ideas and recommendations in a UCC/Senate-ready form. Under these circumstances, whatever the committee came up with what would need to be its own document, one that it would "own" and work hard to get adopted by the Senate. At the same time, at least politically, the committee's proposal needed to be seen as responsive to the Task Force Report and the campus process that had produced it. It needed at least to adapt some of its suggestions and produce a set of proposals that was faithful to the spirit of the report, particularly in its call for something that would be a real departure from LASAR, in short, something that could be seen as proposing a new general education system.

After the round of forums, people wanted to see what the UCC would do. For some time, there was silence from the committee. It did not meet with members of the Task Force to discuss the report until early February. The UCC's initial response was rather tepid, and the meeting with the task force members was a tense, somewhat antagonistic one that no one found satisfactory. Members of the two groups did not meet again until late May. Like the Task Force before it, the UCC carefully guarded its independence as it carried out its appointed task. The UCC prepared an initial informational report for the Senate which described the Task Force proposals and then focused largely on questions and problems that the Task Force's specific recommendations seemed to raise. (The Student Association, declining invitations to meet with task force members, issued a largely negative report.) By early March it began to be bruited about that once again "general education reform was dead." A number of people knew about the measured response of the UCC, and some assumed, incorrectly, that the UCC was in fact hostile to the report and its recommendations. Moreover, many people still thought of the Task Force as the public face of general education reform at Queens College but the Task Force was no longer visible. There was little for its members to do until the UCC came up with something concrete to discuss and act upon.

Appearances to the contrary, general education reform was not dead, though it was in a precarious position. It was clear that the Task Force's hope that a broad set of proposals could be debated and acted upon in the 2004–2005 academic year had been unrealistic, if not naive. It was easy to forget how burdensome the UCC's agenda of day-to-day curricular business was. General education reform was a huge add-on to the committee's workload.

The UCC had to devise a strategy as to how it would proceed and then decide what to recommend and how to recommend it. The UCC's (in the end largely successful) strategy was not unlike the strategy Senator Henry Clay had used to pass the famous Compromise of 1850 that postponed the Civil War for a decade. Initially, all the separate compromise measures had been gathered into one large "Omnibus Bill" which was defeated because the opponents of each particular measure banded together to defeat the whole. The UCC, like Clay, decided to break the report into four areas (corresponding roughly to the four key areas in the Task Force report) and address them one at a time, rather than try to fashion an "omnibus" general education proposal. It was clear to everyone that the most important one was the "Areas of Knowledge." It was also clear that it would take much of the next academic year to get Academic Senate action on a comprehensive Areas of Knowledge proposal. At the same time, it was widely recognized that it would be a serious, if not fatal, mistake to let the year pass without some positive action. Without something concrete to show for the year's effort, the rumor that general education reform was dead could well become prophesy. Accordingly, the UCC submitted a proposal to the Senate regarding the Integration and Synthesis courses. It reduced the Task Force's recommendation that three such upper division general education courses be required to a proposal for one course and called for a program to "pilot" a series of such courses over the next two academic years. The proposal passed the Senate at its last substantive meeting of the academic year. At the same time, the UCC had begun serious work on a proposal for the Areas of Knowledge that it would present to the college at the beginning of the 2005–2006 academic year.

In late May 2005, the College sent a seven-person team to a week-long Workshop on General Education conducted by the American Association of Colleges and Universities (AAC & U). The coordinator of the Task Force led the team, which was composed of the long time chair of the UCC, the Associate Provost, who is a key ex-officio member of the UCC, a second member of the Task Force, and three faculty members who had been active in the working groups. The Queens College team's participation in the AA C& U ended up being a pivotal event in the College's reform effort, less because of what the team learned at the workshop than because of how it coalesced a group. There had been some worry within the UCC when it learned that the College was sending an as yet unnamed delegation to the AAC & U workshop that this might be yet another example of a group outside the UCC entering into the general education reform process just as the UCC itself was hard at work crafting the Area of Knowledge proposals it expected to put before the college community in the fall. It had already drawn up a draft of a proposal. Would this now be shelved when the team returned from the Workshop? The composition of the team somewhat allayed these fears. Even so, most important was the way in which the team came together as a working group. The chair of the UCC presented the UCC's Areas of Knowledge draft to the group. It occasioned intense and often heated debate within the group, but there was at the same time a clear recognition that the document the UCC was working on was an initial version of the one that would be put before the College in the fall. It was decided that as soon as possible after the Workshop members of the team would meet with the UCC to continue the discussions that had shaped much of the work of the team at the Workshop. At that joint meeting, debate continued but with an important underlying amity as it became more and more likely that a final document could be forged that everyone there could support. In fact, several team members worked with UCC members and served as the final drafting committee that over the summer hammered out the final UCC Areas of Knowledge proposal.

The UCC's proposal for Areas of Knowledge requirements closely paralleled the definitions and classifications of the Task Force (which in turn had drawn upon definitions the UCC had earlier proposed.) Students would be required to take eight Perspectives on the Liberal Arts and Sciences (PLAS) courses in five basic categories: Reading Literature (RL-2 courses); Appreciating and Participating in the Arts (PA -1 course); Cultures and Values (CV- 1 course); Analyzing Social Structures (SS 2 courses); and Natural Science (2 courses). The UCC proposal did, however, modify the Task Force recommendations in several ways. It added a second category of requirements to be fulfilled by PLAS courses, which it labeled "Contents of Experience Courses," of which there were three: The United States (US), European Traditions (ET), and World Cultures (WC). It also included two "extended requirements"— Pre-Industrial Society (PI) and Abstract or Quantitative Reasoning (QR)—which could be fulfilled by PLAS courses, courses in a major, or suitable electives. The several PLAS courses, like the Task Force's area of knowledge courses, shared a common, clearly stated overall educational goal. Through them students would "acquire awareness of the connections among different educational goals and the expectations of modern life, of the characteristic modes of study in the several disciplines, and the content of different categories of experience that shape modern academic discourse" (Undergraduate Curriculum Committee 2004, 2).

The UCC rejected the Task Force's vision of the structural relationship of general education to the rest of the college curriculum, particularly its relationship to the academic departments. The Task Force argued that the general education program should be housed in a clearly designated institutional location outside the departmental structure. Such a location was necessary, the Task Force believed, in order to develop and protect general education as a distinctive and crucial part of a Queens College liberal education by providing a counter to the force that today's academic disciplinary specialization exerts on faculty and hence on the undergraduate curriculum. This argument was met with considerable skepticism. Departments objected that the demands of their undergraduate and graduate programs were such that they could not afford to spare significant faculty time for a "separate" general education program. The Task Force tried to counter this objection by pointing out that once introductory departmental courses no longer served as general education courses, departments would not need to offer as many sections of such courses, thereby freeing faculty time for general education courses. Under the Task Force's plan, departments would not stand to lose FTEs but would simply have to reconfigure how faculty instructional time was deployed. This argument might have had some theoretical merit, but it soon became clear that it would be hard to get departments to risk assigning a significant portion of instructional time to specially designated, extra-departmental general education courses.

The UCC adopted a very different strategy. Instead of removing general education courses from the departments, the UCC proposal placed the burden of general education squarely on the departments themselves. Conceptually as well as practically, that is, politically, this was a shrewd move, essential to the eventual passage of the UCC proposal. Under the UCC proposal, the departments themselves had to develop courses that were specifically designed to address and meet the clearly defined general education goals put forth in the UCC Areas of Knowledge proposal. Although a department might elect to permit one of its specified PLAS courses to count toward its major, the UCC proposal did not allow a department to simply mount a general education version of an ordinary departmental course and have it fulfill an area of knowledge requirement. Moreover, the UCC proposal called for the establishment of a general education subcommittee of the UCC, which would review and approve or disapprove all proposed PLAS courses.

The UCC considered this move essential in order to save "the basic concepts of the Presidential Committee's overview." A long-term member of the UCC who has been through innumerable discussions of general education at Queens College explained the UCC strategy accordingly: "We took the idea that the qualities that define general education as a form of liberal education should be explicitly incorporated in specially designated courses to be offered by departments. It would become the faculty's responsibility to explain how and why the subject being taught belonged in a liberal education context." Perhaps most importantly, because the Perspectives in the Liberal Arts Courses would be "departmental courses for which the department remains responsible to the College, the faculty—within the framework of the department—will become formally responsible to the College for the General Education content" (Lidov 2006).

The UCC presented its Areas of Knowledge proposal to the College at the opening of the 2005–2006 academic year, and discussion over it occupied much of the time of the Academic Senate and numerous departmental, student association, and divisional meetings. The UCC strategy proved to be a successful one: The proposal passed at the last possible moment, at the Academic Senate's last business meeting of the year. It passed by a large measure, with only eight dissenting votes (the student members of the Senate voted unanimously for approval). Nonetheless, passage of the proposal only came after intense debate, during which a positive outcome seemed very much in doubt. Some people considered the UCC proposal to be too narrow; they argued that by relegating responsibility to the departments and permitting the substitution of a departmental course for one PLAS course in the areas in which two PLAS courses were required, did not, in the end, represent a significant change or much of an improvement over LASAR. Others argued that the entire structure of PLAS courses, "contexts of experience" courses, and "extended requirements" was too cumbersome and confusing. Others argued that the proposal, de facto, encroached on departmental autonomy and prerogatives and mandated the teaching of vaguely defined "general education" courses rather than rigorous disciplinary courses. There was also some concern expressed largely by students that the new system represented too great a diminution of student choice. Through intense and patient discussion of what the proposal actually would and would not entail, careful "politicking," and effective presidential leadership, a winning coalition was put together. This group was made up of those who supported the UCC proposal because they thought it would require relatively small changes and not threaten enrollments or FTEs; others who thought it opened up the possibility for broader, more meaningful curricular reconstruction; and still others who feared that if the College itself did not come up with a revision of its general education program, change might be imposed from the outside. An important factor in gaining the support of the student members of the Academic Senate was the argument that, even though the new curriculum could not possibly affect them, they had been given a unique opportunity to do something that would have an important and lasting impact on the College.

Getting an institution of higher learning to adopt a major new curricular program such as its system of general education is a complex, difficult, and multi-year process. Formal adoption of a new general education curriculum is only the first step toward deep reform. What a formally adopted proposal provides is largely a framework for change. The nature and extent of the reform depends upon how a new curriculum is developed and implemented, not only what new and revised courses are developed, but also the process by which this development takes place. In the end, whether Queens College's new general education program involves significant change, or whether it adds up to little more than tinkering around the edges of reform, will depend on what happens over the next two to three years. The proposal adopted by the Academic Senate has the potential to go either way. It is certainly possible that departments and divisions will take a minimalist approach: develop a new course or two, revise a few others, and then use existing major courses as "substitutes" for one of the two required PLAS courses. However, the proposal itself also contains an important conceptual opening for a much more far-reaching reform of general education. All PLAS courses are expected to have in common a set of learning goals. A PLAS course must be explicitly designed to introduce students to how a particular discipline creates knowledge and understanding, show them how this knowledge is part of the larger whole called liberal education and, finally, explore how and why this knowledge addresses what William James referred to as "living" questions—how it connects to the students' lives and the worlds they inhabit. The PLAS system does not provide a "core" curriculum, but it can constitute a "common" general education, one that in all its parts or "areas of knowledge" addresses similar fundamental epistemological, intellectual, and moral questions. In short, what needs to emerge through and out of the development and implementation process is not simply a collection of commonly designated courses, but a coherent and connected general education curriculum that is recognized and embraced as such by both faculty and students as significant, meaningful, and essential.

A more radical, far-reaching change at Queens College (and, I would argue, elsewhere), requires the development not simply of a collection of new courses—no matter how innovative and exciting they may be—but the development of a new and different kind of intellectual and educational culture: one, as Judith Summerfield argues in this volume, that embraces general/liberal education as an important organizing framework for undergraduate education and delivers that education to its students. Unless the faculty and institution believe in the centrality of general education to undergraduate education, there is little chance that students will understand it and its courses as little more than a set of opaque requirements to get "out of the way."

However, can such a cultural change really be effected and if so, how, by whom, and by what means? There are formidable obstacles to such a cultural shift. There is the silo-like organization of faculties in departmental structures in which their disciplinary, departmental home is the most salient, if not the only, campus collective to which they feel allied. It should be pointed out here that at Queens as elsewhere there are a number of efforts, many initiated by faculty members themselves—particularly newer faculty—to break out of this isolation and develop a sense of themselves as part of a broader faculty, not simply a collection of individuals who happen to teach at the same college. Another obstacle lies in the emphasis on disciplinary specialization and intellectual production that so profoundly shape how graduate students are socialized into the academic profession. Too often the lesson that is learned and then reinforced in the early, pre-tenure years of an academic career is that one should cleave as closely as possible to teaching in one's discipline, that "service teaching" may be a part of one's responsibilities but is largely unrelated to one's professional identity, development, and achievement and can, in fact, get in the way of it. Finally, there is the issue of whether and how teaching, curricular work, and engaging in the scholarship of teaching and learning are recognized and rewarded by the institution.

These are formidable obstacles but not, I think, insurmountable. In the end, the burden, or perhaps more accurately, the challenge and opportunity for significant curricular change, lie with the faculty. For such a cultural and hence curricular transformation to take place, there has to be significant faculty "buy in" to the potential and possibilities of the new curriculum, a willingness to devote serious time and effort to curricular development. There are several things that augur well for a significant Queens College buy-in at this time. Curricular reform is something newer faculty (and some veteran faculty) often seem to be eager to engage in, but only if it can be undertaken in ways that do not appear to jeopardize their chances for tenure and career advancement. At Queens College more than a third of the full-time faculty have been hired in the past five years, mostly as tenure track assistant professors. Moreover, by 2008 well over half of the college's full time faculty will have been hired since 1998. General education reform provides this faculty with a rare opportunity to actually fashion the curriculum within which many will likely teach for much of their careers. Second, the PLAS program directly addresses the tension between general education and specialization that marks much of American undergraduate education by starting from the disciplinary structures within which faculty are trained and then moving outward to liberal education issues and questions. Moreover, successful general education reform involves a shift in faculty culture in which faculty members see general education as an essential part of their professional identities and responsibilities. The reform effort also needs to be a collective and collegial effort, in which faculty across departments and divisions work together to design new courses and revise existing ones, self-consciously and directly engaging in local, CUNY-wide, and national conversations about liberal education and teaching and learning. This involves providing incentives and venues—stipends, workshops, institutes, and so on—where individual and group efforts, within departments as well as across departments and divisions, can take place. At Queens College—as at many other institutions—the recently created Center for Teaching and Learning, which brings together the WAC program, faculty and course development programs, and the faculty instructional technology lab in a single location, will provide a central venue for the envisioned curricular, faculty, and cultural development to take place. (In addition, CUNY has instituted a program of annual, CUNY-wide conferences on general education that have brought colleagues from across the system onto "common ground" to discuss crucial issues and practices concerning general education.) As the President's Task Force put it in its letter transmitting its final report to the College, "As the faculty takes up the multi-year task of revising the courses and educational practices it calls for, the faculty, inevitably, will become less a collection of individual teacher/scholars largely scattered in particular departments and more a genuine Collegium with a shared vision of general education" (2004, 3).

Is all of this a utopian vision, not fully realizable? Undoubtedly. However, it is certainly one worth striving toward if liberal education is to reconstitute itself, provide our students with a foundation for continuing intellectual and personal growth, and give them the tools for acting in the world as informed, engaged citizens.

WORKS CITED

Gregorian, Vartan. "Colleges Must Reconstruct the Unity of Knowledge." *The Chronicle of Higher Education*, 50.39 (2004): B12.

Lidov, Joel. "Renewing General Education for Students and Faculty." Remarks delivered to the 2nd Annual CUNY Conference on General Education. "General Education and the Disciplines: New Approaches to Old Debates." Queensborough Community College, 5 May 2006.

President's Task Force on General Education. *Toward a Reorganization of General Education at Queens College*. Queens, NY: Queens College, 2004. http://www.qc.cuny.edu/about/presidents_page/GenEdReport.pdf.

Undergraduate Curriculum Committee. *General Education at Queens College: Proposal 2: Area Requirements*. Queens, NY: Queens College, 2004.

Part IV. Stories from the Field

CHAPTER SEVEN

Integration, Socialization, Collaboration

Inviting Native and Non-Native English Speakers into the Academy Through "Reacting to the Past"

ANN DAVISON AND SUE LANTZ GOLDHABER

Queens College

"The Master said, 'If one learns from others but does not think, one will be bewildered. If, on the other hand, one thinks but does not learn from others, one will be in peril.' "
—CONFUCIUS, *THE ANALECTS*, BOOK II.15

THE CULTURE AND THE CHALLENGE: TRANSITION TO THE ACADEMY

Walk into the Queens College cafeteria on any day when classes are in session, and it is instantly apparent that Queens' reputation for diversity is well deserved. Our borough is the most diverse county in the United States, with a population representing 160 countries and more than 60 languages. Students waiting on the cafeteria lines are likely to be chatting in Hindi, Spanish, Hebrew, Arabic, Greek, Korean . . . you get the picture.

Whether they are native or non-native speakers of English, our students are accustomed to ethnic diversity in their workplaces, neighborhoods, and schools. They expect it. Unfortunately, their strategies for adapting to the large-scale mix of languages and cultures on a campus full of strangers often include self-segregation. Even a cursory tour of the cafeteria reveals ingrained seating patterns: Russian emigres in this corner, African Americans at that table, Chinese here, Pakistanis there. (Note: we are indebted to our former student, Miriam Shaleveshili, for carefully mapping the ethnic groupings in the cafeteria for us.) Our significant ESL population, like their counterparts at other branches of CUNY, must struggle to become more proficient in English while making their way in a campus culture that, while tolerant of difference, offers limited opportunities for real integration.

Depending on their scores on the CUNY reading and writing exams (ACT), these English language learners will be placed either in developmental reading and writing courses (as well as a required communications skills course), or in a section of English 110: College Writing. In either case, these students are eligible to register for additional courses throughout the college, and they are expected to quickly acclimate to the rigors of academic work in a new language.

The leap to English 110: College Writing is a dramatic challenge for most students. Why? For native English-speakers making the transition from high school, it is the discovery that what was deemed superior or acceptable writing in high school will not necessarily earn them the expected A or B on their papers. For others, especially our ESL students, it is the realization that they will be writing extensively from the first day and that paragraph development and grammar are not the sole focus of the College Writing class. ESL students enter this course with great hope and much trepidation. While they continue to build academic reading and writing skills, they also need to develop confidence and build their oral skills so that they can become vocal *participants* in the classroom—something expected in every American university.

Eligibility to be fully integrated into the general student population comes with passing the ACT examination with a score of 7 or better. Theoretically, students who pass are competent to take any course in the catalogue, and many of them manage well. What happens, however, to students for whom academic work in English will be a significant challenge for several semesters to come? They are advised to take classes that will give them ample opportunities to practice their English; yet for many, reading and writing in English remain so time consuming that they shy away from courses that require substantial reading and assiduously avoid any course with a writing component. Math, computer science, and accounting courses fill their schedules, while writing intensive courses are put off until impending graduation forces them to enroll. Classes where students can sit comfortably and quietly in the rear are preferred to classes that require oral participation. The problem is compounded because Queens is a commuter school. Students may retreat at the end of the school day to households, neighborhoods, and even jobs where no English is necessary.

At CUNY, all students must pass a rising junior exam, the CPE (CUNY Proficiency Exam), after 60 credits. ESL students without sufficient practice working thoughtfully with complex texts in English are at a serious disadvantage.

The challenges are clear: How do we facilitate the transition from high school to college and from foreign cultures to the language and culture of the academy? What spaces can we create for ESL students where exploring ideas in their writing is given priority over finessing grammar and usage? How do we enable native and non-native speakers alike to increase language competencies (reading, writing, speaking, listening), build their confidence, integrate socially and join what Patricia Bizzel and others have called "the academic discourse community"? What might a liberal education mean for this diverse population?

In 2003, President Muyskens established a task force charged with evaluating the college's requirements, a process that led to reconstituting the curriculum at Queens, broadly, as Perspectives on the Liberal Arts and Sciences. The final report of the President's Task Force on General Education recommends "a stronger emphasis on the Entry Experience for both Freshmen and transfer students . . . and an expansion of two- or three-course learning communities to as much of the entering first-year class as possible" (2004, 5–6). Among the "critical abilities" considered essential by the task force are "written and oral expression" and "understanding and conducting research." The new vision looks beyond acquisition of knowledge and analytical skills. More important is the ability to question critically, to make logical and imaginative connections, and to understand information and experience contextually. As we implement the new curriculum, our students need to become active participants, not passive observers in the classroom, and faculty need to create innovative opportunities for teaching and learning that will enable them to do so.

REACTING TO THE PAST

Krystyna is from Poland. She has been in New York for about two years and is very hesitant to speak, even in a one-on-one conference. Now, however, she must address the whole class. The students are playing a "game" set in sixteenth-century China at the end of the Ming dynasty. In the guise of Confucian scholars, they are advising the Emperor Wan-li on a matter of critical importance, and each scholar has prepared a written "memorial," an argument that makes his faction's case persuasively.

Krystyna understands the political crisis at hand; she has learned about the culture and traditions that established the form and substance of the memorial. In her hand, which trembles a bit, is a written copy of the memorial that will be posted on the Blackboard Web site with all the memorials from the class. She is anxious, but she is determined not to read her text verbatim, which the scholars have been instructed to avoid. Instead, she summarizes her argument from prepared notes, making sure to look up frequently at her audience. In turn, they listen carefully, to learn which position she has taken.

In 2002 several Queens College faculty were introduced to an innovative pedagogy devised by Barnard College historian Mark Carnes called "Reacting to the Past." In "Reacting" classes students recreate watershed historical moments by taking on politically defined roles, strategizing in factions, debating and voting on critical issues.

Each student receives a role sheet that describes his/her social class, occupation, gender, religious or political affiliations and special interests: just enough to enable the students to locate themselves in the game's historical world. As they work through the background reading, their sense of themselves in that world deepens. Most role sheets specify alliances, (e.g., Athenian supporters of Socrates, radical Jacobins), but crucial to each game are several "indeterminate" characters who must be persuaded to cast decisive votes.

In order to publicly and credibly promote their positions, the students need to understand them in the historical and political context of the time. Assigned texts, lecture, and class discussion provide basic information about the circumstances and the philosophical and political principles in play. Because the students know that this newly acquired knowledge is a means to an end, they have an incentive that recalls John C. Bean's observation: "Critical thinking tasks—which require students to *use* their expanding knowledge of subject matter to address disciplinary problems—motivate better study habits by helping students see their learning as purposeful and interesting" (2001, 9).

Once the historical framework has been established, the instructor steps back and adopts the role of Gamemaster, that is, facilitator and arbitrator. This crucial component of "Reacting" is consistent with a learning-centered pedagogy that moves the learning process away from the teacher as lecturer and toward the idea of teachers as "coaches, facilitators who assist students in finding their own meanings and in developing cooperative and supportive classroom communities" (Johns 1997, 9). Donald L. Finkel characterizes this shift away from the instructor as the physical and emotional center of the class: "Instead of mediating between the students and the material, she places the students in direct contact with the material, stepping to one side to permit a direct encounter" (2000, 103).

After reading and writing to expand their roles' personal identities and to define their characters' diverse points-of-view, the students interact in character, giving brief, prepared presentations and contributing to the proposals, counter-proposals and debates that constitute "Reacting" game sessions. The debates require preparation, attention, flexible thinking, and the ability to articulate ideas and arguments. As Francis (a young African American who graduated high school early) put it, the class is "introduced to a whole new system of debate. There can be constant rebuttal that is made up on the spot!"

This is not scripted. The students *create* the historical narrative, collaboratively and competitively, over 5 to 7 class sessions. Students enact, for example, the creation of a French constitution in 1792, the moment of Indian independence from Britain in 1947, or the fate of Anne Hutchinson in Puritan New England.

Sometimes their resolutions mirror the historical record; often they do not. In a "post mortem" session that acts as a coda to the game, the class explores the discrepancies between the recorded past and their own improvised experience. This, in turn, raises larger issues: The nature of the contingencies and factors—some overt but others subtle or obscure—that drive historical events. With a personal stake in the outcome, and having "lived" an open-ended version of the story, "Reacting" students want to know not just what happened, but *why* things turned out as they did. Reflecting on their own motives, and hearing what informed their classmates' thinking and actions, adds a meta-cognitive dimension to the class's intellectual exercise. This is active, engaged learning indeed.

As Stanley N. Katz writes in an on-line *Slate* symposium on reinventing college, "teaching must involve presenting students with problems to solve rather than merely lecturing about those problems" (2005, 3). "Reacting" games promote engagement in liberal education by inviting students to develop an understanding of historical events and the workings of political science by working through *their own solutions* to some of the past's more intractable problems, and then reflecting on what they have done.

"REACTING" AT QUEENS COLLEGE

"Reacting" classes were initially taught at small liberal arts institutions, often, as at Barnard, in freshman seminars. How well would they work in a different institutional setting? When a FIPSE grant funded the dissemination of "Reacting" to a diverse consortium of colleges, Queens—a large, public, urban commuter school—was included at the suggestion of Barnard Provost Liz Boylan. Queens does not have freshmen seminars. We do, however, have an interdisciplinary program, The Freshman Year Initiative (FYI), that has allowed us to adapt the pedagogy to our own needs.

Founded in 1990 by Judith Summerfield, now University Dean of Undergraduate Education at CUNY, FYI places entering students in learning communities for their first semester, enabling them to form the kinds of bonds that do not happen readily on an urban commuter campus. It was originally designed as a fall semester program; however, FYI has been exploring opportunities to offer its resources to transfer students and freshmen who enter in the spring semester.

From its inception, one of FYI's priorities has been to create conceptual spaces, in which students integrate the ideas and information presented in multiple disciplines, anticipating the current general education goals for the campus. To do this, FYI encourages faculty to use the learning communities as innovative sites where they can experiment in partnership with colleagues and students. Indeed, faculty from many departments who have taught for years in our learning communities—including Donald Scott, who, as Dean of Social Sciences, headed the Gen Ed task force—participated in the development of the college's new general education requirements.

Martin Braun, Mathematics Professor at Queens College and FYI's current director, has overseen the introduction of appropriate "Reacting" games into a variety of our learning communities. Faculty members in several disciplines—philosophy, history, drama, sociology, and world studies—have made "Reacting" games an integral part of their courses.

Meanwhile, the intercollegiate "Reacting" community has adopted two new games created by Queens College faculty. Fred Purnell in Philosophy devised a recently published game that emphasizes scientific inquiry by exploring the conflict between Galileo and the Church; and Helen Gaudette and Rebecca Granato, adjuncts in the History Department, are putting the finishing touches on a game that brings students to the Second Crusade, inviting them to "understand the crucial history of crusading, holy war, religious conflict, and politics in the Middle East that will inform their views of those issues today" (Gaudette 2006).

LINKING CLASSES

Each FYI learning community includes English 110: College Writing, the course traditionally thought of as "freshman composition." The single course required of all students at the college, English 110 is described in the catalogue as comprising "The arts and practices of effective writing and reading in college, especially the use of language to discover ideas" (Queens College, 126). Skillful writing is necessary for effective communication, but writing is also integral to learning. As established in the AAC&U report, *Greater Expectations: A New Vision for Learning as a Nation Goes to College*, students need practice in "adapt[ing] the skills learned in one situation to problems encountered in another"; the college classroom needs to become a space which "enable[s] integrative thinkers who can see connections in seemingly disparate information and draw on a wide range of knowledge to make decisions" (2002, 21). English 110 is a flexible course that lends itself to the project of integration, especially when the instructor can draw on the texts and ideas that students are encountering in their other subjects when they design the writing assignments for the class.

Both Sue and Ann have years of experience teaching English 110 and collaborating in interdisciplinary FYI communities, including those in the honors programs at Queens. Sue Lantz Goldhaber's expertise in ESL makes her ideally suited to working with a group of students from a variety of linguistic backgrounds. In addition to teaching ESL reading and communications courses, and specializing in writing, she has served as Assistant Director of Composition and as an Associate Director of FYI, developing an ESL community linked with anthropology and music under a FIPSE grant to include frequently marginalized ESL students in the FYI program. Sue is an active member of TESOL (Teachers of English to Speakers of Other Languages), and has made presentations on ESL related issues in Higher Education at conferences in the United States and abroad.

Ann Davison has been Projects Coordinator of FYI since 2001 and has taught writing and literature courses in the English Department since the mid-1980s. Through FYI, Ann has become active in curriculum development; rethinking the way fundamental literacies are defined and taught at the college level; and exploring pedagogical approaches that engage learners, including the potential of role-play and drama as pedagogical techniques. She has worked with colleagues across disciplines in FYI learning communities, and created courses in the World Studies program—conceived at Queens College as a place to integrate social sciences and the humanities.

In 2003, while we were collaborating on the curriculum for a new FYI learning community, we began to talk about the needs of students in other courses we were teaching. Fifty percent of the students in Ann's English 110 section that semester were designated ESL, and she needed strategies for anticipating and responding to their particular writing issues. This led to conversations about the dynamics in a class of both native and non-native speakers of English.

In our experience, when non-native speakers venture to ask or answer questions in class, discussion is hampered by their English pronunciation and the tendency of many to speak quietly. Furthermore, each student addresses the instructor, who is expected to translate the comments into louder, clearer English. Small group work helps, but there, too, ESL students, accustomed to feeling marginalized, often choose a passive role. In a "Reacting" classroom there are no passive roles. All the students have an incentive to speak up and to listen to one another without depending on the instructor as an intermediary.

What would happen, we wondered, if we were to create two linked courses in the spring semester for first-year students recruited from two groups that, without an FYI learning community, lack an easy way into the social and academic mainstream? This integrated community would bring together and provide a comfortable space for students who often fall through the cracks: ESL students who have already spent a semester in college but who have been on the periphery, in a safe yet isolated linguistic and social environment (e.g., College English as a Second Language classes); and newly arrived freshmen entering in the spring who must navigate the system without the welcoming fanfare given to freshmen in the fall. A new learning community—a shared experience of collaborative learning, in an environment where increasing familiarity enhances conditions for learning—would provide optimal opportunities for students to improve language and fluency through participation and lead to improved academic outcomes for both groups.

Sue would teach English 110; Ann would develop a World Studies 101 syllabus using "Reacting to the Past" games. The two courses could be scheduled on the same day, with an hour-long break between them, allowing for lunch, for tutoring sessions, and for the faction meetings called for by the "Reacting" pedagogy: a logistical challenge at a school without dormitory life. Frankly, we figured it would either be fabulous or a complete disaster.

For the World Studies course, we chose two "Reacting" games. One involves a succession crisis at the end of the Ming dynasty in late sixteenth-century China. Its perspective is non-western, informed by the teachings of Confucius in the *Analects*. Chinese students, therefore, begin with a bit of an advantage. Confucius is hardly revered in China today; still, he is part of their cultural heritage, and they are happy to share their thoughts, particularly on the regrettable position of women in the Confucian hierarchy.[1] The second game takes place in New York City on the eve of the American Revolution, and its core text is Locke's "Second Treatise on Government," followed by a series of colonial pamphlets. For some foreign-born students, this is their first exposure to American history.

Taken together, these games introduce students to foundational ideas by demonstrating essential differences in values, style, and thought processes, while addressing the common issue of an individual's obligations and prerogatives in the civilized world. Because "general education" envisions "broadly interdisciplinary courses aimed at giving students a more sweeping perspective on their cultural heritage" (Katz 2005), our World Studies course serves our diverse student body well.

We have just completed our third semester combining native and non-native speakers in the linked courses. It has been fabulous.

Darya stands nervously at the podium, looking at her notes. Around the conference table, 18 of her classmates watch her intently, expectantly. It is the summer of 1776, and in this crucial session of the New York Assembly, each delegate will cast a definitive vote for reconciliation with, or independence from, Great Britain. Everyone knows that victory for the loyalist or patriot factions hangs on Darya's vote. A first-year, ESL student who initially expressed extreme reservations about her ability to manage the coursework, she has long since gotten over her early anxiety over speaking up in this class. Her nervousness has nothing to do with her imperfect English, and she has become quite adept at finding textual references to support the positions she takes.

In her role as an independent-minded landowner from the Hudson Valley, Darya has been drawn to the patriots' arguments and has consistently voted with them. Now, however, she must explain that she is casting her deciding vote with the loyalists. A vote for independence will mean certain war, and British ships are already massed off Staten Island. She has seen war, she will tell them: the devastation that war brings to families, society, property. She cannot in good conscience allow such a disaster to befall New York, and she has found a passage in James Chalmer's loyalist pamphlet that supports the cautionary position she is taking.

What is particularly compelling about Darya's need to persuasively defend her stance against war is that it is not merely theoretical. Darya was born and raised in Iran, and has childhood memories of Iran's war with Iraq. She is using textual references to speak eloquently from experience, and from the heart.

Only a few weeks earlier, the ESL students were struggling to make sense of the primary English texts. Once merely difficult reading assignments, they have become, as they did for Darya, accessible sources of information and ideas. In the process, the ESL students have been redefined as scholars, able to analyze and utilize English texts, rather than principally being judged by their error production.

In the "Reacting" class, second-language learners enter into an ongoing dialogue with native speakers of English about historical events and related conflicts and develop strategies for resolving these conflicts. They work with primary and secondary sources; they learn discipline-specific vocabulary and negotiate complex linguistic structures; they are required to do extensive writing[2]; and they present oral arguments—some of which are prepared statements; others are given under the pressure of the moment.

Active debate is a required element of the "Reacting" experience. Students quickly discover that in order to fully absorb their roles and successfully enter the discourse community of the World Studies, it is necessary to become actively engaged with the texts from which they will extract their information. They will be graded based on their performance as policy makers, dissenters, or assenters, and their voices are heard in two ways: through debates and comments presented to the class and in their written work defending their positions. As they resolve the virtual historical conflicts, second-language learners leave the margins of the classroom and become active participants. Such practices teach our students strategies for entering into other discourse communities in which a shared knowledge of discipline-specific language, form, and structure facilitates comprehension, dialogue, and active participation.

In English 110 one focus is naturally on language: the importance of being precise, of taking time to select words and define terms; the necessity of using language that describes and conveys what the writers wish their readers to see, feel, hear, sense. Students in Sue's class develop lists of synonyms and determine the value of each one for expressing a particular idea or image. (Imagine the arguments that ensue over what conveys a positive image or a negative one.)

The English class also learns to consider syntax, style, structure, and content in shaping an effective argument. Sue's students practice developing their ideas and illustrating them with focused examples that extend their arguments and learn to integrate research to support their claims. They read about the bombing of Hiroshima from two perspectives: those of a survivor and one of the bombers flying overhead; they analyze the effective elements (which can later be applied to their World Studies arguments). As students improve content, their essays become more coherent, articulate, and informed.

Because the primary texts assigned in World Studies are so difficult for native and non-native speakers alike, they are used in the English class for practice in close reading and for learning strategies for tackling long, dense reading assignments that are essential for academic work. The Confucian analects—concise but oblique, and syntactically complex—are ideal for practice in paraphrasing. Syntactically challenging excerpts from Locke are used to practice both paraphrasing and summarizing. Active reading and annotation are taught in English using the game's texts, an exercise that familiarizes students with the text before they work with it in the World Studies class, and prepares them for English 110's mandatory research project.

Even with these strategies, second-language learners often find themselves struggling with the meaning, particularly of the primary World Studies texts, as well as with the task of formulating and expressing ideas about them in English. In an effort to achieve some parity with the native speakers, they often seek resources online. The Confucian *Analects*, they discover, can be read in Russian; Locke can be read in Chinese. Appropriate, strategic use of translations is yet another practice that will be transferred to their work in other courses.

We are both mindful that students new to college need an introduction to the values and conventions that govern academic citation and plagiarism; and we know that ESL students have the additional challenge of adapting to American academic conventions. For example, what would be considered legitimate referential copying of a master's work in Latin America or Asia might well constitute plagiarism here. The Writing Fellows at Queens College devoted an issue of their annual journal to perspectives on issues of citation and plagiarism, including an essay that explores the assumptions that ESL students often bring to appropriation of texts. "If we are to effectively deal with the matter of plagiarism," notes Mehmet Kucukozer, "we cannot simply moralize the issue and disembed it from the social, cultural and political context from which people originate" (2004/5, 10). Accustomed to different conventions, ESL students may be "criminalized" as plagiarists by faculty who are unaware of the context from which they write. In both classes we make a point of addressing this issue.

Similarly, faculty who are unaccustomed to working with ESL students have difficulty separating the content of a paper from the students' surface errors. The collaborative culture of the class offers students a means to work through some of these issues with the encouragement of their peers. Through English 110's drafts and peer editing, and a few brief formal lessons, attention is given to the students' individual writing challenges. In fact, when they do peer reviews, the native English speakers often face the same challenges that instructors do when reading an ESL paper. Although they help one another with language and grammar issues, they need to practice reading *past* the errors, to look at the content. The ESL students often are able to return the favor by guiding the development of a native English speaker's essay. Eva, a bright young woman from Greece, expressed astonishment at the difficulty she sees American high school graduates having with the basic organization of an essay, something she learned years ago. However, while students from Greece are prepared to organize their papers effectively, they have been taught not to add "unnecessary" and "self-evident" obser-vations that *are* necessary in English to clarify context. The result is prose that is con-sidered too concise in the United States, lacking in detail and development.

Of course, there is more than one way to write in the academy, and different disciplines have distinct styles and conventions. Our students need to practice not just "writing well," but writing effectively in diverse ways. Finding an appropriate voice for academic discourse is an ongoing challenge, so our assignments reinforce the essential idea that style is never independent of context, and that discourse is socially, culturally, and historically located.

Rather than ask students to invent an effective style from scratch—a daunting task for both native and non-native students—in World Studies we ask them to mimic the primary sources. They use Confucian analects to argue for and against the Emperor Wan-li's choice of heir, and when they write "memorials" to the Emperor—stylized, traditional arguments—they reference the *Analects* and the actual sixteenth-century memorials we have as models, mimicking the syntax, the structure and the flowery, flattering language, and inventing metaphors from nature that are right for the period. For many of our ESL students, in particular, this model serves to anchor and guide their writing.

When we move to eighteenth-century America, the language shift is signifi-cant. The students are now literate patriots, loyalists, slaves, and laborers. They write diaries in character and prepare notes for debates in the New York Provincial Congress, where loyalty to Britain and a growing clamor for independence are hotly debated. The primary source models are forceful, direct arguments in pamphlets like Tom Paine's "Common Sense" and James Chalmers' rebuttal, "Plain Truth."

The reading and writing assigned in the linked classes assumes a broad inter-textuality. Discussing text, role, and context, Ann M. Johns notes that "Individual texts are influenced by previous experiences of all kinds [because] experienced readers and writers draw from their previous genre knowledge and experiences to process a text within a specific context" (1997, 35). Such schemata provide a platform on which our students practice accessing and building knowledge.

While we are aware of the value of sending our students to travel and study abroad, we should keep in mind that our ESL students are *already* abroad, and benefit from opportunities to connect their academic work to their personal base of knowledge and their new life experiences. Here is Zhen:

> Maybe it's due to my traditional Chinese background, which pursues harmony and quiet, or maybe because of my anti-quarrelsome personality that made me quite uncomfortable with arguments at the beginning of this class. Chinese people value relationships among each other very much, they think argument or quarrels will undermine their friendly relationships, and that always needs time to heal scars in the heart of each other.
>
> Not until later, when some told me "argue without anger" did I understand that this was the American way. I must fight for my role, my stand, since I was in America. I constantly told myself not to devote too much emotion into argument. Business is business, which would be divided from my own life.
>
> America, New York, big cultural compounded society. I love it! Most important, I am proud that Chinese culture could be known by people from all over the world.

Students routinely bring their cultural knowledge to the game situations, as Deepa did when she excitedly explained to the class that the Stamp Act is alive and well in India, which has its own problematic history of British colonialism. Li Hui, too reserved to participate much in class debate, and needing to bolster her class participation grade, volunteered to teach the class about Chinese writing. Eva, reflecting on the prospects for colonial victory against the British, observed that the colonists would have the advantage of fighting to protect their homeland, just as her fellow Greeks fiercely resisted the Ottoman Turks for centuries. Several students pointed out that Americans encountered similar resistance in Vietnam, and now in Iraq. It is hard to tell who is more engaged by the American Revolution game, the native speakers for whom American history is coming to life (and is far more complicated than they thought), or the foreign-born students who feel that they are discovering something important about America and New York.

"Reacting" classes provide opportunities for students to share such knowledge, to use personal experience as they work with and produce new texts. According to Johns, "Central to reading and writing as viewed in a Socioliterate perspective is the contention that all literacies are, in fact, social, intertextual, and historical. The languages, cultures, literacy experiences, roles, and communities of readers and writers, as well as the immediate context, are critical influences on literacy development" (1997, 16). This orientation to language and writing contributes significantly to second-language learners' reduced levels of anxiety and builds the confidence of all our students in the academic setting.

Once the roles are assigned in the games, the students approach the readings—both primary and secondary—as interested parties, looking for anything that will help them understand their characters and circumstances.

As Confucian scholars, they do not think of the analects as arcane and alien constructs. They make sense of the analects as they are learning about Chinese culture, and they know that the analects will be their principle reference and support for the verbal and written arguments they offer to the Emperor during the China game. As colonial citizens, they appreciate the fully developed logic of John Locke, and pore over their texts, looking for passages that support their claims. They have both the incentive and the satisfaction beyond that of completing an assignment, and they experience the value of informed discourse. Use of textual references, much like the use of specified style, builds their confidence. There is little fear of "being wrong" when they can rely on a shared assumption that, in this context at least, Confucius and Locke are always right.

The English 110 curriculum deepens the cultural contexts for the "Reacting" games through the reading of texts that grapple with social issues from diverse cultural perspectives. The students discuss readings by Amy Tan, a contemporary voice that offers a new perspective on Chinese culture and traditional ways of thinking. An animated discussion related to Chinese tradition and culture ensues, and Chinese students find that they have an unaccustomed authority. Qian had been in the United States for only five months when the semester began and would not initially presume to speak, but he became an active participant in response to his peers' questions, eagerly clarifying misconceptions of Chinese culture.

Later in the semester, the English class—having read Locke and Paine in World Studies, and being engaged in debating the merits and conditions of citizenship, freedom and independence in the colonies—considers Martin Luther King Jr.'s *Letter from a Birmingham Jail* and does a close reading of *The Declaration of Independence*. When it is time for them to cast a vote in the Provincial Congress supporting or opposing independence from Britain, the students know what is at stake, and how these events will form a distant but critical frame for the American civil rights movement.

One of the essays assigned in English asks students to research an historical event. The second-language learners often select something from their native histories and a new kind of cultural exchange takes place as students begin to experience one another in the context of their places of origin. Deepa, for example, wrote a dramatic piece about the religious riots pitting Sikhs against Hindus in India in 1984, as told to her by her uncle, who had been severely injured in the aftermath of the rioting. This and other pieces elicited strong responses from the other students, who drilled the writers about their topics. "Reacting" takes many forms.

SECOND-LANGUAGE ACQUISITION

Lev Vygotsky's sociocultural theories revolutionized our understanding of how we develop and process learning. His theories look at the internal thought processes of social and cultural experiences to describe how cognitive learning takes place.

Vygotsky identifies a Zone of Proximal Development (ZPD) as "the distance between the actual development level as determined by independent problem solving and the level of potential development as determined through problem solving . . . in collaboration with more capable peers" (1978, 86).

Our linked classes provide such a venue for our ESL students, a space where second-language learners collaborate with peers who have greater linguistic competence. Furthermore, the academic and social collaboration that takes place makes students allies in a variety of ways, breaking down linguistic barriers and some of the negative stereotyping and isolation that ESL students often experience in their other classes alongside native English speaking students. Marysia Johnson argues—following Vygotsky—that this socialization is essential to second-language acquisition (SLA).[3]

We establish a Zone of Proximal Development in English 110 when students brainstorm for ideas before embarking on an assignment; share and challenge points of view from their explorations of and responses to literature; critique and defend drafts of essays in peer editing sessions. In the World Studies course, the ZPD emerges through the challenge of the "Reacting" games and the opportunity they give second-language learners to take risks first in a safe environment (what Steven Krashen calls removing the "affective filter" that prevents students from effective learning) (qtd. in Johnson 2004, 48) and finally in the unsafe zone of possible error production when they debate.

At their best, the debates are passionate but reasoned, and grounded in historical facts and textual references. Moreover, as Mark Carnes notes, "push[ing] the students into distant worlds" makes the practice of reasoning and speaking skills more effective; "There, free from the constraints of their own sense of self, they find it easier both to explore new and challenging ideas and to talk about them" (2005, 11). Here is an example: Angel, from the Dominican Republic, told us he would never have dreamed of speaking up anywhere but in his Spanish literature classes. However, there he was, a fervent Loyalist, holding forth with passion, conviction, and notable eloquence on the necessity of reconciling with Great Britain.

This brings us to liminality: "that threshold region where the normal rules of society are suspended or subverted. Liminal settings are characterized by uncertainty and emotional intensity, by the inversion of status and social hierarchies, and by imaginative expressiveness" (Carnes 2004, B7). "Reacting" classes become liminal spaces as soon as the games begin and the instructor steps to the margins, retaining only minimal authority. Interacting in roles in this charged liminal space alters and heightens perception. As Louis said about his vicarious experience of New York on the verge of revolution, "*Being there*, so to speak, really brought home quite forcefully the danger, and the fear, that social and political upheaval entails." Carnes demonstrates that when students are removed from "the rigidity of social structures and the rules of daily existence, liminality gives them the freedom to invent new solutions to old problems, or to regard familiar things in new ways" (2004, B7). We are reminded here of John Dewey's observation that "Only by wrestling with the conditions of the problem at first hand, seeking and finding his own way out, does [the student] think" (1916, 188).

To be sure, not every student fares as well as Angel, Louis, and Darya did. We have shy students for whom going to the podium remains difficult. (Sometimes their peers stand next to them for moral support.) We have had tears. The fear of public failure can oppress any student, but non-native speakers are particularly vulnerable to revealing, in Carnes's phrase, "the insufficiency of their understanding" (2004, B6). Instead, collaboration in the "Reacting" games allows students to create what Lee Shulman winningly calls "a *marriage of insufficiencies*," in which, through social interaction, they can "work together in ways that scaffold and support each other's learning, and in ways that supplement each other's knowledge" (2004, 559). Native speakers offer more capable models of English discourse, while second-language learners bring a vast experience of life and, often, enhanced critical thinking skills to the marriage.

All students entering college are undergoing a *rite of passage*, characterized by changes in place, age, or status, and second-language learners experience this dislocation on two levels. According to Victor Turner, shared liminal experiences foster "intense comradeship and egalitarianism. Secular distinctions of rank and status disappear or are homogenized" (1969, 359–360).

The goal of the Freshman Year Initiative's learning communities at Queens College has always been to facilitate a transition to the academy through socially and academically integrative, communal experiences. The liminal "Reacting" experience, built on teamwork, alliances, personal goals, collective strategies and the experience of theater, creates a deep sense of community. Whether they are struggling with the English language, or with adapting to college, or both, "Reacting" games offer our students a shared sense of excitement and possibility, risk, novelty, and being in the same weird boat. Absorbed in their character roles and bolstered by textual resources and support in literacy practices, they are emboldened to throw themselves into their debates with passion, flair, and a remarkable lack of self-consciousness. They come to class to listen intently and respond to each other. In this version of Vygotsky's "Zone of Proximal Development," second-language learners begin to ease past the inhibitions of shyness and linguistic self-consciousness that hamper their developmental potential in more isolated learning environments. At the end of each session, they behave like a theater troupe after a successful performance, leaving in integrated groups, laughing and kidding each other casually in English.

The collaboration happily spills over into the writing conferences that Sue holds each week. We have moved from requiring students to attend a mandatory conference to seeing students regularly join their classmates' conferences, forming, with their professor, roundtable discussions of their peers' papers. For instance, Alex, a painfully shy Taiwanese-American, sits quietly to the side while Zhen, a Chinese immigrant, reviews her paper with Sue. As Zhen struggles to revise and edit, Su Min, a Korean, and Andrei, from Russia, gather around. Alex begins to make suggestions and evaluate Zhen's ideas. She listens attentively, and at the end of the session they leave together to grab a bite and continue working on Zhen's draft. The students have become "active agents in the process of their own learning" (Shulman 2004, 559).

In fact, the five principles—"activity, reflection, collaboration, passion and community"—identified by Shulman as essential in overcoming "amnesia, illusory understanding, and inertness" (2004, 558) in the classroom, are all present in our linked courses.

In the liminal world of "Reacting," students have the freedom to creatively engage in "the messy, ambiguous, and context-sensitive processes of meaning making" (Bruner 1999, 5). Native and non-native speakers alike do not grasp everything at once. They bring whatever they take from the readings and lectures to the game, where, as in Bruner's model case of text interpretation (1999, 6), they begin to form hypotheses about the historical moment. This dynamic, in turn, enriches their understanding of their place and perspectives in the imaginatively reconstructed world. Gradually they develop a way of knowing that—because they have inhabited it and acted on it—they are not likely to forget.

Virtually, it is the spring of 1776. Francis and Maria, in the role of slaves owned by New York City colonists, are petitioning the Provincial Congress to consider emancipation. After all, the colonists have a lot to say about freedom, liberty, and the rights of man.

Earlier today, Francis's English class has studied a Langston Hughes poem, "Theme for English B," whose theme of identity and challenge to whites for respect speaks to Francis personally as well as to his role as a slave seeking emancipation. Having asked Sue's advice ("Langston Hughes wasn't born in 1776. May I use his poem? And how would I cite it?), Francis has spent his lunch hour reworking the poem, keeping its theme but adapting it to his conception of his colonial character.

When Francis and Maria make their dramatic plea, everyone recognizes the source.

Although their petition will fail (the colonists are not prepared to give up their property or to acknowledge the humanity of their black slaves), Francis and Maria have the satisfaction of having made their point in a clever, creative way.

We have taught these linked courses three times now. Twice we were fortunate to begin with lively groups of outgoing students, inclined to participate from day one. One class, however, was a particularly interesting and instructive challenge. The students were passive, shy, and reticent; only two or three were willing to raise their hands in either course for the first several weeks. Afterwards they told us that the diversity of the class, exceptional even for QC, had initially been a shock. (For ESL students who have been here a very short time, NYC's famous diversity is itself a shock.)

We were seriously concerned, but bonding became noticeable by mid-semester, as soon as we finished the first "Reacting" game. The dynamics of the group had changed: Reflecting their shared feeling of accomplishment in successfully getting through the game together, the students had moved from tentative, uncertain ground to a communal space where they were interacting easily, entering and leaving the classrooms in small, fluid groups, and seeking each other out for help in revising and editing the final drafts of their papers outside of class. They were going to lunch together and forming what have turned out to be lasting friendships. Peer reviews, debates, research and new reading, writing and critical thinking strategies converged, as the barriers to linguistic fluency and academic achievement fell away.

CONCLUSION

We think of our linked courses as a springboard into the mainstream of the academy for our ESL students. Here they leap into the unsafe zone of speaking and writing in their new language by taking an active role exchanging knowledge, exercising their critical thinking and developing their writing. In terms of the College's new general education guidelines, they offer an entry experience in a two-course learning community where "critical abilities"—written and oral expression and conducting research—are priorities. The demanding yet complimentary pair of courses sets a high bar in terms of expectation, and serves as an excellent foundation for both the ESL students and their peers.

Our ESL students tell us that they work hard; that they are becoming stronger readers and writers; that they have become more comfortable speaking in their other classes; and that the support that they get in English 110 for the World Studies work is invaluable. So far our assessment has been anecdotal and experiential, but we have begun to collect data on our students, tracking their academic progress, noting the types of courses they take to fulfill college requirements and checking their scores on the CPE. We are holding focused interviews with former students, to hear how well they have fared in their mainstream coursework. As the semesters go on, we plan to look at participation in campus activities and retention rates at Queens and in college altogether.

At the end of each game, Ann asks our students to "go meta" (Bruner 1999, 10, 58), reflecting on their personal experiences in and out of their roles. Vasiliki, a young Greek woman, sums up our objectives nicely:

> I learned learning. I learned how to learn about history and culture.
>
> I learned to give equal importance to both sides of the story. I was motivated to find out more about what we were doing, on my own.

Also, I had sometimes a difficulty distinguishing reality with re-acting reality. I was very passionate about it and I felt sometimes that I was actually the person I played. So, I learned a lot about myself, how I reacted to pressure, how I had to control my emotions and how real experiences in my life played a role in the experience of these games.

Like the self-segregated students in our Cafeteria, "American citizens increasingly inhabit intellectually gated communities. Untested and unchallenged, ideas devolve into opinion; 'political discourse' becomes a contradiction in terms" (Carnes 2005, 1). The experience of our students in the linked World Studies and English courses has helped transform this intelligent but tentative cohort into independent thinkers and learners; the ESL students are gaining a new voice, becoming fluent in English and, together with our native speakers, learning the language and culture of the academy. Beyond their years in college, we hope that both groups will be able to participate in the intellectual debates that our democracy needs.

As we continue the process of imagining what a liberal education can be for our increasingly diverse students, we should think of our ESL students as a resource. Shulman points out that the "Process of knowledge growth, criticism, and development in the academy leads to the achievement of new understandings, new perspectives, or new ways of interpreting the world" (2004, 550). Indeed, that is precisely what our students discover with and within each other: a new way of constructing knowledge and language, and multiple ways of seeing the world across the disciplines, across new languages, and through the newly encountered cultural lenses of their peers.

NOTES

1. Louis, a student from Singapore, wrote, "Reading Confucius was quite a revelation: having grown up in a culture where Confucian values are prevalent—e.g., respect for your elders, deference towards figures of authority—having those values decontextualized was a bit of a shock."
2. They write about the texts they are reading; they write down points of argument that they will make; they write to develop their character roles. They draft two Chinese memorials, which are formal arguments and, if more practice is needed, another argument about the American political crisis. For their midterm they write short essays. They might be asked to connect the traditional Chinese values they have been living by with contemporary conditions in China as reported by *The New York Times*; they might read a short story from the Ming period and identify the many cultural elements that are embodied there. At the end of the semester they are asked to compare and contrast (a mode taught in English 110) some of the values, ideas and cultural practices evident in the disparate worlds of the two games.
3. For a detailed discussion of Vygotsky's sociocultural theory and second language acquisition, see Johnson, *A Philosophy of Second Language Acquisition* (2004).

WORKS CITED

AAC&U. *Greater Expectations: A New Vision for Learning as a Nation Goes to College.* Washington, DC: Association of American Colleges and Universities, 2002.

Bean, John C. *Engaging Ideas.* San Francisco: John Wiley & Sons, 2001.

Bruner, Jerome. *The Culture of Education.* Cambridge: Harvard University Press, 1999.

Carnes, Mark. "Inciting Speech." *Change: The Magazine of Higher Learning,* 37.2 (May 2005): 6–11.

———. "The Liminal Classroom." *The Chronicle of Higher Education,* 8 October 2004, B6–B8.

Dewey, John. *Democracy and Education.* New York: Macmillan, 1916.

Finkel, Donald L. *Teaching with Your Mouth Shut.* Portsmouth, N.H.: Boynton/Cook, 2000.

Gaudette, Helen. "Re: Reacting Perspectives." E-mail to A. Davison. 24 April 2006.

Johns, Ann M. *Text, Role, and Context.* Cambridge University Press, 1997.

Johnson, Marysia. *A Philosophy of Second Language Acquisition.* New Haven: Yale University Press, 2004.

Katz, Stanley N. "Does College Need to Be Reformed?" *Slate,* 15 November 2005 http://www.slate.com/id/2130158/.

Kucukozer, Mahmet. "Plagio: A View of Plagiarism from Abroad." *Revisions: A Zine on Writing at Queens College,* 2.1 (Fall 2004/Spring 2005). http://qcpages.qc.cuny.edu/Writing/zine.htm.

The President's Task Force on General Education. *Toward a Reorganization of General Education at Queens College.* By Donald Scott et al. September 2004. http://www.qc.cuny.edu/about/presidents_page/genEdReport.pdf.

Queens College. *Queens College 2003–2005 Undergraduate Bulletin.* New York: Queens College, The City University of New York.

Shulman, Lee S. *The Wisdom of Practice: Essays on Teaching, Learning, and Learning to Teach.* San Francisco: Jossey-Bass, 2004.

Turner, Victor. "Liminality and Communitas." *The Ritual Process: Structure and Anti-Structure.* Chicago: Aldine Publishing, 1969.

Vygotsky, Lev S. *Mind in Society: The Development of Higher Psychological Processes,* edited by Michael Cole, Vera John-Steiner, Sylvia Scribner, and Ellen Souberman. Cambridge: Harvard University Press, 1978.

WORKS CITED

CHAPTER EIGHT

Our Mission at Hostos

Charting a Course to Self-Empowerment

ROBERT F. COHEN AND KIM SANABRIA

Eugenio María de Hostos Community College

If it is true, as Zora Neale Hurston asserts, that "ships at a distance have every man's wish on board" (1989, 1), then Hostos Community College embodies the vision of success that all sudents carry in their hearts. One needs only to enter the doors of Hostos to understand how powerful this dream can be. The special desires of each individual, multiplied by a population of over four thousand students, create a pulsating current, wherein each traveler sees the college as a kind of buoy guiding them toward the realization of their hopes. No newcomer to the buildings can ignore the power of this dynamic.

Students at Eugenio María de Hostos Community College, which was founded in the South Bronx in 1968 and named after a Puerto Rican educator, writer, and visionary, are more than willing to tackle the challenges this voyage represents. Laden with hope, many of them are entering an unfamiliar educational terrain, either because they come from countries with different educational infrastructures or because they have not had access to educational opportunities within the United States itself.

The college has a wonderfully diverse population. 55.3% of our students are foreign-born; 60% are Latino, mostly Dominicans, with many Puerto Ricans and an increasing number of newly arrived students from Central and South America. Another 29.7% are black. Women account for 72.3% of the student body (2005 statistics from the Office of Institutional Research, Hostos Community College). Some are graduates of New York City high schools who switch seamlessly from Spanish to English and back again; some are seeking to be doctors, lawyers, engineers, or journalists; some are recent immigrants and second-language learners seeking a more secure future or fleeing countries torn by poverty, war, or violence. Some are raising families and building a new life for themselves and juggling this responsibility while studying and working in a garage, a restaurant, a hair salon, a foyer. Some are well on their way to becoming nurses; others have plans to go to business school or pursue careers in early childhood education. Some are very involved in the community and volunteer their time with the disabled or in after-school programs.

However, despite the rich tapestry of experiences that they bring to the college, our students' knowledge and experiences are undervalued in American schools. This lack of recognition is unfortunate because few among us can compete with our students in naming a novel written in Chad, in reciting a poem by Pablo Neruda, in listing government leaders in Ecuador, Colombia, or Puerto Rico, in speaking four African dialects, or in understanding the power of the story of *Las Mariposas*. Discussions about subjects like these reverberate along the college's corridors and contribute to the college's stimulating and vibrant atmosphere. Somehow, when we evaluate the skills our students have yet to acquire, we must also leave room to admire their verve, appreciate their life histories, and embrace them for the considerable knowledge that they acquired in the different worlds they inhabited before coming to Hostos Community College.

Accompanying our students' vision and commitment is a sobering reality. They are, as a whole, among the poorest of New York residents, and many of them represent a segment of society that has lacked extensive exposure to the benefits of a formal education. According to recent census data provided by Ed Morales in his *New York Times* article "Nickels and Dimes," the South Bronx remains the nation's poorest urban county (2005, 14: 1, 8). Strikingly, only 7.7% of the Dominican population over the age of twenty-five, born on the island but now living in New York, have a college degree or more, and 56.2% have less than a high school diploma (New York City Department of City Planning 2004, 152).

These incontrovertible facts are critical to our mission. If our students are not fully equipped with the skills required of them to enter the academic discussion, they will be unable to respond adequately to the subject matter that we present to them or see themselves as part of the academic setting. In addition, they will also lack the tools needed to construct a future for themselves, and will be denied the academic certificates and diplomas required for better positions to which they are entitled. As a result, they will be constantly barred from the rewards of economic security and a higher degree of comfort in life that they so urgently seek. While nobody would argue that the purpose of education is merely to get a better job, we are cognizant of the college's mission, which is to provide access to higher education leading to both intellectual growth and socio-economic mobility. Entrusted with this hope, we educators must lay the groundwork for students to grow academically, giving them a passport to a better future. This is our goal.

Nevertheless, this eventual achievement entails great challenges. As students move from familiar ground to a world riddled with obstacles they have never before encountered, they are catapulted into new expectations and demands that inhibit their movement. Entry tests are undeniably the most visible stumbling blocks for Hostos students. Of the entering freshmen at the college, almost 85% must enroll in developmental English/ESL courses and over 50% in developmental math, because the placement tests administered at initial registration determine a lack of preparedness in reading, writing, or math. Although these standardized tests suggest that a significant percentage do not have sophisticated English language skills and may not be equipped for the expectations of college life, students tend to perceive these tests not as gateways, but as amorphous and arbitrary nets holding them back from realizing their dreams. Despite the high degree of frustration that characterizes their lives as many of them take these examinations over and over until they make the grade, it is to our students' credit that a far-reaching vision of advancement and potential enables them to tackle the tests again. However, behind the backdrop of the statistics and failure rates lies another, less measurable brake on our students' progress: the erosion of their self-confidence. In the end, considering that putting a dream to the test is the most important task that anyone can face, we are doubly charged with supporting our students' quest, and we cannot afford to tolerate their failure in this endeavor. Helping our students prosper and succeed is ultimately the measure of our efforts as educators.

Indeed, what Hostos students undergo in a more dramatic way than many of their counterparts at other colleges is a radical reorientation of their educational perspective, along with a confrontation with their own strengths and weaknesses. While they pursue their studies, they therefore tread a reflective path, one which asks them to analyze the significance of their progress at every step and to consider their own responsibilities, evolution, and potential. In fact, the motif of reflection embraces various beliefs that we ourselves hold about the educational process. First, self-assessment, that confrontation with ourselves that we experience whenever we look closely and honestly at our own efforts, should be a constant exercise, because this practice allows us to evaluate and direct our learning. As the universal emblem of the truth and a lens through which we often focus on our future dreams and aspirations, the "mirror" also encompasses our belief in the need to strive toward our personal best, because seeing ourselves also entails seeing who we want to become. In short, peering into our own reflection permits us to reflect back and examine ourselves more critically as we project ourselves into the future. Surely, if our students learn to exercise such judgment, they will be better equipped to negotiate the challenges of this new environment.

Educators must also undergo a reflective process as they seek to understand the complex challenges that their students face, and they respond by evaluating the effectiveness of the programs and initiatives that they are implementing. Our own partnerships in the realms of teaching, writing, and editing have benefited considerably from such a process. We, the authors of this essay, have been close friends and colleagues for almost twenty years. Our backgrounds in linguistics, translation, and foreign language acquisition cemented our relationship all the more because we immediately found common ground in our professional endeavors. Although we both moved to Hostos to become tenure-track faculty members of the *Department of Language and Cognition*, we met at Columbia University's *American Language Program*, where we collaborated on materials development and curricular changes that have recently come under the rubric of "General Education." We have both been very active writers of textbooks in English as a Second Language at various levels, from beginning to freshman composition. Furthermore, our recent collaborations as editorial consultants for two textbook series in Turkey and the United Arab Emirates have given us greater insights into the benefits of learning academically focused, interdisciplinary content that permits students to explore themes across the curriculum.

We are convinced that when people study a full range of subjects, they cultivate a better understanding not only of their chosen field but also of its significance within the full scope of acquired human knowledge. Thus, inherent in our work is the understanding that a liberal education gives our students an opportunity to examine a diverse range of subject matter. This diversity stimulates their imagination, appeals to their common sense, cultivates their global awareness, and enables them to pose questions and find solutions to universal problems that concern us all. Throughout this process, students not only achieve academic success, but they also emerge from our doors as more empowered citizens of the world. We must debunk the myth, an entrenched vestige of outmoded notions of educational philosophy, that academic proficiency is a prerequisite for liberal arts instruction. On the contrary, although some may presume that language proficiency in reading and writing is a goal to be reached before students are exposed to meaningful content, recent pedagogical theory suggests otherwise. Indeed, a curriculum that does not divorce skills from content, but instead allows the integration of the two, gives students a sense of purpose and direction.

Briefly stated, the content-based instruction model, which forms the backbone of the programs we describe below, prepares students for the courses they take in the academic content areas. It addresses these fundamental requirements:

- our students' need to develop linguistic competence, not just to pass tests but to contribute their own voice to the academic forum;
- their need to cultivate the skills that will enable them to navigate the college environment;

- their need to become familiar with academic content from various disciplines.

Although this model reflects a current trend in English language-learning pedagogy, it naturally embraces the spirit of General Education principles. Through content-based instruction, students focus on interdisciplinary modular units that permit them to study in depth all kinds of academic material. In sharp contrast to the older "skills-based" models of instruction, in which reading, writing, speaking, and listening courses were taught in isolation of one another, the integration of these skills is essential to the success of all our students. The model benefits not only those who are still taking developmental courses, but also those who have made the transition into the regular college sequence.

At Hostos, various programs have been engineered to take both our students' needs and challenges into consideration and help them to emerge as empowered learners and competent participants in the academic arena. In the six years that we have been faculty members of the college's Department of Language and Cognition and active participants in college-wide endeavors, we have seen the school undergo a major transformation that has enabled it to serve its students better. We are proud to say that we have participated in this renaissance through our contributions to several significant initiatives, such as the development of the content-based *ESL curriculum*, and the creation of the *College Enrichment Academy* and *Honors Program*. These programs reaffirm our belief that all students, especially those who are at the entry point of their academic journey, can benefit from multifaceted instruction yielding a strong combination of background knowledge and core competencies, which form the tenets of the General Education initiative. The three programs are not necessarily sequentially linked, even though they do intersect at various points as students progress in their skills. Nonetheless, they all subscribe to a similar pedagogical philosophy and take into consideration the realities of the Hostos population.

ESL CURRICULUM: DEPARTMENT OF
LANGUAGE AND COGNITION

Of the difficulties that our students bring with them, the one that is easiest to single out is their failure to pass reading and writing skills in English. If they fall below the threshold of the minimum competencies stipulated by the university, they are in fact unable to proceed with their academic programs because they are not permitted to register in content area courses required for their majors. However, our students arrive at the college with such complex linguistic backgrounds that simple questions about their language proficiency or language dominance are often by no means clear-cut. Appropriate placement in language sequences, either English or ESL developmental classes, is a monumental task that forces us to consider myriad factors such as the students' age at their time of arrival in the United States, the number of years they have spent in the country, the language they speak at home, the culture or peer group with whom they identify most closely, and so on. This lack of homogeneity creates a serious dilemma, leading to difficult choices at the institutional level. A particularly complex group is our burgeoning population of "Generation 1.5" students, U.S. educated English language learners whose oral and writing skills are at opposite ends of the spectrum. As for all students, these students need to be assured that they will receive a closely tailored program that will allow them to pinpoint their areas of weakness and go forth with confidence. It should be noted here that Hostos is unique not only among CUNY schools, but among colleges across the nation, in its bilingual mission. Therefore, students who do not yet command English may take advantage of the opportunity offered by the college to take content classes in Spanish. However, this is a transitional model, and as students advance in their English proficiency, they need to take more and more courses in English that reinforce their second-language competency.

Once our students are in classes, we must continue to make sure that our curricula form the proper guideposts toward their goals. In this process, we insist that the key ingredients to our students' success—language, skills, and content—be intertwined. It was with the imperatives of such thinking in mind that the *Department of Language and Cognition* recently revamped its ESL curriculum by replacing the former skills-based approach with a content-based model, which allowed us to incorporate the three parallel elements referred to above. This new curricular structure was realized through the concerted efforts of a committee of devoted colleagues who recognized that just as we are asking our students to become reflective learners, we, too, had to engage in careful examination of the responsibilities and impact of our educational strategies. Of course, the spirit of this evaluation continues, as we explore ways to cement a more collaborative relationship with our colleagues in the English Department and the Modern Languages unit.

The new curriculum in our regular ESL Program takes its cue from our reputed Intensive Program, which for many years has successfully prepared students for their careers through content-based instruction. The coordinator of this intensive fifteen-hour a week English immersion course selects outstanding students from among our regular ESL population through a competitive procedure and gives them the opportunity to progress through the ESL sequence at an accelerated pace, that of two semesters in one. Considering that people achieve proficiency in a language at different rates, this course obviously is not appropriate for everyone. Most students need to follow the path of our regular ESL sequence, and even the four-semester itinerary mapped out for them, which culminates in their eventual acceptance into

Expository Writing (Freshman Composition), once they have passed the ACT reading and writing examinations. This seems for many to be quite a rocky road. Students entering at the lowest level take twelve hours of courses per week: *ESL in Content Areas I* for six hours and *Literature and Contemporary Issues for ESL* for six hours. They then move on to a nine-hour block, with *ESL in Content Areas II*, at six hours a week, and either *Contemporary Issues for ESL II* or *Literature for ESL II*, at three hours each. The advanced level follows suit, with *ESL in Content Areas III* at six hours a week, and either *Contemporary Issues for ESL III* or *Literature for ESL III*, at three hours each. Upon completion of this level, exceptional students are given the opportunity to take the required ACT examinations. Those who pass both exams go on to take *Expository Writing*, thereby joining their non-ESL counterparts. Those who do not pass follow the regular sequence, a combination of *Basic Composition*, at six hours a week, and *Foundations of Critical Reading*, at three hours a week, and then take the aforementioned ACT exams.

In the ESL classes, students focus on modular units that permit them to study in depth all kinds of material related to such areas as immigration, the environment, first amendment rights, family structure, business ethics, and philosophy. Concurrently, depending on their level of language proficiency, they may also take courses in English or Spanish in early childhood education, sociology, political science, and other disciplines. The success of such an approach is guaranteed because the students' motivation is heightened all the more when they see that the content of their language classes complements the themes of their future majors. In addition, we must not forget that in an atmosphere in which content information is valued, where students participate in the discussion of existing ideas and the birth of new ones, their critical thinking skills are constantly being put to the test. Undoubtedly, as ESL students explore the full range of academic disciplines studied at the university, they become more able to negotiate the challenges of a university education.

This strategy provides our students with a means of becoming familiar with the discourse, methods, and concerns that are idiosyncratic to the various disciplines across the college curriculum. Although, ideally, a visitor to these classes might believe that the "content" is the driving force behind all the lessons, the astute observer will soon come to realize that "language" is being consciously taught as teachers deftly weave necessary grammar elements, rules of pronunciation, and ways of recognizing word forms into the "discussion" at each given level. Indeed, despite the fact that techniques for vocabulary building and syntactic control are being taught through thematic context, in response to the needs of the content that is being studied, it is important to understand that the teaching of particular linguistic tools at a particular time is not at random. For instance, if students do not learn the present tense, past tense, and the future tense in the lowest level, they will not be prepared to go on to the next level, where more complex verb tense structures are learned. Similarly, if they do not learn how to form questions with "Wh" question words in the lowest level, they will not understand how to distinguish a question from a noun clause in the next level. In the same vein, if students do not learn first how the use of the negative prefix "un" can reverse the meaning of the adjective "prepared," they will not be ready to learn how adding the suffix "ness" to that newly formed adjective will convert it into a noun. Because the scaffolding of grammar lessons and vocabulary-building initiatives is essential for effective language teaching, a definite schedule specifying the linguistic tools that students are required to master from level to level is woven into the logic of the curriculum. Ideally, students learn to appreciate the wholeness of this approach when they realize that they need a particular structure or word to express what the content compels them to say.

The value of improved linguistic competence within the academic context goes hand in hand with the cultivation of skills that will ensure success in the college environment. Time management, academic preparedness, and learning to use resources correctly are among the factors that guarantee a successful college experience. However, beyond these so-called "study skills," we have found that in assigning tasks, we must provide structured tools and mechanisms to allow students to build the academic competencies, or cognitive skills, which form the foundations of inquiry. For example, it is not enough to ask students to "read this essay" or "come to class ready to discuss Chapter X," because we commonly find that students skip tasks they perceive to be too easy, skim readings without weighing the significance of the ideas they present, fail to grasp the main points, or see connections between them, avoid the more difficult pieces altogether, and fall back on personal experience too readily. To address such deficiencies, we have designed our curriculum so that students are taught to perform the above tasks well. For instance, we teach them to advance from reading for main ideas to reading for specific details, and to be able to distinguish purposes of inference, and to analyze tone, audience, and language. It is our hope that as they learn to conduct vocabulary searches, answer multiple-choice questions, take notes, cite, paraphrase, summarize, read related material, prepare to lead class discussions, or construct reactions to the class material, they will become aware that the skills they are practicing will serve them well as they advance in their academic programs, read longer and more complex material, and prepare more detailed written assignments. This specific focus on skills, with an attendant increase in academic competence, also leads to a heightened sense of self-esteem and students' ultimate engagement in the academic forum.

In order to understand fully what we mean by "content" and its "connection" with the linguistic and cognitive tools that students must acquire, we will briefly describe how one of our modular units is orchestrated at the lowest level. Students read a text about a true story, "The Baby Jessica Case": Baby Jessica's biological parents, the Schmidts, would now like to raise this two-year-old girl, who thus far in her life has only known her adoptive parents, the De Boers. Detailed information is furnished pertaining to why Cara Schmidt gave Jessica up for adoption, how her life was when Jessica was born, and how it is now. The same updates are also provided for Dan Schmidt and Roberta and Jan De Boers. Because students are not familiar with the outcome of the story, the task they are presented with is to decide who should have Jessica. Should the child stay with her adoptive parents, the De Boers, or should she go back to live with her biological parents, the Schmidts? The objective of the unit is therefore the writing of an opinion essay in response to this question.

Apparently, many layers of scaffolding are required in order to prepare students for the writing task. The activities that precede the actual writing of the essay are "integrated-skills" discussions that come to life through reading, writing, listening, and speaking. As they prepare this essay, the students are differentiating between facts and opinions, because encapsulated in their thesis is an opinion based on real information that they have learned. They are also practicing summarizing and paraphrasing the readings that they have done together, and by so doing, learning skills that will be essential for their future academic development. They are using new vocabulary—*adoptive parent, biological parent, suburban*, and so on. In addition, as students consider the Baby Jessica story itself within the context of adoption, they practice the use of modal auxiliaries, such as *should* and *ought to*. The groundwork for the writing task has already been laid through extensive class discussions, lists of ideas, and supporting details that have been justified and expanded through paired and group discussions. Furthermore, they have examined lexical and syntactic models, as well as written work that can show them the basic tools needed to organize and elaborate on their thesis through topic sentences and paragraph development. As they brainstorm possible outcomes to the Jessica case—by writing sentences such as "If Jessica stays with the De Boers, she will live a comfortable life" or "Cara Schmidt will be very happy if Jessica comes back to live with her"— they are practicing the present real conditional with *"if"* sentences and correct tense sequencing. This activity not only provides grammar practice, but also embeds reasoning that will ultimately lead to the preparation of body paragraphs. As teachers provide the necessary models for language, form, and content, students imitate the models, and through this mirroring, they succeed in making the necessary progress.

Thus, in this example, the cognitive tools and the language tools are combined in sophisticated and meaningful assignments. This approach represents an ambitious undertaking for students at this beginning level. Similar units throughout the ESL sequence engage the students accordingly with increasingly complex material. In all our courses, language is not the end in itself, but rather the means by which students explore academic subjects worthy of their attention.

COLLEGE ENRICHMENT ACADEMY

Complementing credit-bearing courses of the developmental English/ESL sequences is the *College Enrichment Academy* (CEA). This program is free of charge, and it provides an additional forum for students to practice their language skills, gain familiarity with college procedures and expectations, and expand their knowledge base through the study of interdisciplinary content. The program, funded by a Title V grant that was awarded to Hostos in 2004, carries no academic credit. It is held on the weekends during the fall and spring semesters for a total of 24 hours, and also during the intersession periods (June, July, and January), for a total of 48 hours. Spaces are available for approximately five hundred students per year, and their participation is entirely voluntary. Once they are registered in the program, they are exposed to an intensive course of studies, working in groups of about twenty-five people and studying with both instructors and tutors. Attendance is strictly enforced in order to allow students to retake one of the "exit tests" referred to previously. Although the CEA's mission is enrichment, not test preparation, students who have joined the program thus far have been showing significant passing rates on their reading, writing, and math examinations—not surprisingly perhaps, because their participation in the program means that they are being exposed to an additional learning experience that complements their regular class work.

The CEA is organized thematically by topics that revolve each session: *Art, Personal Success, Health and Medicine, Education, Science and Technology, Immigration,* and so on. These themes are broad enough to allow us to explore different angles and subtopics, and they can grow in different directions, according to the interests of various groups. Students in the program read articles and journal entries related to the topics, write about questions emerging from the material, go to guest lectures and visit museums or other institutions. They also engage in a common reading with other program participants. For example, during the recent session on *Health and Medicine,* the six concurrent classes considered questions related to diet and exercise, child obesity, bird flu, hospital reform, alternative medicine, and insurance practices.

The topics always include a significant number of reading and writing assignments, and the main focus is on language development because this is the area that really prohibits movement through the college sequences. However, during the intersessions, students also read about math themes—fear of math, women in math, and so forth—and study challenging problems in math in small groups. The groups become so intrigued with the material that even students who once hated math start to like studying it with their peers and with the program's tutors. Naturally, some students who may be weak in English are quite competent in math, or vice versa. The smile on the faces of students who suddenly become their group's instructor for polynomial or quadratic equations demonstrates that they are envisaging themselves in new roles. The sessions also allow us to pinpoint areas of difficulty that may be holding certain students back in their math sequences. The students are also given practice in the computer lab and may take advantage of personalized academic advisement.

The first benefit of these CEA sessions is that students are able to practice their skills in a different learning environment. There are no grades and no tests for the class, so the students' focus is squarely on the material under discussion and the progress that they are attempting to make. As students read and discuss material on the topic of the month, they acquire new vocabulary, evaluate different viewpoints, participate in debates, practice note-taking, answer multiple-choice questions, learn essay organization, and take timed essay simulations of the actual tests they subsequently need to pass. In the session on *Health and Medicine*, for instance, many students did not know what alternative medicine was or had never heard of acupuncture; few were familiar with the "placebo effect," but some who had taken a course in ethnicity and illness were eager to share their understanding of the Hippocratic Oath. Their engagement with the material is unquestionably high. For instance, in one recent session, a young woman came to class every Sunday morning straight from an all-night shift at the hospital. Despite her tiredness, she enthusiastically contributed to the class, reacting to the *New York Times* special issues on patient complaints from the perspective of someone who really knew what she was talking about. The students had no trouble exercising critical thinking, finding weak points in the writers' arguments or juxtaposing one argument—that "nurses in most hospitals are greatly overworked"—with another—that "a nurse's responsibility is to treat people, not just illnesses."

Just as in the ESL program, the emphasis on grammar and vocabulary fades into the background as the students fight about the patients' bill of rights or write letters about soda machines in the hallways of our elementary schools, and yet there is real language learning going on here, fed by the teachers, tutors, other students, and the material itself. Even more importantly, this program establishes a community of learners. Within rough guidelines, the CEA admits students from a variety of classes, language backgrounds, and levels of language proficiency.

In the same session on *Health and Medicine*, the students read *Tuesdays with Morrie*, the touching story of the friendship between Mitch Albom, the author, and his dying professor. When at the end of the six weeks, we watched the incredibly moving film of the story, the level of engagement in the material was at its highest. The tears demonstrated the power of the real lessons we had learned: We need to "connect the dots" between reading, writing, and thinking; literature can touch us, ignite our imagination, and illuminate our lives; and we are all enriched by sharing our perceptions. There are other intangible offshoots of an engaging academic experience. For example, a professor from the Nursing Department visited the class and saw the students fired up in a discussion of flu vaccines. He was so enthralled that he sat in the class for two hours. The students, believing that he was another student, were eager to share their own ideas with him about hospital practices and doctor/patient relationships, and when they learned that he was a professor, became so proud to have been able to discuss such sophisticated content with an expert in the field. As a result, not only was their confidence level boosted, but this interchange triggered their expression of interest in applying to the nursing program and seeking him out as a mentor. Acquiring new study habits and practices helps people to envisage themselves differently, and the goals of the program—to increase language use, skills, and content—found their apogee in a fledgling community whose worth continued to grow far longer than the scheduled twenty-four hours of the program itself.

HOSTOS HONORS PROGRAM: LEADERSHIP DEVELOPMENT INSTITUTE

The learning community model is also the prelude for entrance into the *Hostos Honors Program*. Starting in June each year, students who are exempt from or who have passed out of the developmental sequence are invited to participate in the *Leadership Development Institute*. This is a five-week intensive program in which they enjoy the building of community, not only because they study shared content together, but also because they get to know each other as human beings. Although students in this cohort have gone beyond the scope of the developmental rubric, they benefit from the program in the following ways: They attain a stronger background in English and math; they achieve an enriched awareness of diverse ideas and cultivate an understanding of the many issues that our society confronts today; they engage in collaborative approaches to solving issues of public concern; and they become aware of the different ways in which they can be of service, not only to the college community itself, but also to the community at large. Of course, achieving these ends can only be possible through a curriculum that helps us to realize these objectives. Throughout the *Leadership Development Institute*, students question their values, their hopes, and their dreams as they re-evaluate not only their ways of thinking but also their ways of behaving toward one another as human beings. Since the program was established, the main thrust of our curriculum has come from one very provocative question: "What does it mean to be human?" As students consider this question, other questions such as "What is a leader?" "What is a hero?" "What is an educated person?" come to the fore. Students test their answers to these questions as they try to create their own definitions and support them with examples. Throughout this inquiry, they read and discuss material related to the following themes: *Leaders in our Society, Science and Ethics, Prejudice and Stereotypes, The Values of Indigenous Peoples,* and *Technology and Modern Life.*

Seven different learning "formats" give body to the structure of the *Institute*. Throughout the session, students address the themes mentioned above by participating in (1) *Intensive Discussions*, generated in response to readings, viewings of films, and talks of guest lectures. The value of these discussions is reinforced as students (2) *Meet a Leader!* Leaders such as environmental activists, documentary filmmakers, and personality theory psychologists have added a rich and colorful texture to the discussions of recent institutes. The "dialogue" continues as students themselves lead and participate in (3) *Conflict Resolution Simulations* that exercise their leadership and critical thinking skills. To heighten students' awareness of their inner creativity as thinkers, the (4) *Math Component* has students go beyond the traditional math curriculum and engages them in games of logic, teaching them to have fun with numbers as they consider such questions as the "history of π." In this continual process of self-empowerment, students also share their own personal life experiences with the group as they assume center stage and take their (5) *Place in the Sun*. Related to this self-affirming activity is the (6) *Weekly Reflective Journal* that students write in regard to their total Institute experience. In addition, participants enjoy (7) *Field Trips* to such venues as a community garden (e.g., Genesis Farm) or *Pacem in Terris*, the home of artist and sculptor Frederick Franck in Warwick, NY.

We hope to achieve through these formats what we want our students in all our programs to realize—that the abstract concepts that they may explore in liberal arts courses are not abstract at all when they revolve around everyday problems.

We have found that students derive a lot of benefits from this summer experience. Not only do they develop more confidence in their ability to pursue academic work, but they also construct strong bonds with other students and teachers that continue to have a positive effect on them as they continue their course work during the regular academic year. Most importantly of all, they find themselves as people. One student remarked: "For the first time in the two years I have been in this country, I have felt at 'home.'" Another recommended: "The *Institute* shouldn't even be called an institute. It's like a family to me." Reflecting the rigor of the curriculum, another said "Every day that I take a seat in the *Hostos Honors Institute* is a challenge." This sentiment is echoed in a further comment, "I feel as if I have moved from one level of education to another within this short period of time." Finally, commenting on the power of a cohesive support network, students stated that "Sharing your experiences, strengths and hopes with others is always positive: it lets you know that you are not alone," and "The seminar helped me to acknowledge that sometimes people act the way they think they are, instead of acting the way they are."

Undoubtedly, as can be seen from these students' comments, this process of self-examination is a very important aspect of the learning experience. We realize that if a learner does not become responsible for the learning process, he or she will never be able to truly progress. Plutarch's axiom, "A mind is not a vessel to be filled but a fire to be ignited," explains the intent of our commitment at Hostos. Not only must we furnish our students with the skills they need in order to do college work, but we must also help them to cultivate a vision of who they can become. Without intense reflection, how can this be possible?

We have seen many changes take place at our school. The three programs we have described, brought into being under the leadership of the Provost and Vice President for Academic Affairs, Dr. Daisy Cocco de Filippis, have the potential to help our students transform their lives, and they mark the first steps of a longer journey. Undoubtedly, because these programs reflect the principles inherent in the General Education initiatives that are now being discussed throughout CUNY, it is our hope that along with the knowledge that our students will acquire under our direction, they will become not only the guardians of the past and the present but also the guarantors of humanity's future. On another level, it would truly be wonderful if every student who entered the developmental English/ESL sequence and participated in the enrichment program were to eventually enter the *Honors Program* and graduate with an "H." In fact, to our great delight, we can honestly say that because of the efforts of many of our dedicated colleagues at Eugenio María de Hostos Community College, more and more of our students are beginning to fit this profile.

WORKS CITED

Hurston, Zora Neale. *Their Eyes Were Watching God*. New York: HarperPerennial, 1998.

Morales, Edward. "Nickels and Dimes." *New York Times*, 9 October 2005, Section 14: 1, 8.

New York City Department of City Planning. *The Newest New Yorkers 2000, Immigrant New York in the New Millennium*, October 2004: Table 6–2, 152.

Office of Institutional Research. *Fall 2005 Databook*. New York: Eugenio María de Hostos Community College, 2005. http://www.hostos.cuny.edu/oaa/oir/databookfall05.pdf.

CHAPTER NINE

The Shakespeare Portal

Teaching the Canon at the Community College

CRYSTAL BENEDICKS

Queensborough Community College

A recent "open mic" poetry reading at Queensborough Community College, where I teach composition and literature (Shakespeare, this term), recently sparked a vigorous debate on the faculty Listserv about what students should learn, what faculty should teach, and what freedoms of speech should be protected on a college campus. At the event, some students read poems in the spoken-word hip-hop tradition, angering some faculty members who were offended by what they perceived as the racism, homophobia, and sexism of the genre. One faculty member, defending students' rights to explicit language, wrote "Talk about poets with potty mouths, have you read Shakespeare? That Mercutio is a trash talker!" Another, questioning the role of hip-hop in the college curriculum, argued that "Queensborough may be the only place where students will have the opportunity to experience Yeats or Shakespeare or Dante," so why "waste" class time studying popular culture? Picking up on this, another faculty member suggested that Queensborough consider adopting a "Great Books" program, where the question of what counts as "great" would be open for students and faculty. Others responded that teaching the intricacies of a line of poetry and examining the conventions of a literary tradition—be it hip hop or a Shakespeare play—is the real work of the curriculum.

As a new faculty member at the beginning of her career as a scholar, I also quickly came up against questions about Shakespeare and the role of canonical literature in the Queensborough classroom. In a composition course I teach, the class was discussing an essay by social critic and educator Mike Rose, problematizing canonical approaches to teaching literature and writing. We ran into trouble when I realized that the students did not share an understanding of what "canonical literature" is

> Name a "Great Book," I said.
> > That's easy: Shakespeare.
> Name another.
> > Silence.
> > Finally: *The Da Vinci Code?*

Shakespeare has a high profile at Queensborough. The Theatre Department is about to launch a production of *Romeo and Juliet*. Posters, advertising a new club for students interested in performance, show a black-and-white photo of "Shakespeare" as a young man, dressed in a black tee-shirt and tattoos. "Why are you using complicated words like that?" I heard one student ask another during peer review, "What are you, *Shakespeare?*"

Asked to reflect on his reading habits, one student in the Composition I class I am currently teaching writes:

> I don't like the books which don't challenge my mind to analyze the words and meanings behind them; although sometimes the difficult books can get annoying, I'm up for the challenge. I can't say that I have read all of Shakespeare's writing, but I have read the Bible a lot.

Saying "Shakespeare" is saying a lot. He is so iconic that the word "Shakespeare" comes to mean both the man and the writing (thus, "Shakespeare" is a "what" rather than a "who" for the students doing peer review, and "Shakespeare" is also an appropriate answer to a question that asks students to list titles of books). For the students I have quoted here, he is simultaneously representative of a kind of writing that is at once foreign and unnatural (*what are you, Shakespeare?*), emblematic of what it means to be an educated reader (*I don't like the books which don't challenge my mind*), and a figure ripe for appropriation and adaptation (the performance club's vision of the tattooed artist, or the theatre department's production—advertised on a poster decorated with sailor-tattoo style hearts and daggers). For the professoriate, meanwhile, "Shakespeare" suggests ongoing curricular debates over what ought to be taught in college.

At the poetry reading, students and faculty read poems in at least four languages (and more if you count dialects). In order to understand the roles Shakespeare plays, it is necessary to look at the literacies Queensborough students bring with them to college, to the classroom. Although all CUNY colleges are often discussed in terms of the remarkable diversity of their students, Queensborough Community College is a special case. While many CUNY colleges enroll one race or ethnicity predominantly (Hostos Community College is mostly Caribbean, John Jay College is mostly

Latino/a, and so on), Queensborough Community College is balanced almost equally between white, black, Asian, and Latino/a students. The result is often a truly generative mix, an environment that challenges received ideas about what college is, whom it is for, and what it ought to teach. Such an environment—composed of a set of conditions that constantly forecloses the possibility of conclusions, of easy resolution—seems to me to get at the heart of what a truly liberal (which is to say, liberatory) education ought to deliver.

From this mesh of voices, conflicts, and cultural disconnects, Shakespeare emerges as an unexpected and highly contested bit of common ground. On a campus where students come from everywhere and racial friction is sometimes as chaotic and disruptive as it is productive and enriching, Shakespeare stands out as the one element of the western high art tradition that everyone knows, or has at least heard of. Most students have read at least one Shakespeare play in high school, but even if students have no firsthand knowledge, Shakespeare is a cultural icon everywhere: They know Shakespeare through movie adaptations, magazine articles, advertisements. It is no fluke that the students in my Composition class only got as far as Shakespeare in listing the classics: Shakespeare is perhaps the only standard western classic they are all bound to have heard of. Only *The Da Vinci Code*, still at the top of bestseller lists, has a profile as visible.

Shakespeare's high profile on the Queensborough campus is nothing out of the ordinary. The student who wrote about Shakespeare and the Bible side-by-side was accessing a long American tradition of locating the two at the heart of what it means to be literate. His words echo those of John Quincy Adams in the late eighteenth century:

> At the age of ten I was as familiarly acquainted with [Shakespeare's] lovers and clowns as with Robinson Crusoe, the Pilgrim's Progress, and the Bible. In later years I have left Robinson and the Pilgrim to the perusal of children; but have continued to read the Bible and Shakespeare. (Levine 1988, 16)

Several decades later, German poet and scholar of American folklore Karl Knortz wrote:

> If you were to enter an isolated log cabin in the Far West, and even if its inhabitants were to exhibit many traces of backwoods living, he will most likely have one small room nicely furnished in which to spend his few leisure hours and in which you will certainly find the Bible and in most cases also some cheap edition of the works of the poet Shakespeare. (Levine 1988, 18)

The Queensborough student, who is Latino and who also works as a salesman in a start-up company, Adams, who served as the country's president, and the typical backwoods American pioneer are united in their reading habits: Shakespeare and the Bible. These are at once the sacred texts and the common texts.

In *Highbrow/Lowbrow: The Emergence of Cultural Hierarchy in America* (1988), Lawrence W. Levine, from whom I have taken the above quotations, argues that Shakespeare was not always the embodiment of high art. In nineteenth-century America, he posits, Shakespeare was understood as popular culture, although, as in the case of John Quincy Adams, the nation eventually "grew up" to separate Shakespeare from the popular novels of its cultural infancy. Every pioneer would have owned some Shakespeare—available in cheap editions—and every nineteenth-century theatregoer would have seen Shakespeare performed alongside vaudeville acts. The slippage from Shakespeare to *The Da Vinci Code* would have been no slippage at all to nineteenth-century American audiences, who saw *As You Like It* alongside "a most magnificent display . . . of the Science of Gymnastics" or *Richard III* with "A NEW and ORIGINAL Patriotic Drama in Three Acts . . . [with a] Grand Military Tableau!" Or *King Lear* followed by *Love's Laughs at Locksmiths; or, The Guardian Outwitted*" (Levine 1988, 22–23).

Levine argues that modern cultural historians often look back on such pairings and see "highbrow" Shakespeare linked to "lowbrow" vaudeville. However, Levine holds that these categories had not yet become hardened into opposition: Shakespeare really was popular culture. Here Levine makes an important distinction: "Popular culture" is now taken to imply something easily accessible, even trashy, whereas Shakespeare, in the nineteenth century, was simply popular, in the sense of "widely read." "Popular," not yet a tainted word, signified that Shakespeare was conceived as widely available, open to all.

For Levine, Shakespeare's availability had a lot to do with his place in the curriculum. In a culture largely based on oral traditions, a culture that prized rhetoric and looked up to the statesmen who could deliver intricate and moving speeches, Shakespeare was taught as language rather than literature. Excerpts from his plays were taught to schoolchildren as rhetorical exercises to be memorized and read aloud. However, by the turn of the century, Shakespeare's curricular place had shifted from the child's rhetoric reader to the university's literature classroom. For a variety of reasons—from the influx of languages that came with late nineteenth- and early twentieth-century waves of immigration, to the changing role of the theatre as center of literary rather than "popular" entertainment, to the wane of melodrama as a dominant genre and the shifts in acting style away from the bombastic and toward the contemplative—Shakespeare's role as master of English rhetoric as well as his accessibility to mass audiences had begun to fade. Levine writes: "By the turn of the century Shakespeare had been converted from popular playwright whose dramas were the property of those that flocked to see them, into a sacred author who had to be protected from ignorant audiences and overbearing actors threatening the integrity of his creations" (1988, 72). By 1882, A. A. Lipscomb was able to predict that Shakespeare "is destined to become the Shakespeare of the college and university, and even more the Shakespeare of private and select culture" (Levine 1988, 73).

The Queensborough curriculum enacts this contemporary understanding of Shakespeare, to the extent that "Shakespeare" comes to stand for that other slippery term, "liberal education." At Queensborough, there is only one non-survey, single-author course on the books: Shakespeare. The curricular justification for the course is that it fills a transfer requirement mandated by Queensborough Community College's sister senior college, Queens. Students planning to major in education at Queens College can take the Shakespeare course for transfer credit. It also fills a graduation requirement needed for the Liberal Arts and Sciences associate's degree program at Queensborough. It is expected that such Liberal Arts and Sciences students will go on to Queens College or another four-year school. Assigned the course number 611, Shakespeare sits at the top of the English curriculum. There are no higher numbers.

Many assumptions about Shakespeare's role in education, about the liberal arts, and about the relationship between senior and junior colleges are implicit in the curricular logic of this course. First, the course catalogue imagines Shakespeare as a gateway course through which students on the verge of moving from the community to the senior college must pass. Second, to become a teacher, you must know Shakespeare. Third, Shakespeare is an integral part of what it means to be liberally educated—even to the point where the curriculum offers no other options for in-depth study of a particular author or grouping of authors. Finally, Shakespeare is provided for those students who are "going on" with their liberal arts educations. Shakespeare is not primarily intended for the student nurses, the technology students, the student scientists, or the students on explicitly career-bound tracks (except, of course, teachers). An asterisk in the course catalogue marks it for special interest to liberal arts students and future educators.

All of these curricular questions and assumptions highlight the Shakespeare course as a portal through which students can pass to go from being novices in the university to full-fledged members, that much closer to the senior college, the liberal education ideal, and that most humanistic of all professions: teaching. Shakespeare is assumed to have a transformative power. Studying Shakespeare's plays or sonnets changes students and puts them closer to the center. The question gets more complicated when one begins to ask what exactly Shakespeare is conceived as a portal *to*. For some of the faculty I have quoted here, it is a portal to the Great Books tradition, which, it is assumed, students "need to know." For others, it is a problematic relic that does not speak to student experience. For some students, it is an entry to the very center of literary culture, while for others Shakespeare is a compilation of foreign and over-elaborate language. More complicated still: Who will pass through the Shakespeare portal? Is it only for those on their way out, those who will go on to pursue a higher degree?

Levine traces Shakespeare's transition from a generally known aspect of nineteenth-century culture to a bastion of high art. That is, in Levine's configuration, Shakespeare served as America's general education—that which everyone was assumed to know—before he was reified as America's liberal education—that which marks one as especially well versed in traditional western expression and thus linked to "timeless" moral and civic values. Standing as he does here at Queensborough, on the curricular border between community and senior college, general education and liberal education, the figure of Shakespeare allows us to examine the porousness of those boundaries and to pose questions about what we, as educators, mean by "liberal education" and how it is different from what we call "general education." In a sense, those distinctions are as flawed as the distinctions between "high" and "low" art: Although all these categories carry undeniable cultural significance, they are also invented categories whose borders are open for contention, especially on the college campus, where students perform hip hop in the Quadrangle and Shakespeare in the Theatre.

I find that the students currently enrolled in the Queensborough Shakespeare class came themselves with a wide range of goals and expectations. It is a full class, with over thirty students. A few plan to major in education at Queens College next fall, but many more are simply liberal arts students in the sense that they have focused broadly on general education during their years at Queensborough and plan to major in the humanities at a four-year college. Several are not sure what kinds of careers they will pursue—and this is not something one hears often at a community college, where the majority of students focus on career preparation and where the curricula are increasingly designed to support professional education. Some students told me they were there because they needed another liberal arts and sciences credit for graduation, and this class fit their schedules. One man will enter the Police Academy soon; he passed the qualifying test two years ago, but he needed sixty college credits to enroll. He thought it might be useful to learn something about drama and performance. Another student is finishing up her time at Queensborough and plans to transfer to a medical school to become a doctor. A young musician in the class knows Shakespeare through musical adaptations; she plans to transfer to a senior college to pursue a degree in music. One student is writing his application to Binghamton University in upstate New York, where he wants to earn a doctorate in Classical Language and Literature. For some of these students, especially those from working-class or immigrant families, the cultural access that Shakespeare promises is potent. Teachers and educators, the keepers of the curriculum, cannot afford to ignore this potential or let it go unexamined.

There is also another type of student enrolled in Shakespeare—not anything I expected. Two retired primary-school teachers who had once attended Queensborough, older than the rest of the class by four decades or more, are auditing the class. One middle-school teacher on sabbatical has signed up: He has authored a book due out very soon about writing pedagogy, and he is under contract for another. These students are also teachers, all spending their free time reading Shakespeare. They do not need the credits: They are here for joy. That, too, is a potent motive for study.

This is an odd class in that the students do not share a mutual identity as Queensborough Community College students: They are visitors and they are those on the cusp of going. The class is defined by its peripheral relationship to the college. On the first day of class, all students pointed out their area of interest and why they had enrolled in this Shakespeare course. Over and over we heard "I'm transferring to—, I'm transferring to—; next year I'll be at—." We study Shakespeare in a liminal space; the curriculum tells us that Shakespeare will usher us through that space. But how?

What is Shakespeare for? This is the question that drove my preparation for class over the summer, and that I now think of in the context of the students enrolled in this class—their plans and their reasons for being there—and also in the context of the curriculum at Queensborough Community College. There are a lot of other questions embedded in that one question: What does it mean to teach Shakespeare—the most canonical of the canonical—at a community college? The canon is often problematized among the professoriate, but students are not often brought into the conversation (my own experiment with this, recorded above, proves it is difficult to do, but the question of what ought to be taught in college is not one we should keep from college students). What do students mean when they say they are "reading Shakespeare?" What kinds of relationships are there between the way the curriculum imagines Shakespeare—as a course for those who are headed for the "big leagues"—and the way students imagine the uses of the course?

Most of the students in this Shakespeare class, like the student who wrote about liking challenging books, are dedicated. In almost a decade of teaching—as an adjunct and now a full-time assistant professor, at senior colleges in Manhattan and at community colleges throughout the boroughs—I have never encountered a class where the discussions flow so easily and where the level of engagement is as high. Taken together, these students refute the notion that community college students "can't" read Shakespeare, or that such courses are best kept where they are usually found—in the upper division at senior colleges.

For me, the question is about how studying Shakespeare "delivers" the liberal arts promise, for the assumption made by students, professors, and course catalogue alike is very much that it does. I find it difficult to believe that knowledge of Shakespeare's writings is transformative in and of itself—especially for a student population that shares little of Shakespeare's heritage and largely identifies itself outside of the charmed circle of English classics. Moreover, I do not share the belief that Shakespeare is the "best" writer we have had—or even that it is useful to make "best of" lists.

So I do not believe Shakespeare is a magic Liberal Education bullet. However, I do think that there is immense value in reading a resistant text. Shakespeare's stories and his sense of psychological realism are broadly appealing, but his language is several centuries old. It is not just that: He writes out of an Elizabethan aesthetic that prizes artifice, complicated structures, and elaborate ornamentation: the opposite of what we value in writing today, in the age of "effective" communication and "clear" writing. Sitting down to read something so foreign, something that shares little of our contemporary aesthetics, demands what I think is at the heart of a liberal arts education: a refusal of the notion that reading is a goal-oriented transaction where the idea is to "get" the answers. Reading Shakespeare demands a level of comfort with epistemological uncertainty, a willingness to find new styles of reading and paying attention that respect complexity and welcome the unexpected.

In Shakespeare class, we start every day with a discussion of what it was like to read the play at hand. We talk about reading strategies: One student reads aloud when she finds herself getting confused, another tries to read each play twice, another rents the movie, another consults Sparknotes.com (an Internet reading guide) to understand the plot. Some students purchased the plays in a new edition called "No Fear Shakespeare," which gives Shakespeare's original text on one page, and a modernization on the opposite page. My hope is that by openly discussing the reading guides that are often criminalized in classrooms, we can refute the assumption that they are "illegal" because they "give away the answers for free." I want students of Shakespeare to understand that the benefits of having read Shakespeare do not come from being able to summarize three main themes in *Hamlet* or the role of irony in *Macbeth*, or grasping the plot of *Richard III*. Rather, the goal of reading Shakespeare is to learn how to read Shakespeare, to engage with a challenging text not to mine it for answers, but to understand and appreciate the complexity, the uncertainty.

We talk about different ways of coming to understand Shakespeare: through performance (a group performance is a significant part of the grade; students make interpretive choices during the rehearsal process, and afterwards lead a class discussion on the interpretations they have launched), through radically different film versions of the same play, as well as through literary analysis and close reading. We raise the issues we encounter in reading: how to handle the cognitive disjunction that occurs every time you look down at a footnote or flip back to the Cast of Characters to remind yourself who someone is. In paying attention to the way we read Shakespeare, we come closer to being aware of our own learning and assessing what it is we are doing.

In the course of studying Shakespeare's plays, we also study Shakespeare as cultural icon. We watch scenes from Baz Luhrmann's postmodern vision of *Romeo + Juliet* set in Miami Beach; Tim Blake Nelson's *O*, a reimagining of *Othello* centered on a modern boarding school's basketball team; Michael Almereyda's production of *Hamlet* as a capitalist distopia; and Akira Kurosawa's cultural translation of *Macbeth* into a Samurai movie, *Throne of Blood*. Through focusing on the ways Shakespeare is appropriated today, we interrogate the various cultural uses of canonical literature, unmooring Shakespeare from his distant origins and contextualizing his writings in the literary debates taking place today. In fact, many students arrive in the Shakespeare classroom already having experienced these film versions. They come with an understanding of Shakespeare as culturally "up for grabs" in a way that is closer to the nineteenth-century notion of Shakespeare as a poet of the democracy than to competing notions of Shakespeare as sacred literary giant. As Levine reminds us, the split between a reified Shakespeare-as-art and a popular Shakespeare whose work is available for broad appropriation and consumption is relatively new, and is not something we are obliged to enact in the classroom or in the curriculum.

Judith Summerfield began the General Education Project at CUNY, as she recounts in her introductory essay, by asking participants to recall a liberally educative moment. Mine centers on the Shakespeare class I took in college. I do not remember which play we were reading or what we were talking about, but I do remember it was one of those "good" classroom conversations, where we were responding to one another and arriving mutually at new ideas. The professor, caught up, stood up from his desk and went to the chalkboard. However, the conversation had gotten too complex, and he could not think of how to represent it. He ended up drawing a line on the board, as if to emphasize a word that was not there. For me, this meant that the importance neither lay in the conclusion nor in the thrust of the conversation but in the fact that we were having it, that we were grappling with language and ideas. For me, this moment was liberally educative because the text had been opened up for debate. More precisely, the meanings we were arriving at in that class did not come hierarchically from Shakespeare, or even from the teacher-as-explicator, but from our mutual interaction, our willingness to enter into and "own" Shakespeare's words. In the process, we were circumventing a stultifying sense of Shakespeare as cultural monolith and actually engaging in the meaning-making process, in the democratic sense Levine describes. That is what the professor underlined, and that sense of critical engagement with a text is what I hope is emphasized in my Shakespeare class at Queensborough as well.

WORK CITED

Levine, Lawrence W. *Highbrow/Lowbrow: The Emergence of Cultural Hierarchy in America*. Cambridge: Harvard University Press, 1988.

CHAPTER TEN

A Shared Classroom

General Education at Baruch College

DAVID POTASH

Hunter College

Institutions may be ranked by endowments, SATs and faculty scholarship, but they present themselves to their students primarily through their courses. A course is a structured and regulated exchange between an institution, a faculty member, and a student. A course defines a realm of knowledge, navigating disciplinary strictures and departmental prerogatives and accommodating, to varying degrees, the multiple demands of the curriculum and the varying aspirations of students. The offering of a single course represents hundreds upon hundreds of decisions by faculty, students, staff, and administrators. Every course needs the evaluation and approval of disciplines, departments, committees and other bodies, and the enrollment of students. In such ways courses, the daily interactions of students and faculty, collectively define an institution; they are lived and learned. What takes place in a classroom between student and instructor is at the very heart of higher education. In theory, the experiences, actions, thoughts, and work that radiate from a course, coupled with the larger curriculum, reflect and reinforce institutional priorities; in practice, the lineaments between a course and a program and broad institutional goals are not always clear or strong.

Just as faculty are located within disciplines and departments, so, too, are courses. The process of course development and evaluation normally requires local or departmental concern. Without departmental support, courses usually die. Consequently, courses incorporate disciplinary and departmental priorities, and they seek student learning primarily along disciplinary lines. The agenda of a department, however, may not necessarily directly advance the broader aims of a college or complement the post-collegiate aims of a student. The learning goals of general education, which most of us in higher education find so difficult to define, pose particular challenges because they do not emerge directly from a department or discipline, though they usually are achieved while in simultaneous pursuit of disciplinary aims. General education goals are not necessarily the same as disciplinary learning goals. Rather, students benefiting from a robust general education know things and are able to do things that reach across and through disciplines and departments; their knowledge is not grounded in a readily recognized structure. One of the key challenges of general education is the coordination and pursuit of learning goals that may or may not be normally located within a discipline or department.

In the spring 2005 semester I taught an upper level undergraduate history course, "American Foreign Relations in the Twentieth Century," at Baruch College. An examination of this one course, looking at why it was offered, what it was about, why students took it, and what I wanted the students to learn, opens a window on many of the issues central to general education at Baruch. My multiple roles at the college similarly offer multiple perspectives from which to address these issues; from 2000 to 2005, I served as Associate Provost for the teaching and learning environment while regularly teaching as an adjunct in the Department of History. I was deeply involved in issues of student learning and helping the college develop learning goals and assessment plans, working with faculty and staff to determine what we really thought students should learn and be able to do because of a Baruch education. Broad concerns with students' knowledge and abilities, coupled with a conscious effort to develop skills relevant to business students and the business school, played a prominent role in History 3420. The course was very much a consequence of Baruch's initiatives and plans; even more, the college's priorities and the course reflect many of the current debates about general education and its relationship with the disciplines and the baccalaureate.[1]

Located in several buildings along Lexington Avenue in mid-Manhattan, Baruch is a senior college in the City University of New York. It enrolls approximately 12,500 undergraduates and 3,000 master's level graduate students, offering the BBA, BA, BS, MA, and MS degrees. Importantly, Baruch's culture has been shaped by a shared sense of mission. Long ago City College's downtown campus and the site of its business school, Baruch's identity has been closely linked for many years to business education. Baruch's undergraduate students over the years have reflected the demographics of New York City's public high schools: They hail from families of modest means and are often recent immigrants to America. Baruch offers these students an education and the opportunity for economic advancement. It is, for many, a clear path to the middle class and potential prosperity. While Baruch's faculty, staff, and leadership are aware of the institution's role and importance to these students, there is also a shared realization that the college is not, nor or should it be, about vocational education. Student advisement repeatedly stresses the distinction and faculty members throughout the college reinforce the importance of the arts and sciences. Slogans used for a recent fundraising effort illustrate that tension: "Baruch means business" generated internal criticism, but "Baruch: where the American dream still works" was well received.

Baruch is an unusual institution of higher education, different from any other in the United States because of its size, business focus, and structure. In fact, no other college or university in the nation graduates anywhere nearly as many business students. Baruch is organized into three schools: the Weissman School of Arts and Sciences, the Zicklin School of Business, and a School of Public Affairs. The Zicklin School of Business and the Weissman School of Arts and Sciences each house more than 215 tenure-track faculty members. Accredited by AACSB, the Zicklin School of Business's reputation has grown as it has recruited productive scholars and competed in rankings and other measures of quality. The Weissman School of Arts and Sciences, originally organized with a service role, has become academically stronger and much more active in recent years. Across Baruch, scholarship is valued, but so, too, are student learning and success. All three schools have outstanding faculty members with international reputations, and all rely more than they want to on adjuncts to teach the students who crowd the college's halls. Nonetheless, overall the college's public identity is associated with business.

Baruch offers a fascinating laboratory to examine the relationship between general education and undergraduate professional education. Because of the college's uncommon structure, the regular priorities of academic schools are reversed, and business receives the lion's share of attention and external support. More than 85% of all undergraduates at Baruch seek the BBA and major in business. However, the AACSB and business education best practices mandate that at least half of a student's course of study should be in arts and sciences. For freshmen matriculating at Baruch, those broad curricular requirements mean that students focus on arts and sciences during their freshman and sophomore year, whereas they study mostly business during their junior and senior year. Overall, student activity is greater in the arts and sciences, but because of the college's organization, much of the arts and sciences curriculum can be understood as general education.

Baruch constantly wrestles with curricular issues and learning issues, as do most institutions, but the exchanges at Baruch are particularly difficult to resolve because of the relationship between the school of arts and sciences and the school of business, which faces pressing requirements of external accreditation. Faculty and school cultures, as well as the college's administrative organizational structures, both help and hinder this complicated interaction, which is fraught with challenges to school, departmental, and individual faculty members' prerogatives. The Zicklin School of Business needs students well schooled in the arts and sciences, but the development and delivery of the arts and sciences curriculum are the purview of the Weissman School of Arts and Sciences. Communication, cooperation, and trust are essential for the relationship to work, the college to move forward, and the students to succeed. A fundamental objective of my administrative responsibilities was facilitating positive relationships within and between the schools, pulling together stakeholders from across the college community.

Baruch's leadership has long recognized the power of inertia and the difficulty of ongoing curricular evaluation and change. Internal committees and college-wide initiatives repeatedly promote broader discussions. For most faculty members, scholarship and teaching provide ample demands, and both of these activities are closely intertwined with the discipline and the department. As at most institutions, curricular changes are usually driven by changes within the field as new scholarship is disseminated and evaluated. Upper level courses tend to change more frequently while entry level courses are more stable. Most senior faculty members prefer teaching graduate or upper level courses while entry level courses are more frequently assigned to adjuncts and junior faculty. Adjuncts lack the standing to propose course revisions, and more often than not junior faculty are encouraged to focus on scholarship, not curricular development. As a consequence, lower level courses, the courses comprising general education, usually suffer from haphazard or inadequate curricular development. The delivery of base level courses may receive attention, particularly if students are having difficulty making progress through a departmental sequence, but it is rare for the content of lower level courses to receive systematic attention. Because changes in general education require school-wide and college-wide attention, mechanisms that call for faculty to look outside of their departments are essential. At Baruch, the common core curriculum has been a recurring focus of concern and debate from faculty and administrators across the institution.

Baruch's common core is perhaps the most salient example of the interaction of business and arts and sciences. Baruch's 2001 iteration of the core, implemented in conjunction with other major efforts in curricular revision, assessment and student learning, attempts to provide undergraduates with breadth and depth. A three-tiered set of requirements and goals, the common core asks that students take introductory courses in the key disciplinary areas of arts and sciences (Tier I and Tier II). The desire to expose students to different disciplines and departments was also a salient feature of the earlier core. The significant change in the 2001 core was adding an arts and sciences minor as a requirement. The minor, colloquially known at the college as "Tier III," consists of one introductory and three upper level courses, one of which is usually a capstone. Initially located only in the departments, Tier III now includes interdisciplinary programs.

To summarize, Tier III consists of advanced arts and sciences courses offered in a sequence by arts and sciences faculty for students who are primarily interested in business. Faculty across Baruch shared the belief that undergraduate business students would greatly benefit from a more in-depth understanding and appreciation of a subject within the arts and sciences irrespective of area or discipline. For whatever reason—the structure of the college, the composition of the committees, an unwillingness of faculty to reach across disciplines, or some combination of other factors—faculty resisted the call for specific discipline-based learning goals. Instead, the plan assumes that student learning anywhere in the arts and sciences would carry with it something greater than just mastering content.

Implementation of the common core affected many of the college's practices, changing enrollment patterns as well as the interaction of faculty members across schools. Within the Weissman School of Arts and Sciences, demand for seats in upper level courses increased dramatically. Departments and programs labored to shape meaningful minors, bearing in mind budget and staffing constraints. The college was also challenged to create a curriculum and requirements that would not impede students' progress toward the degree. Left for the departmental curricular committees to determine was the exact composition of Tier III, nine to twelve credits of curricular programming that would best serve the students. Some departments, such as psychology, opted for a unified capstone experience. In mathematics, the capstone was eschewed for advanced work in a selection of upper level courses. The Curriculum Committee looked for ways to accommodate disciplinary and departmental wants within overall college goals, some of which were changing because of learning outcomes assessment. Flexibility was essential, for the departments' plans were, in essence, creating new standards of competency.

The Curriculum Committee did agree, however, that all of the minors should attempt to incorporate communication as a learning goal and that the departments should strive to develop communication intensive courses, or CICs, in Tier III. The focus on communication was an expression of a long-standing Baruch priority to improve its students' communications skills, an aim actively supported by the Zicklin Curriculum Committee. In fact, international business education organizations consistently stress the importance of developing strong communications skills at the graduate and undergraduate levels. At Baruch, the challenge was met head on: Written and oral communication is part of the college's basic core requirements and emphasized throughout the curriculum through the work of the Bernard L. Schwartz Communication Institute, which also oversees the Writing Across the Curriculum (WAC) program.

Reporting to the provost's office, the Schwartz Institute directs resources to schools, departments, and faculty members, trains and supervises communication consultants, researches communication related data and issues, and provides a public forum for examining communication issues in academia and business; its mission is to improve the written and oral communication of Baruch's students. Faculty, working with communication experts from the Schwartz Institute, established guidelines for the development and assessment of communication intensive courses (CICs). The courses are offered throughout the curriculum, with more support directed to targeted courses that reach the highest possible number of students. While much work was done with writing in conjunction with CUNY's WAC initiative, oral communication was not neglected. A required interdisciplinary capstone course in business received the greatest degree of attention. In this capstone, the students, all seniors close to graduation, give presentations which are taped and reviewed. As the Institute's mission stresses the importance and value of developing written and oral communication, the Weissman Curriculum Committee believed that CIC guidelines would provide a useful template for Tier III courses. In practice, the Weissman Committee did not require that the CIC guidelines and practices be followed explicitly.

Baruch did not embrace outcomes assessment on its own but instead came to accept and use outcomes assessment deliberately and in conjunction with external pressures. Initially, it took hold in areas that saw professional growth and requirements dependent upon assessment. Through the demands of AACSB reaccreditation, the Zicklin School of Business was required to develop and implement a plan that would assure student learning. My understanding of the needs of business pedagogy and learning was greatly influenced by participation on the Zicklin School of Business's Curriculum Committee and its Committee on Learning Assurance. External stakeholders were consulted about the optimum balance of generalized and specific skills; these and other measures regularly pressure business schools to question their curricula. Surveys of employers, for example, reveal a strong desire for graduates who possess basic abilities and temperaments suited to the workplace: Employers want graduates who have good interpersonal skills, writing and speaking abilities, are effective working in teams, and demonstrate integrity and a strong work ethic. These are laudable outcomes, but they do not map neatly into a traditional curriculum or program. Teamwork is neither a course nor can writing be assigned solely to the English department or speaking to the department of communication.

Within Zicklin, eight learning goals were collectively identified after analysis of individual courses, programs, and majors. Of the eight learning goals, students' written and oral communication skills were the initial focus of the business school faculty. Participation, expertise, and data from the Schwartz Communication were essential.

Following a pattern common in academia, the adoption of assessment moved more slowly within the Weissman School of Arts and Sciences. No external accrediting body demanded the speedy implementation of an outcomes assessment plan, allowing more time to question basic foci. As a member of both groups, I tried to keep both working along similar paths.

All of these issues were factors in determining what courses I would teach. Like all adjuncts, I taught what was needed. The history curriculum at Baruch consists of a limited number of introductory level courses followed by a wide range of courses at the more advanced level. For Tier III, the department allows students to enroll in a combination of these upper level courses; a capstone seminar that emphasizes historiography issues ends the sequence. History is a popular minor, which means that more upper level courses are needed. After consulting with the department's chair and several colleagues, I decided to try my hand at History 3420, American Foreign Relations in the Twentieth Century. It had been years since the course had been run and without a current syllabus, the course needed to be redesigned. The task appealed to me, particularly as it allowed me to try to shape the course with an eye toward the broader challenges facing the curriculum: assessment, student success, and the relationship between the business of arts and sciences—general education—and the demands of an integrated business education.

When Tier III was first implemented, many students grumbled and considered it just another hurdle that the college had placed in the path to a degree.[2] After all, Baruch already had a rigorous set of required courses in place. Students who hope to major in business are required to complete an eight-course pre-business curriculum consisting of English Composition, Calculus, Business Law, Statistics, Micro and Macroeconomics, Introduction to Computing, and Principles of Accounting. A minimum grade point average for these courses is required before students can declare their intent to major in a business discipline. Once the major is approved, students face an additional set of business base courses. Prior to Tier III, few students sought a minor. With very few degrees of freedom in students' course of study, an additional requirement was viewed skeptically.

The students' perspective is understandable. What is the benefit of another requirement and why attend college? For most of us who work in academia, the value of higher education is closely linked to the creation and sharing of knowledge. College is a period of growth and personal development, an important phase in the formation of a well-educated adult. For most students, a college degree is a necessary step before securing a good job, even though it is not always clear how exactly a baccalaureate prepares students for the workplace. The baccalaureate, nevertheless, is a reliable path to financial opportunity and stability. As a student once explained to me, his degree was an investment in himself. In 2005 the U.S. Census Bureau provided average salaries on the basis of degree: $27,915 for a high school diploma, $51,206 for a bachelor's degree, and $74,602 for those with an advanced degree.[3] Most college students I taught at CUNY were very much cognizant of the financial consequences of an education.

Colleges face an array of challenges reconciling students' vocational expectations with pedagogical aims and intellectual aspirations. Rarely do we see faculty at four-year institutions define their broad function as the creation of workers. Instead, we take pains to make it clear to students in a variety of ways that higher education is not vocational. We do not train; we educate. We do not provide jobs; we provide an education. Some two-year colleges, specialized schools and programs are very effective at mission-driven education that produces employable graduates. On the other hand, the concept does not always rest as comfortably with many of us employed in four-year colleges. In other words, when those of us who teach in the arts and sciences face the demands of the market, we are forced to reconfigure our thinking and our pedagogy.

The tensions between vocational desires and education aims are revealed in the very basic structures of higher education, which valorize the creation of knowledge over its dissemination or use. The more theoretical the endeavor, the more cultural capital we tend to assign to it. At most institutions, for example, the business school is an appendage of arts and science. Along similar lines, departments and disciplines describe fields of scholarship, not pedagogy or method. Moreover, departments and disciplines almost always define the major, not a putative future employer of graduates. Courses, especially in the arts and sciences, more often than not map a body or range of academic knowledge, not employment. Students major in English and Psychology, not in "working in a small advertising business" or "finding success in a large corporation." Admittedly a smaller set of undergraduate majors, such as accountancy or pre-law, point to specific career paths. However, these majors are rarely in arts and sciences. They also have less cultural capital and are situated closer to the periphery in academic circles.

Consider the undergraduate major, which we expect to define expertise and authority. Majors do chart well-recognized bodies of knowledge, but not as areas that an undergraduate can ever master. The faculty and the department or institution, not the student, hold and direct the powers inherent in the definition of a major. Majoring in one area, by its very nature, claims to develop in-depth knowledge. The major almost never, on the other hand, gives students adequate knowledge or skill for a career. Students are aware of this reality, too, and it is revealed in their language; a biology major will not call herself a biologist and a political science major will not describe himself as a political scientist. Students, nonetheless, want majors and ways of defining themselves and their studies. They seek direction and specialized knowledge; expertise carries with it status and personal validation. Majors are also important to students for how they describe their studies to others and the market; many believe it is necessary for the successful navigation of the post-collegiate world. Departments face a similar complicated relationship with the world of work when it comes to defining, evaluating, and selling an undergraduate major to an institution and students. Majors, therefore, can be understood as an intellectual space demarcated by faculty for one set of criteria on which students ascribe interest and possible career goals, which are based on a different set of criteria. It is a very complex series of exchanges. At Baruch, few students sought arts and sciences majors; business was paramount. Tier III, on the other hand, meant that all students would obtain a minor in the arts and sciences, and as a minor, it meant more than an elective; it would be the consequence of student choice. The minor is neither fish nor fowl. It makes no pretense at deep disciplinary expertise, but instead it is assumed to be an indicator of a student's interest and, perhaps, a more intensive general education experience. The arts and sciences Tier III minors at Baruch also function as indicators of how the departments and programs explain themselves to a student population more interested in a business degree.

As I interpreted it, Tier III's effectiveness depended, in part, on students' understanding of its aims. Therefore, I sought to define disciplinary learning goals for my course through readings, exercises, and studies, and simultaneously to attempt to cultivate students' secondary level knowledge of the discipline through discussion and other readings. Comprehensiveness would be impossible, so I decided to try to make sure that the students would gain a sense of the critical debates within the field. For my course, that meant that a goal was that students would be able to highlight major issues of agreement and contestation in U.S. foreign relations. This aim, I imagined, would complement the more general goal of helping students to make more sophisticated connections between disciplines and discourses. I hoped that the course's pedagogy would allow for different student interests while maintaining a shared focus on thinking about what and how things were learned. Learning, in other words, might be more meaningful to the students if it took place on multiple levels and if it had the potential to reinforce itself through student awareness.

Although planning for my course initially followed traditional lines, inspiration came as I sat with the Zicklin School of Business Learning Assurance Committee evaluating student presentations. As part of its assessment and reaccreditation process, the business faculty labored over how best to define and assess effective oral communication. Setting goals must precede assessment, and establishing consensus about what made for effective oral communication was surprisingly difficult. Some faculty put great stock in the value of diction and clarity. Other faculty on the committee wanted an emphasis on exposition and organization, and others saw the exercise as important in the development of persuasive skills, which are extraordinarily useful in a business setting. Our discussions took a new tenor after the Schwartz Communication Institute showed videos of Baruch students giving business presentations. The students mostly appeared to be well coached, but the impact of their presentations was often weak or hard to gauge. The students seemed to be making presentations primarily because they had been told to do so, not because they wanted to or because the presentation emerged organically out of class discussion. I wondered if students saw a meaningful goal in the exercise. For some presentations, the enterprise appeared empty. It reminded me of an unsuccessful lecture, with an instructor repeating information to an uncaring group of students. I then realized that oral communication for faculty could be quite similar to oral communication for instructors, and that effective communication might share similar traits. At that moment I decided that oral communication would be the key to my history class.

I altered the course's requirements and structure, trying to turn it into a large seminar. I wanted to share the responsibility of teaching and learning with the students. Oral communication would serve as a vehicle for students' learning as presenters and for students' learning as active listeners or audience. I decided that the students would not be presenting for the sake of making a presentation; instead, they would lead the class in 15 to 25 minute segments to further our knowledge of American history. Leadership in the classroom would be shared, and I would help to integrate the learning goals of all presentations. Furthermore, I decided to bring the students in on the plan from the beginning, explaining what we were doing and why we would be doing it. For example, the final grade for the course, a good indicator of how students would spend their time, was altered to make the new goals clear:

- Research paper of 8–10 pages (25% of final grade)
- Presentation/lesson plan (20% of final grade)
- Participation including short writing assignments and feedback/assessment of colleagues' presentations (20% of final grade)
- Midterm essay exam (15% of final grade)
- Final essay exam (20% of final grade)

Class preparation was refashioned, too. I created a detailed timetable for the term with an expanded list of potential topics for every class session. The document was akin to a highly detailed syllabus: Each class, except those set aside for reviews or examinations, had readings and two to four key events or issues attached to it that would help to illustrate the more general topic. The readings ranged from general texts to primary sources available online. I wrote outlines for each class, sketching out lectures and assignments, and developed items that I expected to cover in class discussion. For class twenty-two, for instance, I planned to draw students' attention to the Military Industrial Complex, the debates surrounding the end of atomic testing in the atmosphere, and the U2 spy plane. However, I also was aware that how that specific session would play out would depend upon whether any students were interested in researching and presenting on one of those topics and our consequent collective planning.

Once the semester started the first few class sessions were not unusual, save that I shared the detailed listing of topics with the class and tried on a few occasions to explain the course's broader pedagogical goals. Over the first two weeks of the term we worked to establish a common vocabulary and understanding of foreign relations, as well as a heightened awareness of different schools of scholarship about foreign relations. I also incorporated a few assignments that encouraged group work and student participation in an effort to break down some of the barriers between instructor and student. By the third week of the semester we started talking about class presentations and the work that they would require. Most of the class was organized into pairs. The students then selected a presentation topic from the detailed list. Some made the choice immediately; for others, there was significant back and forth in class and in a Blackboard discussion group. For example, returning to class twenty-two, no one voiced interest in examining the military industrial complex or the end of nuclear bomb testing in the atmosphere, but one student was keen on giving a presentation about the spy plane. The goal of the exercise, I emphasized repeatedly, was neither an oral presentation for its own sake nor for students to read material and then repeat it back to each other. Instead, it was about students engaging with history in a different manner, teaching one another and learning from each other. The students were asked to research and summarize material, to be sure, but the real effort, I told the class, would come in the determination of importance and relevance. Students also realized that the research necessary for their presentation could be useful for their research paper, another requirement in the course.

Each team was required to provide me with

- a paragraph outlining the learning goals for the presentation;
- an outline of the presentation; and
- a bibliography of sources approximately ten days before their scheduled presentation.

Students were surprisingly good about getting their material to me in a timely fashion, in part because of their anxiety about an oral presentation and in part because I emailed each team about the need to coordinate their presentations with my lecture. Every class with a student presentation required some last minute adjustments on my part. When possible, I tried to share my learning goals for the session well in advance with the students who were presenting.

Basic exchanges about sources and research were very similar to interactions I have had with students in other courses. What stood out was helping each team understand the goals of their presentation and the concept of learning goals; students grappled with issues of intentionality. I told the students that repeating information that could be gleaned by reading would not make for a successful presentation and most students understood the warning. Students can be sophisticated evaluators of teaching, and they know when teaching is active and engaged and when it is perfunctory. I challenged each group to make their presentation special, asking them "What one thing would you want your classmates to remember about your topic and presentation at the end of the semester?" It is a question that I also asked myself about the course.

Further, I sought to professionalize the students' presentations by expanding the evaluation process. Research indicates that deeper learning takes place when students reflect upon it, and hence I created a simple peer evaluation form, borrowing from materials developed by the Schwartz Communication Institute, the discussions in the Zicklin Learning Assurance Committee, and Baruch College's student evaluation of faculty. The form asked students to evaluate a presentation on its organization and supporting materials, and to assess a speaker's voice, physical presence, and overall effectiveness. In the absence of a student pilot, the class tested the instrument on me, evaluating a lecture that was part of one class. My presentation that day was not particularly effective; the students knew it and rated it as such, so I had some confidence in the process and the form. We discussed the evaluation in the following class and the students made a number of helpful suggestions about the form itself. The peer evaluations were not factored into grades, but the students nonetheless seemed to take them very seriously. I reviewed all evaluations before giving them to the presenters. The quality of comments remained thoughtful, positive, and appropriate throughout the course, and I believe that the process raised the quality of student work.

It was a fascinating course to teach on many levels. Students seemed to engage with their material in exciting ways, and I would like to believe that the oral presentations were partly responsible. The student who presented on the U-2 spy plane, for example, visited the *USS Intrepid*, an aircraft carrier museum on the west side of Manhattan that houses an SR71 Blackbird. He took digital photos of the plane and incorporated them into his presentation, describing to the class what the spy plane looked and felt like. The students who presented on the Battle of Stalingrad, both émigrés from the former Soviet Union, contrasted the history they had learned in Russia with the results of their research in the United States. The student who presented on the Battle of Iwo Jima came to class in a uniform and addressed his classmates as though he was preparing a group of Marines for a landing on the island. The concept was his alone and his execution was outstanding. I am sure that all of us gained a new and deeper understanding of World War II in the Pacific. Most of the other presentations were more traditional, but almost all were delivered with enthusiasm and intensity. For example, the students who discussed the CIA sponsored coup in Iran were emotionally invested in their issue and desperately wanted the class to make connections with current U.S. foreign policy in the Middle East.

Was the course effective? It depends on one's criteria. I found the quality of student work, especially the presentations, to be good and in a few cases, excellent. From my perspective as a teacher, class discussion and levels of engagement among the students were very high. The students' evaluations of the course, as well as an anonymous questionnaire I gave them in addition to the college's standard instrument, were positive, and most believed that it had a positive effect on their communication skills. I cannot prove that it did so; I did not set up the course with a formal pre- and post-assessment. My intuition and instincts as an educator are that the course did have a positive effect and that the students took great pride in their work. A good number of students in the course, I would wager, will remember it down the road, both in terms of American foreign policy and history, and in terms of public speaking. What I see as important were many of the smaller comments and actions that serve as anecdotal evidence that the students were thinking and learning in a positive and supportive environment. I plan to share leadership with students in future classrooms along similar lines.

Some educational theorists argue that learning takes place with certain kinds of discomfort. The vast majority of the students in the class expressed unease and voiced complaints about creating a learning goal for their presentation. This part of the task, more than any other aspect of the assignment, challenged them. Most of my pre-presentation meetings and communications with the students focused on their presentation goals. The students said that it was surprisingly hard, and several noted that it forced them to think differently about historical material. The students who presented on Ho Chi Minh, for example, read several biographies and were not sure how to deal with reliable but conflicting historical scholarship. They eventually decided to emphasize the political nature of Minh's life and his manipulation of his image. In contrast, the team who made a presentation on Henry Kissinger faced similar tensions in the historical record and decided to be uniformly critical. I was comfortable with both approaches, not necessarily because I would have taught the material the same way, but because I required the students to support their arguments with research, scholarship, and facts. Moreover, because I was sharing, not ceding, the classroom, I had ample opportunity to balance emphases whenever I thought it appropriate.

Students were required to email me a short post-presentation note, describing their opinion of the assignment and what they thought worked and what did not. More than a few noted that the exercise gave them a different perspective on teaching, and this comment also was made several times in the classroom. I believe that this is additional reason to believe that the experiment was worthwhile. Effective learning is strengthened when students are able to think critically from alternative viewpoints, and everyone in my course at one point or another had responsibilities as a scholar, as a teacher, as a colleague, and as a student.

On reflection, sharing took place in many ways and on many levels. Classrooms are sites of multiple exchanges that generate multiple meanings; I conceptualized my course with several of these in mind. Most saliently, the course belonged both to history and Baruch's common core. History has clearly defined disciplinary goals, methods, and practices, and these normally determine most of a course's intent.

The core curriculum or general education is fuzzier and less transparent. Without the authority of a discipline or the institutionalized power of a department, general education was left in many ways for me as instructor to define and discover. The core curriculum's learning goals rest above and between and among the disciplines. The majority of students in my course registered because they needed to fulfill the common core requirement, and they were interested in history.[4] Most were business majors. No one expressed a desire at the beginning of the term to bolster their oral communication skills. The class as a whole, nonetheless, proved quite willing to work hard to meet all of the course's goals, even in non-historical areas such as oral communication. Communicating all of the course's aims and making them explicit in activities, assignments, and grading, was instrumental in engaging students and creating a positive learning environment.

The course was a shared exercise in yet another way: through my dual role as instructor and administrator. My firsthand involvement in developing college priorities and assessing student communication within the School of Business were unique to the Department of History, if not to most of the School of Arts and Sciences. This was not because the college was lax in issuing reports or sending emails; inter-school and inter-departmental communication steadily increased in volume and importance as the new core curriculum was implemented and evaluated. Information was readily available, but for most faculty members, news about college committees and assessment initiatives was of limited value. With multiple claims on their time, why should a faculty member in the School of Arts and Sciences pay attention to how student presentations in an upper level business course were being evaluated? After all, the matters of primary importance to a faculty member, including promotions, tenure, and most of the curriculum, is mediated through the department and discipline. On the other hand, my wider experiences and knowledge of college issues had a profound impact on what I wanted the students to learn, what I taught, how I taught it, and my understanding of Baruch's broad goals for its common core and general education. Moreover, my standing as an administrator with college-wide duties gave me information and a perspective on the curriculum and students that could not help but affect my teaching.

A course is only truly brought to life through the interaction of students and the teacher. Similarly, while general education may be described in bulletins and catalogs, individual faculty members—full-time and adjunct—define it through the books they assign, the discussions they lead, and the tests, exams, and papers they require in courses. Traditional departmental and disciplinary priorities and structures do not necessarily help the development of general education, even though faculty invariably must approach their teaching assignments in general education through a disciplinary lens. Disciplinary and general education goals ideally are complementary, but it takes planning and a willingness of all involved in the course. For general education to take root and flourish, instructors have to open their classroom to influences beyond the department, especially the goals of the larger institution.

NOTES

1. My deepest gratitude goes to the faculty, staff, and students of Baruch College. In particular, special thank yous are due to Myrna Chase, David Dannenbring, Mikhail Gershovich, Carol Morgan, Phyllis Zadra, and the faculty in Baruch's Department of History, who consistently treated me as a valued colleague. I am grateful for the assistance of Carol Berkin, Julie Des Jardins, Thomas Heinrich, Katherine Pence, Tansen Sen, and Cynthia Whittaker, all of whom played a role in the development of the course. Cheryl Smith made extensive suggestions for the improvement of this chapter, and her help was invaluable. I am also indebted to Vita Rabinowitz at Hunter College. Among the many supportive colleagues I have encountered at CUNY, I want to single out Judith Summerfield and Crystal Benedicks for their outstanding efforts with this project. Above all, though, I thank the students in the spring 2005 History 3420 course, whose good humor, hard work, and willingness to try something new made it all worthwhile. For copies of the course syllabi or other course materials mentioned in this chapter, please email me at: David.Potash@hunter.cuny.edu.
2. I spoke with students in my classes and in academic support centers; few saw the need for another requirement or understood its intent.
3. http://www.census.gov/Press-Release/www/releases/archives/education/004214.html.
4. I know this because I asked the students; I regularly peppered the class with questions, emails, and surveys of one form or another.

CHAPTER ELEVEN

Putting It Together

General Education at LaGuardia Community College

PAUL ARCARIO AND JAMES WILSON

LaGuardia Community College

DOT BY DOT: SETTING THE SCENE[1]

In his masterwork painting, *A Sunday Afternoon on the Island of La Grande Jatte* (1884–1886), Georges Seurat experimented with a form of painting called *pointillism*, which he believed would establish a whole new way of creating art. Rather than melding the colors and lines on the canvas, he argued that the viewer's eyes would connect the painted dots, as it were, and generate a fully integrated and vibrant image. Standing at some distance from the painting, which hangs in the Art Institute of Chicago, one can almost feel the warmth of the sun mixed with the cool breeze blowing off the Seine as the twenty-odd subjects of the painting relax in the still, natural beauty of the park. However, on closer look, we see the smooth texture of a woman's dress has not been created with long brush strokes, but with a series of painted dots. The gentle curves of the landscape are created from sharp, jagged specks of light and dark colors. The cool, still water is made up of thousands of brusquely applied blues and whites that practically vibrate when scrutinized. Out of the thousands upon thousands of individually applied dabs of paint used to produce the work of art, Seurat has created a harmonious, coherent whole.

When a group of faculty and administrators set out to create a general education program at LaGuardia Community College, we also sought to create a coherent whole out of a myriad assortment of individual parts. In its contradictory complexity and sense of harmony, Seurat's painting is an apt metaphor for our program. On the surface, LaGuardia's general education program may not seem to have much in common with *A Sunday Afternoon on the Island of La Grande Jatte*. LaGuardia is not far from a river, but ours, the East River, does not have the romantic connotations of the Seine. The surroundings of our college would never be described as pastoral. The college is in the heart of industrialized Long Island City, Queens, and its tranquility is disrupted every thirty seconds with the passing of a 7 or N/R elevated train. Whereas the subjects populating Seurat's painting are a generally homogeneous group, LaGuardia is one of the most ethnically and racially diverse colleges in the country: Among our 13,000 degree students, approximately two-thirds are foreign born, and of these, almost half have been in the United States less than five years, representing over 150 countries and speaking over 110 different languages. Seventy-nine percent of our students are minorities; 60% are first-generation college students; two-thirds of entering students report a family income of $25,000 or less. In fact, if one were to capture an image of LaGuardia, it would not be reflected by stillness and relaxation, but of a swirl of movement and bustle produced by the energy of thousands of students negotiating the demands of school, work, and family.

There are, however, a number of similarities between the painting and our general education initiative. Our students, courses, activities, and programs are as diverse as the varied, individual dots of color on the canvas; nonetheless we have been able to bring an order to the whole. Perhaps most importantly, just as Seurat's technique has the viewer connect the dots rather than the artist doing so himself, we have striven to provide opportunities for our students themselves to connect the dots: to make meaningful connections among their different courses, between their curricular and co-curricular experiences, and between their school work and their lives.

In this essay, we invite the viewer to step forward and take a close look at our program. Examining the work up close raises questions about the pedagogical choices that were made and the ways in which they contribute to the unifying goals and outcomes. These are questions with which we are still grappling. In addition, different from Seurat's painting, our program is neither a completed, unchanging work, nor was it created by a single artisan. Each dot and brush stroke in LaGuardia's general education program reflects the diligent work of a college administrator, faculty, student, or academic support personnel. We, the authors of this essay, are just two of the hundreds of individuals involved in the creation of the general education program at LaGuardia. We represent two different perspectives, and the main body of the essay reveals our two different viewpoints, voices, and academic experiences. Paul Arcario, Dean of Academic Affairs and formerly a professor of English as a Second Language, took the lead in the original design and administrative implementation of the program. James Wilson, an English faculty member with background in theatre and African American literature, created and taught a curriculum applying the various components of the program objectives. Of course, our own perspectives are influenced by all of the people with whom we have worked, and their work is intricately connected with our analyses and narratives. Our essay shows the methods we use to create a program with assorted elements and components, and how we are, individually and collectively, putting it together.

INTO THE WOODS: ENTERING THE GENERAL EDUCATION CONVERSATION

In the opening sections, Dean Paul Arcario discusses the issues facing the college as it began to pull together various initiatives into a comprehensive program.

> What creates the common experience in general education? Is it that all students must experience the same courses (that is, the core)? Is it that all students must achieve the same aims (common outcomes)? Is it that students must share the same college experience regardless of major (learning communities, clusters, or something else)? What should students experience in common through general education has been asked philosophically (mission and goals), substantively (great books, core curriculum), structurally (distributional requirements, articulation agreements), and experientially (learning communities, freshman seminars). The issue of commonality begs the larger one: What makes for a coherent curriculum and a meaningful experience in general education?" (Johnson and Ratcliff 2004)

The above quote touches upon many of the questions that confronted us as one of the first community colleges to join the CUNY General Education Project. Were we to focus on the "what" of liberal, or general, education: deciding upon a body of knowledge and specific courses for all students? Certainly the issue of whether students should all experience the same courses was paramount in those initial CUNY conversations. Moreover, would this mean ending up in the thicket of academic "turf" battles over distribution requirements? Would the whole project play out at the level of arguing whether we should require students to take World History or American History? Alternatively, were we more interested in the "how" of liberal education: facilitating particular approaches to teaching and learning? There was also much talk at the CUNY-wide meetings of general education being fragmented, and a consequent call for more integrative learning. However, what exactly did that mean? Of particular concern for the community colleges, how were we to provide general education for all of our students, particularly given that core or distribution requirements derive from a senior college model not always applicable to all of our degree programs? In dialogue with our CUNY colleagues, we began to frame our answers to these questions.

At LaGuardia, we first reconsidered the definition of general education as it applies to the community college. While it is the community college "Liberal Arts" degree programs (our AA in Liberal Arts: Humanities and Social Sciences and AS in Liberal Arts: Mathematics and Science) that correspond most closely to what has been traditionally defined as general education at the senior colleges, we did not want to equate "general education" with only these Liberal Arts majors. Rather we wanted a model that would provide each and every major with a common general education experience. Could we achieve this goal through uniform general education course requirements across all majors? Although such a distributional system is the norm at 90% of senior colleges (Astin 1993), it is difficult to accomplish at a community college. Associate's degrees (at least at CUNY) are generally capped at 60 credits, and each major needs to include general education courses appropriate for the discipline, and these often vary by major. In fact, designating general education courses on a program-by-program basis is a typical pattern among community colleges (Zeszotarski 1999). As a result, if we try to define general education at a community college as a set of specific courses that all students have to take across all majors, the number of such courses tends to be small indeed. With this difficulty in mind, we began thinking it would make more sense for us to design a comprehensive general education program around a series of competencies or proficiencies required across all majors, rather than around such a limited number of required courses—but what would be key would be developing those competencies tightly linked to discipline-area content, as the last thing we wanted was to work on competencies in isolation.

At the same time, other issues, demands, and projects were coming into play. We were grappling with designing and implementing an outcomes assessment plan as mandated by our accrediting agency; a major Title V grant enabled us to adopt electronic portfolios (ePortfolios) as the basis for the plan. A Task Force was re-examining our developmental education programs with the goal of improving student learning outcomes; simultaneously, we were designing a comprehensive first-year experience program as a collaboration between the divisions of Academic Affairs and Enrollment Management & Student Development. In fact, we were selected as one of ten colleges nationally to participate in the "Integrative Learning: Opportunities to Connect" project sponsored by AAC&U and the Carnegie Foundation. As work on these initiatives progressed, the pieces of our general education program began coming together. Conceiving of general education as competencies across the curriculum would allow for a uniform outcomes assessment process in each major: Each and every program would take responsibility for graduating students proficient in those competencies. Perhaps more importantly, an across-the-curriculum approach would support broad-based faculty exploration of how competency development could at the same time facilitate discipline-area learning, for example, through such pedagogies as "writing to learn." Aspects of our definition of "integrative learning" thus began to emerge: Writing, we told our students, was not something just done in English class, and making oral presentations was not just for speech class, but rather these skills also needed to be developed in the context of the disciplines. As LaGuardia graduates, students should be well on the path toward writing and speaking as members of their chosen field. By the same token, faculty teaching business or computer courses, for example, would not leave writing instruction solely to the English faculty, nor speaking solely to the Speech Communication faculty. We wanted this kind of integration to extend to developmental education as well. With the majority of students at LaGuardia—and most community colleges—needing developmental education, we felt that linking skills and the disciplines should become a key element in our general education program.

HOW DO I KNOW: OUTCOMES ASSESSMENT AND CORE COMPETENCIES

As LaGuardia's outcomes assessment plan was being thought out, a number of goals emerged. We wanted a plan that would first and foremost help us improve student learning and that would designate common outcomes we would strive to achieve across all programs so that all of our students would benefit. We wanted to capture the student learning and development that in our heart of hearts we knew was occurring, but that was not always revealed by standard measures such as graduation rates. Moreover, we wondered if we could design, in Lee Knefelkamp's (1989) words, assessment that would be "transformative":

> . . . assessment is transformative, and whether or not we're comfortable with it, assessment is about revolution. If we really listen to students and take them seriously, then our teaching and learning methodologies will change . . . Finely tuned assessment efforts help keep us from being self-satisfied or complacent about the workplace we love . . . Through assessment we challenge ourselves to rethink our ways of teaching, structuring the curriculum, working together, and even knowing itself. It provides a means for self-correcting action and for the continual expansion of our thinking about the idea and purpose of higher education. (22)

We began by deciding with the department chairpersons upon a list of general education core competencies required in each and every major:

- written communication
- critical thinking
- critical reading
- quantitative reasoning
- oral communication
- research and information literacy
- technological literacy.

In establishing these general education core competencies, and approving them through college governance, the faculty members have taken responsibility for reinforcing these competencies within each particular discipline as part of an across-the-curriculum approach. For each competency, faculty members would be supported through professional development seminars offered by our Center for Teaching and Learning. It is precisely this sort of experimenting and assessing on the part of faculty—engaging students in the kinds of writing, speaking, quantitative reasoning, or research skills necessary in their respective disciplines and exploring pedagogies that might better promote these skills—that can refine and deepen our thinking about teaching and curricula. In addition, the "productive" nature of many of these competencies meant that faculty in all the disciplines would end up designing many more opportunities for students to actively (re-)produce knowledge whether through writing, speaking, or project-based work. This approach is potentially transformative given the so-called "generation effect," namely, that "having to produce information leads to better learning than being presented with information" (deWinstanley and Bjork 2002, 22).

Using ePortfolios for assessment would allow us to achieve another of our goals: that of capturing a rich, longitudinal picture of student development and learning. As faculty worked to enhance learning through assignments calling for more extensive writing, critical reading, quantitative reasoning, and discipline-based research, we would collect and evaluate this work through electronic portfolios. We therefore specified a minimum number of "ePortfolio courses" in all curricula where student work would be put into their ePortfolios: basic skills and introductory courses to capture baseline data; the urban studies course (a requirement in all majors) as a mid-point; and a capstone course as the end-point. These ePortfolio courses require that students' assignments be deposited in their portfolios; this work is used to assess student mastery of competencies required in the major, as well as selected general education core competencies. Thus, the urban studies ePortfolio course has been designated as an official point in the curricula where writing, critical thinking, and critical reading (we ultimately combined these into one "critical literacy" competency) is to be reinforced and assessed; all urban studies courses are therefore now running as "writing intensive" courses. The capstone ePortfolio course includes at least one assignment or project designed to reinforce and assess the critical literacy and the research and information literacy competencies (again serving as a designated writing intensive course). At this point, we are still in the process of deciding upon other designated courses in which the remaining core competencies will be incorporated into the portfolio and assessed. As a major comes up for program review, faculty will be able to collect a sample of student work from their portfolios, affording a record of student learning from the first semester through graduation. Assessing an actual body of student work against the faculty-developed rubrics for each core competency tells a program whether or not students are achieving the required levels and if not, where improvement is needed. Recommendations from these program reviews can then become part of a program's strategic plan goals.

SHOW ME: STUDENTS BUILD THEIR ePORTFOLIOS

To get students started with their ePortfolios, a template was designed guiding students to put a Welcome page, an About Me section, educational goals, and course work into their portfolios. As they progress, students add to and refine their portfolios, developing exactly the kind of complex, rich record of learning we are seeking to document. Faculty can look at a portfolio such as the one done by Charles Mak, a Fine Arts major, and assess the development of artistic technique based on the digital photos he includes of his portraits, anatomical drawings, and still-life paintings. In addition, in collecting his work Charles engages in the kind of analysis that supports learning by posting his own self-assessment of his growth in his portfolio. Lee Shulman's restating of this process is very much to the point:

> As Dewey observed many years ago, we do not learn by doing; we learn by thinking about what we are doing. Successful students spend considerable time, as Bruner calls it, "going meta," that is, thinking about what they are doing and why. (2004, 559)

Thus, ePortfolios not only serve as the mechanism for collecting student work and making it accessible to faculty for assessment purposes, but they are also designed to guide students themselves in the process of reflection and self-assessment of their learning, as Charles does in assessing his growth as an artist:

> During fall of 2004, I've noticed various improvements in my drawings because of constant practice. My whole perception of subject matter changed, seeing subjects more abstractly rather than figuratively. As a result, a transition in my style formed, from a naturalistic to a combination of realistic and abstract. Subsequently, my technique also altered using more of a painterly approach in drawing.

With each iteration of his ePortfolio, Charles is able to document his growth further—concurrently providing faculty with greater insight into, and a rich record of, his development:

> This year [2005] I strive to try something different. Last year was interesting with development in style and technique, but a time comes when all must change. Since I've gained a better understanding in composition, my next goal is to improve in contrast. Because I possess a sensitive touch, my work leans more on the bright side. Achieving a higher level of contrast will be enjoyable for me, especially when it involves manipulating materials. Smudging, rubbing the medium through physical contact, and other rendering of material is a new technique for me, which I've always wanted to develop.

At the same time, the reflective writing assignments called for in the ePortfolio provide Charles with additional practice engaging in the discourse of his profession, as his use of terminology demonstrates (e.g., "abstractly," "realistic," "painterly approach," "contrast"). For all students, and in particular nonnative English speakers, mastering discipline-specific and academic discourse is a challenging, and essential, part of their education.

We have also found that ePortfolios engage students in making personally meaningful connections between their academic and life experiences. In her welcome page, Sandra Rios reflects back upon the construction of her portfolio over the course of several iterations. Like many students, she begins her portfolio with what she knows, that is, personal experiences, not yet relating them to academic experiences:

> In that first ePortfolio I wrote about Palmira (Valle), the city where I was born in Colombia, and I wrote about Medellin, where I used to spend my vacations of school. Also, I wrote about my family who were already here when I came to this country, and I wrote about the cultural assimilation process I was going through. At that time, I included a lot of pictures of my beautiful country Colombia, and some of myself.

As Sandra progressed, she started including course work in her portfolio and began to connect her academic life with life outside of school: In this case, the first connections are to her family. We have found this to be very common: Students initially are most excited about using their ePortfolios to show their families what they are doing in college—perhaps not surprisingly given that the majority of our students are first-generation college-goers:

> The second time I was asked to develop my ePortfolio, I decided to include my academic work and goals that would make my family proud of me. In my second ePortfolio, my priority was to focus on my personal growth in my school work and what I was learning at LaGuardia.

For her next version, Sandra reports on a favorite project—one that allowed her to connect what she learned in college with a friend's real-world business. She then writes about how the process of collecting and presenting her work has helped forge her identity as an emerging professional:

> I decided to use my ePortfolio as an opportunity to show and demonstrate all the skills that I have learned throughout my journey at LaGuardia Community College. I decided to post some of my essays and multimedia projects that I have completed in some of my classes. One of my favorite projects is this web page I did for my friend's computer repair business to use on the World Wide Web. All together, my third ePortfolio demonstrates me as a professional who is looking toward her future and who has many goals to reach.

Encouraging reflection and integration through the ePortfolio process is not always easy. While students such as Charles Mak are moving in the right direction, many others need more structure and guidance. As we move forward with our ePortfolio project, it remains a challenge for us to develop the portfolio pedagogies and assignments that will assist students in thinking more deeply about their own learning. In fact, the ePortfolio project also represents an opportunity for us—faculty and administrators—to conduct an inquiry into the notion of reflection (which has become a rather loose and hazy term in education): Can we articulate a clearer definition? How exactly does reflection facilitate learning? What types of reflection best assist learning? How can reflective learning be taught through ePortfolios and other means?

In the meantime, we are encouraged by some of the early outcomes of our ePortfolio initiative. Last year, five thousand students engaged in actively building their ePortfolios (with the eventual goal of reaching all students). Feedback shows that students are highly enthusiastic about their ePortfolios:

- Students who have developed an ePortfolio score higher than both the LaGuardia and national means on a number of key indicators on the nationally benchmarked Community College Survey of Student Engagement (CCSSE), including synthesizing ideas, writing, working effectively with others, and making judgments about the soundness of information, arguments or methods.
- Students who have developed their ePortfolios rank the College higher on a number of indicators on the ACT Opinion Survey, including quality of instruction, whether they would advise a friend to attend LaGuardia, and whether they would choose to attend LaGuardia if they could start college over.
- Pass rates in ePortfolio courses exceed non-portfolio courses by almost 6%.

ALL ABOARD: THE FIRST YEAR EXPERIENCE

As an entry point to higher education for many students who might not otherwise have access—with the majority being first-time college-goers—we felt that the creation of common, shared experiences that foster a greater sense of community and connectedness to the college was a central aspect of general education. Establishing a common reading (in fact, seldom done at community colleges) would create a shared intellectual experience that would immediately establish an academic tone for our new students, setting a particular expectation for them upon their entry: that the ability to read critically is a key to their academic success. A faculty committee selects the book each year, chosen to be accessible to students in basic skills and rich enough in content to exploit in discipline-area classes as well (selections have included *Having Our Say: The Delany Sisters' First 100 Years*, Esmeralda Santiago's *When I Was Puerto Rican*, Tamim Ansary's *West of Kabul, East of New York*, *The Laramie Project* by

Moises Kaufman and Members of the Tectonic Theatre Project, and Art Spiegelman's *Maus*). All incoming students receive the book free of charge at registration, and faculty members are given a gratis copy as well. A small faculty team is compensated each year to create a Web site and study guide for the book, with links, ancillary resources, suggested assignments, and essay topics. A series of common reading events is also held each year, ranging from a field trip to El Museo del Barrio to a multimedia and dance presentation on Afghanistan and the Islamic Diaspora. In addition, students have had book discussions over lunch with the college president, entered our annual essay contest, and had the opportunity to meet and question the authors on campus.

The common reading is also used as the basis for faculty-led discussions during Opening Sessions for New Students. This event is designed to give new students a feel for what college will be like. Indeed, the essence of what college is "like" is their engaging with faculty in the world of ideas. To create this intellectual tone, the day is set up as an academic conference with a plenary session, concurrent workshops, and small-group colloquia with faculty members. Workshops are led by LaGuardia faculty and students on topics such as leadership, women's issues, communication, student clubs, student success stories, community activism, and diversity. Each year thirty to forty faculty members have volunteered to lead the colloquia, which are small-group discussion sessions on the common reading. Students consistently rate these faculty-led discussions as the most significant part of the day.

> *Professor James Wilson is among many faculty members who incorporate the Common Reading selection into their freshman classes. In the following section, he describes how he integrated* The Laramie Project *into a first-year learning community linking his developmental writing class with General Psychology and a freshman seminar.*

In 2004–2005, the common reading was *The Laramie Project*[2] by Moises Kaufman and Members of the Tectonic Theatre Project, and it is based on the murder of gay college student Matthew Shepard. The play's examination of a community struggling with the impact of an act of horrific violence on its collective consciousness, as well as its focus on diversity and acceptance were perfectly suited to the main themes and motifs of the learning community. The text served as a lynchpin for the learning community I was teaching, as it provided the basis for textual analysis and expository writing assignments in basic writing, and in the Freshman Seminar, the play served to initiate conversations around hate speech and social acceptance. In General Psychology, the play also led to an examination of research methodologies. (The members of the theatre company completed their own extensive research on Laramie, Wyoming, in the aftermath of Shepard's murder.) The play also provided the jumping-off point for a semester-long course research project in which students focused on a community and college issue, such as racial profiling, homophobia on campus, and respect for religious diversity.

As a way of connecting the students to the larger college community and their own academic pursuits, I invited a former student, who had completed basic writing the year before, to perform selections from the play in my class. In addition to representing characters from the play, the student, who was close to graduating and transferring to a prestigious New York City four-year college, represented to the beginning college students in the learning community the potential for success at LaGuardia. In the question-and-answer period that followed the performance, for instance, many of the students asked him about his ability to juggle work, family, and school responsibilities. Candidly, he informed the class that being a full-time student had been particularly difficult as he came from a working-class Caribbean family whose other members did not completely understand what it meant to be in college and did not always provide the emotional support he needed. Furthermore, they did not fully approve of his desire to pursue acting, especially when it meant that he would be playing "a gay" in the college's fall 2004 production of *The Laramie Project*. The student's commitment to his learning, as well as the palpable pride he took from acknowledging his placement in basic skills courses to successfully completing several honors-level courses, demonstrated that these were mere obstacles that he handily overcame.

All that said, when the learning community instructors began planning the courses, we knew there would be many ways in which the common reading could help integrate the curriculum, but we were concerned about the reactions the students might have over the issue of homosexuality, which is a major component in the play. However, our emphasis on the text as an academic object of study seemed to diffuse any adverse reactions. The responses to the play reflected the range of the students' racial, cultural, and religious backgrounds, but we were impressed with the ways in which the students maintained a respectful and intellectual approach to the subject matter. Their responses, which often lacked polish because they had not yet fully developed their ideas, were often sophisticated, moving, and honest. In a BlackBoard discussion thread, for example, one student focused on the impact that words and language may have on the eruption of physical violence. He explained:

> Sometimes, [words] may be stronger and more cruel than physical [violence]. Using of offending words about gays have affected and built many people the wrong and bad ideas about gay people unconsciously. It's like [the] influence of TV. For instance, many TV shows are showing only thin and tall [girls] all the time, and fixing audience's point of view about the [beauty], tall, blonde, and buxom. Words and languages also work like that unconsciously.[3]

For many students, popular culture and gender images, areas in which they were far more comfortable, provided access to the text and its themes. The play, which is a hybrid ethnography, living-newspaper, and drama about a community's response to homophobia, was unlike any other assigned reading the students had encountered in their high school English classes. The relative openness of the BlackBoard forums allowed them to apply their own experiences and backgrounds in a safe arena.

In another interesting exchange, a young Muslim woman countered her classmate, who, she thought, had implied that Matthew Shepard somehow deserved what he got because of his "sinful lifestyle." Framing her points in her religious faith, she wrote:

> The only person [sic] that can decide that [homosexuality is a sin] is Allah. You can't just say it is WRONG the way you did, because it will hurt other people. I dunno maybe i don't get what you are saying, or maybe you won't get what i am saying either.

Discussions focused on religious beliefs tend to be one-sided and can shut down dialogue, but the student's posting notably demonstrates her willingness to acknowledge that she misunderstood her classmate while also recognizing that her own words may be misinterpreted as well. Rather than cutting the discussion thread, the student allows possibilities for further conversation. (The first student did not, however, take her up on this.)

As these responses show, the play proved to be an ideal starting point for the semester. Although Laramie, Wyoming, is seemingly in a different universe from Queens, New York, the text opened spaces for an important discussion about highly sensitive social issues in an academic context. The play's presentation of various viewpoints allowed the students to draw upon and interrogate their own cultural, religious, and personal responses to the play while weighing these against the responses of their classmates.

SIDE BY SIDE BY SIDE: BASIC SKILLS, GENERAL EDUCATION, AND LEARNING COMMUNITIES

Mention of Professor Wilson's learning community brings us to a central issue in community college education: A large part of who we are and what we do at LaGuardia has been defined by our basic skills courses—typical of the function of community colleges on the whole. In fact, according to LaGuardia's most recent institutional profile, over 80% of the students require basic skills instruction in at least one academic area (i.e., writing, reading, math) with 25% placing into ESL courses (LaGuardia Community College 2006). How could basic skills instruction therefore not be a part of what we consider general education? However, basic skills and general education are not typically discussed in the same academic milieu. Basic skills tend to reside in the outskirts of a college curriculum and are taught in a set of "pre-college" courses that students must successfully complete before moving through a selection of discipline-specific major courses—which is also the case at LaGuardia. Basic writing, basic reading, and ESL are taught as no-credit courses and are prerequisite for many introductory courses in the social sciences, humanities, and allied health programs. They also serve as the prerequisite for the foundational freshman composition course, or as it is typically called, "College Composition." This designation itself implies that students in basic skills are not yet freshmen and are *pre*-college students, leading to the traditional attitude that, as Bruce Horner argues, such instruction occupies "the province of teachers and students placed at the bottom of the academic institutional hierarchy" (1996, 199).

Basic skills are often taught in isolation using a "skill-and-drill" methodology, which detaches them from the students' career and academic aspirations. Hence, students do not see how the skills are relevant to their own learning. Not surprisingly, many students regard these pre-college level courses as fillers. It is no wonder that retention is at its most precarious at this time in a student's college career—at the moment when students should be most strongly connecting to their college life, they are made to feel not quite a part of it. Barbara Gleason articulates quite succinctly the challenges students face in being both literally and figuratively "college students" while in the process of fulfilling their basic skills requirements. In "Remediation Phase-Out at CUNY: The 'Equity versus Excellence' Controversy," Gleason writes:

> Students who had failed the reading and/or writing skills tests were barred from enrolling in many core curriculum courses at most CUNY colleges. These students often found it difficult to enroll in enough classes to achieve full-time status and thus qualify for financial aid, and even when they did enroll in enough class hours to be considered "full-time," they were often accumulating very few credits during their first and second semesters of college because remedial classes carried only partial credit or, especially since 1995, no credit. (2000, 490)

Indeed, first-year basic skills students often complain that their course work is simply a rehash of their high school or equivalency courses, and they do not feel connected to the college, their classes, or their academic aspirations. As one of our students put it, "I left the college because all the courses were wasting my time. I was doing remedial classes."[4]

General or liberal education, on the other hand, may be defined not only by the mastery of a set of discrete skills or knowledge sets, but by the individual student's ability to make connections between courses, disciplines, and college experiences. On its Web site, the American Association of Colleges and Universities (AAC&U) explains, "Characterized by challenging encounters with important issues, a liberal education prepares graduates both for socially valued work and for civic leadership in their society. It usually includes a general education curriculum that provides broad exposure to multiple disciplines and ways of knowing, along with more in-depth study in at least one field or area of concentration" (2006). However, in what sense could basic skills fit this definition of general education? How could we incorporate multiple disciplines, challenge students, and foster connection-making in the arena of basic skills, and, of course, ensure that the basic proficiencies were being acquired? Our answer has been to contextualize skills development within disciplines. We believe that academic skills are best acquired in a college setting in which students can apply their developing skills to the academic subject matter at hand, rather than in the framework of a model that assumes skills instruction in all cases occurs separately from and prior to discipline-area instruction. In fact, this argument has been supported by researchers who have conducted "meta-analyses" of the literature (Boylan and Saxon 2002). Thus, Grubb argues strongly for "differentiated forms of developmental education," that is, differentiated in the sense of being specifically connected to different discipline areas. Advocating for the creation of "developmental courses that are hybrids" of basic skills and discipline-area perspectives, or learning communities that link the two, Grubb further argues that such differentiated approaches also "address the motivational issue of students coming to colleges, intending to pursue some academic or occupational program, and then finding themselves in developmental courses with no obvious connection to their intended goals" (2001, 14).

In fact, LaGuardia has a long and successful record of integrating basic skills and discipline-area instruction—albeit for limited numbers of students—through our first-year learning communities. We do not think the teaching of basic skills has to be (nor should it be) separate from general education or major-area objectives. Moreover, without disregarding the importance of proficiency in writing, reading, and math, we argue for an integrated approach so the students may have meaningful opportunities to apply basic skills as they develop them. The College's Department of Education and Language Acquisition has taken the lead in expanding this approach, typically offering twenty or more sections each semester, pairing ESL with courses such as Accounting, Introduction to Business, Introduction to Computers, Introduction to Sociology, and Biochemistry. For non-ESL students, the College's "New Student House" model—our earliest basic skills learning community model—creates a full-time program linking two developmental courses with a discipline-area course as well as the New Student Seminar, taught by a counselor. Faculty members collaborate to produce an integrated curriculum that includes joint projects, library instruction provided by one of the college librarians, a library project, and field trips. A unified curriculum is constructed through themes, such as Immigrants in the United States and The Women's Rights Movement in Early Nineteenth Century America. First-year learning communities also serve non-basic skills students: Liberal Arts majors are required to participate in a "Liberal Arts Cluster." These learning communities also use a theme to integrate English Composition, a research paper course, and an Integrating Seminar hour with two courses from various disciplines in the humanities or social sciences.

Nevertheless, despite the success of this approach, our learning community offerings have been, in fact, limited, serving a relatively small percentage of our incoming students. Expanding learning communities would thus indeed be an experiment in merging general education with basic skills. In addition to growing the learning communities, we also knew that a first-year general education program could be improved in other ways: Some elements of the first year were still fragmented (e.g., extra-curricular activities are not well-integrated with the curriculum), and most students were still not receiving enough information about career development as indicated by their freshman survey responses. To address these issues the College has instituted a "First Year Academy" model in order to create a cohesive and comprehensive first-year experience for students. Linking student development services with curricular offerings, the Academies center the first-year experience around the major, while at the same time initiating development of the general education core competencies as well as fostering interdisciplinary connections between basic skills, the major, and liberal arts courses. Based on their major, all incoming students are placed in one of three Academies (Business/Technology; Allied Health; Liberal Arts). Functioning as a "school-within-a-school," each Academy offers a discipline-specific New Student Seminar; a newly developed career development course for each Academy in the second semester; and an array of co-curricular activities that contribute to student success and development, all centered around the disciplines in each Academy (e.g., career orientation events in health fields; study skills workshops utilizing health-related materials; speakers from the health professions).

Each Academy also offers learning communities that link developmental courses with credit-bearing courses in the disciplines. In addition to embracing existing ESL, New Student House, and Liberal Arts Clusters, the Academies created new learning communities with a particular focus on basic (non-ESL) reading and writing. These communities are currently offered to potential majors in business/technology, liberal arts, and allied health, and are designed to put students who require basic skills courses in contact with their majors upon entering college and give them the opportunity to satisfy at least one major or general education requirement in their curriculum. In addition to linking a basic skills requirement with a course in the student's intended major, the learning communities also include a freshman seminar that offers academic and career-choice guidance, and the ePortfolio studio hour. The faculty within each learning community work together to make explicit and implicit connections between the class sections ensuring that basic skill development evolves from discipline-based themes and issues rather than through discrete skill-directed classes. Most importantly, these learning communities can provide the basic skills students with the opportunity to be college students, both in name and through meaningful intellectual and social experiences.

We have been pleased with the success of our first-year programs. In fact, LaGuardia is one of only 13 colleges nationwide to be recognized as an "Institution of Excellence in the First College Year" by the *Policy Center on the First Year of College*, in recognition of some of the outcomes we have been able to achieve:

- In 2004, the College conducted a massive quantitative study of over ten years of data on ESL learning communities. The data showed ESL students in pairs (in which students are "mainstreamed" into discipline-area courses earlier than usual in their academic careers) overall do as well as or better than non-ESL students and ESL students taking those discipline-area courses in a non-paired mode later in their academic careers. In addition to higher grades, there was a statistically significant relationship between passing and participating in a learning community course; that is to say, students were more likely to pass a particular course (whether a content, basic skills, or ESL course) when the course was in a learning community.

- Recent assessments of New Student House and Liberal Arts clusters, which analyzed data collected over an eight-year period, demonstrated improved outcomes in these communities. Students in New Student House passed the basic reading and basic writing courses at higher rates than students who took both courses in the same semester, but not in the House setting. Passing rates for Freshman Composition offered in Liberal Arts clusters were ten percent higher than in stand-alone sections. In addition, data collected since 1996 show that pass rates for the ESL course offered in ESL New Student House on average have exceeded those for the same level ESL course not offered in the House by 10%.

- For the newer learning communities developed in conjunction with moving to the Academy model, data are preliminary, but encouraging at this point: the FY Academy reduced the failure rate by 9%, the course attrition rate by 6%, and the semester-to-semester attrition rate by 6%. In addition, student ratings of their Academy experience on key questions from the Community College Survey of Student Engagement (CCSSE) exceeded both the LaGuardia and national means.

MOVE ON: A FACULTY PERSPECTIVE ON
BASIC WRITING AND GENERAL EDUCATION

In the following sections, Professor James Wilson describes his experience developing and teaching a First-Year Academy learning community.

In the spring semester of 2005, I taught Basic Writing in a new Academy learning community, which also included General Psychology, a Freshman Seminar, and an ePortfolio Studio, a weekly one-hour workshop that introduced students to the rudiments of the electronic portfolio system and assisted them in developing their own ePortfolios. One morning, not long after the students had read excerpts from Freud's *Interpretation of Dreams* in my class and discussed elements of psychoanalytical theory in their psychology course, I introduced a collaborative learning activity that asked the students to apply concepts of Freudian theory to practical situations. Subsequently, they would write an essay of about 300 words using the ideas they generated in their small groups.

In preparation for the activity, I asked the students to arrange the desks into small clusters. I lent a hand and made sure there were no more than four desks per cluster; I helped students align the desks so that the front edge of each faced the others and just barely touched; and I was sure to distribute the clusters throughout the entire classroom, making certain there was sufficient space between them so I could move easily from group to group. Truthfully, my meticulousness that spring morning was no different from any other as the class prepared for the group work.

We were just about ready to commence with the activity when I noticed that one cluster of desks did not seem quite right: It was off by just a hair. I asked the students sitting in the group to move the offending desks a little bit closer to the wall. Really, just a fraction of an inch if they didn't mind. They complied, and as they did, one of the students in the group looked up at me with an expression of pained sincerity borne of tragic epiphany. "Professor," he said drawing upon his recently acquired knowledge of psychoanalysis, "you haven't moved out of the anal stage."

The moment was, as those credit card commercials say, priceless. Not only had the student applied the concept correctly and brilliantly to the particular situation (as well as to my own psychic development—which must remain the subject of another essay), but in his single utterance, he encapsulated the central point of learning communities in general and LaGuardia's general education program in particular. That is, the philosophical foundation of both programs at LaGuardia is grounded on the position that students should demonstrate the ability to make connections between courses, disciplines, and their own college experiences. At the same time, the instance also reflected the possibility of successfully linking complex disciplinary content within the context of a basic skills course.

Heretofore the English Department had linked only a relative handful of basic writing courses with discipline-area courses, mostly in the New Student House model, which offered only two or three sections a semester. The challenge of expanding our learning community offerings has to be seen in the light of other concerns that emerged just prior to this initiative. A CUNY mandate in 2000 declared that students could only exit out of the basic skills courses upon passing a CUNY ACT retest in each remedial course in which they were enrolled. This requirement has had a tremendous impact on the Basic Writing curriculum in LaGuardia's English Department, whose philosophy has been analogous to the AAC&U's definition of general education. The CUNY ACT Writing exam, for instance, is a one-hour, timed, standardized writing exam (and graded by normed faculty on another CUNY campus). LaGuardia's English program, however, emphasizes the process of writing, integration of various viewpoints, a student's engagement with a topic, and clarity of expression over a student's ability to demonstrate "minimal competency" in a sixty-minute, non-course related writing test. Faculty members in the English Department were rightly concerned that the implementation of the ACT Writing Exam as an exit requirement would force them to "teach to the test" and focus on grammar and mechanics at the expense of the writing process. Indeed, it seemed that the department was revisiting familiar pedagogical squabbles.

Historically, both at LaGuardia and elsewhere, the skills-versus-process debate has been central to the basic writing discourse and is directly related to the role of general education in a community college. I would argue, based on the research of the last thirty years, the two programs do not need to be mutually exclusive. In fact, Mina Shaughnessy, who is regarded as one of the principal architects in the development of the basic writing movement, proposed building an integrative, process-oriented approach rather than a program focused entirely on "skills" and language "correctness." She did not claim, however, that grammar and mechanics had no place in the basic writing curriculum. She wrote, "I am not of course suggesting that it is debasing education to help a student gain control of Standard English and the mechanics of formal writing but only that the effort to do this quickly can lead to it exclusively, which means almost inevitably the neglect, at a crucial point, of the deeper and ultimately more important resources our students bring to the classroom."[5] One way to tap into the "more important resources" that the students bring to their basic writing classes in the age of the ACT might be to connect the course explicitly to their interest in a particular discipline. At any rate, I would soon find out.

YOU COULD DRIVE A PERSON CRAZY: CREATING A BASIC WRITING AND GENERAL PSYCHOLOGY COORDINATED SYLLABUS

The title of the learning community I taught was "Beyond Dr. Phil: Psychology and Communication in the 21st Century," and the focus of the linked courses was on developing students' analytical, organizational, and communication proficiencies, using introductory psychology material as the basis for writing and class discussion. The merging of Basic Writing: English 099 with a science-based, highly analytical course (and one which normally has a basic writing prerequisite) was not at first sight an impossible partnership, but it was certainly fraught with difficulties. First, the English Department at LaGuardia has very specific guidelines and goals for the Basic Writing curriculum. In particular, these include the following:

- The creation of a body of well-written and revised college-level work that reflects students' development as writers (based on the development of a thesis using specific examples, logical organization, and clear, correct written English) over the course of the semester.
- Successful completion of the CUNY ACT Writing Exam, which demonstrates students' abilities to write an argumentative essay in one hour.
- Successful completion of the departmental Exit Exam, in which students write a 300 (minimum)-word essay in response to a text that is cross-graded by other Basic Writing instructors.

Although the course as defined by the English Department is not intended to be a traditional "skill-and-drill" course, there is not much room in the curriculum for discipline-specific exploration and analysis. Critical thinking and reading are important components of the course, but faculty are asked to give students a great deal of support in the writing process, including pre-writing strategies, drafting, and revising in addition to the requirements stated above. For this reason, integrating themes from psychology and topics from the allied health sciences offered a unique set of challenges in designing the course. The CUNY ACT writing exam, for example, is based on a hypothetical community issue and asks students to demonstrate writing proficiency using fully developed reasons and examples from personal and/or observed experiences. Writing in the social and applied sciences tends to be more theoretical and text-based. Could the courses teach to both writing aims?

The next main challenge was finding ways to integrate the goals of Basic Writing with General Psychology. Because this course has a Basic Writing prerequisite (which is waived for students taking the course in an academy learning community), instructors of General Psychology expect the students to already have proficiency in topic development, essay organization, and language fluency, the three main areas of consideration in a semester-long basic writing class. The students in that course are expected to read and respond to articles in professional journals and are required to write a ten-page research paper. Furthermore, the course textbook is, to say the least, daunting in both heft and reading-level, and the authors of that text could never be accused of pandering to their readers as evidenced by the depth of analysis and range of examples they provide. I was not being facetious when I, who took several psychology courses as an undergraduate, told my teaching compatriot, "I'm glad I didn't have to take this course. I would have been lucky to get a 'C-.' "

At the same time, the psychology instructor was rightly concerned about "watering down" the curriculum to accommodate the needs of the basic writing students.

She argued convincingly that the grade on the students' transcripts would have to reflect the academic equivalence of students who did not take the course in an academy learning community. So, in the preceding semester, we, along with the freshman seminar instructor (a college counselor), spent many hours exploring ways to successfully integrate the learning objectives and course outcomes while also assuring the students would have a level of success and academic gratification. We did not want to build either the students (or ourselves) up for failure, but we also knew that the linked courses would require academic commitment, intellectual rigor, and endless amounts of energy. The endeavor looked like it could be a tremendous success or a spectacular failure.

In our fall meetings, we created a title, "Beyond Dr. Phil," which we hoped would be catchy enough to attract students, and one that would also allude to the academic, non-pop cultural approach to psychology. We then wrote a common statement that gave an overview of the academy learning community and the goals of the linked courses. Because this was the first time the academy would be offered, we were not sure what kind of response it would get, and we participated in a great deal of course-promotion. We reprinted our statement (with a photo of a smug, shrugging Dr. Phil prominently displayed) along with the chief "selling points." These included:

- Linked courses for greater understanding
- Greater likelihood of passing exit exams
- Closer relationship with peers
- More individualized attention
- Greater access to technology instruction
- Improved retention

We hoped we were not peddling a bill of goods.

Next, we began building the courses themselves, focusing on the explicit intersections in the content and assignments, and discussing how the linkages could enhance the students' chances for success across the learning community. The three main junctures were the college's common reading that semester; community health concerns; and an introduction to Freudian theory of psychoanalysis.

MERRILY WE ROLL ALONG: MOVING
BEYOND THE PERSONAL AND INTO THE PUBLIC

Building on the links that my use of the Common Reading (*The Laramie Project*, described earlier) formed between the students and the main courses in the learning community, I chose a text that would provide a foundation for the exit requirements of English 099, including the CUNY ACT re-test, which asks students to respond to a community issue, and the Department Exit Exam, which requires that students write a 300-word analytical response to a text. The collection of essays contained in *Health Views*, edited by Marjorie and Jon Ford (1998), offered a mechanism for preparing the students for these requirements and also maintaining a connection to the interdisciplinary focus of the learning community. *Health Views* includes essays on a range of topics such as anorexia, depression, effects of sports on young girls, and the ways in which women doctors are changing the medical field. These worked quite well with the psychology curriculum because in that class, the students examined personality traits, body image concerns, and neurological imbalances. In addition, whereas the online and class discussions encouraged the students to explore their personal reactions to *The Laramie Project* based on their own experiences and perspectives, the assignments connected with the articles in *Health Views* asked the students to engage with the material as psychological cases and as research findings.

In "The Novice as Expert: Writing the Freshman Year," Nancy Somers and Laura Saltz argue for the importance of allowing students to write about their own lives and identities in relation to particular assignments. They also conclude, however, that "when students only use writing to study themselves, they become stuck as writers, unable to move forward. Only those students who were able to find a way to connect their interests with those of a discipline, to look beyond the personal to the public, were able to move from being a novice to an expert" (2004, 148). Basic writers in particular tend to have a harder time moving from writing about their own experiences and reflections to critically engaging with texts.

My intention was to help familiarize students with the ACT structure and prompt guidelines while also asking the students to engage with the class readings. At the same time, the issues pertained directly to the topics that the students were discussing in their Psychology and Freshman Seminar classes. At this point in the semester, the students began to make their own organic connections between the courses. That is, when I asked them to respond to an essay by William Styron on coping with depression, many of them injected their essays with information they had learned in their psychology course. In an online peer critique activity, for instance, two students drew upon their knowledge of the physiological basis of depression, which, they argued, could have something to do with a person's level of serotonin. Offering feedback on her classmate's essay, one of the students advised her partner to reconsider the diagnosis that might lower a depressed person's serotonin. She wrote:

> you make a good point but diagnois [sic] cannot cause a drop in sertioin [sic] levels lol. only gentics [sic] can do that . . . REMEMBER THAT FOR PSYCH CLASS!!!!!!

By the middle of the semester, we were encouraged by the fact that the students themselves were forging the links between the courses. In the beginning of the term we made intentional connections, but as we hoped would happen, the disciplinary bridges were gradually constructed by the students themselves.

AH, BUT UNDERNEATH: FREUD'S INTERPRETATION OF DREAMS AND PSYCHOANALYTICAL THEORIES

Near the end of the semester, I created a unit that concretely linked the work students did around Sigmund Freud's theories in their Psychology class. Building on their exploration of psychoanalysis, I asked the students to read two chapters from Freud's *Interpretation of Dreams.* The text was particularly challenging because it was very different from the kinds of work they had read up to that time in the basic writing class. Freud's language tends to be rather ornate and filled with specialized vocabulary, and the students claimed that it required a wholly different way of reading from how they had done it previously. Immediately after reading the excerpts, the class showed a great deal of resistance through a chorus of "I don't understand," a litany of "this is stupid," and worse, the dreaded silence originating from fear of saying something wrong. As the three-week unit progressed, however, the class discussions and writing became livelier and self-assured as the students came to terms with Freud's language and ideas.

For the first writing activity in the unit, I asked the students to interpret one of their own dreams using Freudian theory. While some of the students were not willing to fully accept Freud's theories as "truth," they were willing to engage with them. One student, for instance, shared her interpretation of a dream in a BlackBoard discussion thread. She wrote:

> In my journal I described a dream that I have for many years, me standing on the top of the stairs and wanting to jump. I eventually jump, but I feel scared and afraid, and while I'm in the air it feels like I'm flying. Freud would probably say that I have sexuals [sic] frustrations and that it has to do with someting [sic] that happened to me when I was little, but in my opinion this dream presents [my] confronting my fear of hights [sic], which I'm consciousely [sic] not aware of.

This student, along with many others in the class, demonstrated an impressive ability to show that they understood the theories (e.g., the dream rooted in subconscious sexual desires and childhood experience), even if they maintained a critical distance from them.

The next activity in the unit asked the students to reflect outward and apply their analytical expertise to hypothetical scenarios. In order to facilitate this activity, I asked the students to imagine they were in a Parisian *café*, which for our purposes, was represented by several small clusters of desks with large newsprint. Dubbed the *Café*

Sigmund Freud, the room's layout was supposed to evoke the setting of a French restaurant or coffee shop where early twentieth-century philosophers, poets, and mathematicians scrawled their own work and ideas on the paper covering the tables. Each "*café* table" in the classroom included a question or problem about which the students brainstormed their responses on the newsprint. In the rotating groups, the students responded to the different topics as well as to the responses of the previous group(s).

The inquiry-based prompts I posed were both text-based, requiring the students to support their arguments with quotes and examples from Freud, and ACT-like, asking the students to consider a specific audience. For example, two of the questions included:

- Your friend Dora has been extremely anxious lately, and she is having bad dreams that have caused her many sleepless nights. She is considering seeing her doctor to get a prescription for sleeping pills. You, however, recommend that she see a Freudian psychoanalyst to help her analyze her dreams and find out what's causing them. *What reasons, supported by specific examples from Freud's* Interpretation of Dreams, *would you give Dora for going to the psychoanalyst instead of getting the sleeping-pill prescription?*
- Using his analytical tools for interpreting dreams, how might Freud explain the following dream:

  > Fritz, a 53 year-old teacher, dreams that he is teaching his math class wearing only his glasses and skimpy, red jockey shorts. The students don't seem to notice and take attentive notes during the class. Fritz, however, is deeply embarrassed and desperately tries to hide behind a lectern, which keeps moving away from him across the floor.

In the subsequent class, I posted the students' responses to the questions on the classroom walls. They (and I) were impressed with the sheer number of ideas they generated, and they agreed that the activity was a productive way to wrestle with the topics and to get multiple perspectives before approaching the intimidating first draft of an essay. Their next essay assignment asked them to deal with one of these questions in depth. Because they had already grappled with Freudian psychoanalysis in several different contexts, the students' responses reflected an impressive authority and genuine engagement with the assignment.

WITH SO LITTLE TO BE SURE OF: CONCLUSIONS AND HYPOTHESES

If the story of this Allied Health basic skills learning community were to be reimagined as a Broadway musical or Hollywood film, it would probably conclude with a ragtag group of racially and ethnically diverse students singing a moving anthem along the lines of "To Sir, With Love." Another possibility would be that the ragtag group of racially and ethnically diverse students would make a dramatic and tearful goodbye to the teacher, who, of course, is leaving to help another ragtag group of racially and ethnically diverse students. However, the semester did not end in this fashion at all. Although I cannot quite dispel this dramatic narrative form completely, the ending was indeed a happy one.

I find that it is always difficult to gauge the effectiveness of one's teaching because there are so many factors that play a part in the development (or lack thereof) in a student's academic progress. Chemistry, the indefinable element that forms a cohesive bond between the students and the instructor, certainly plays a major role. The skills the students bring with them to the classroom and that are nurtured in other classes simultaneously also cannot be ignored. Of course, the methodology that works brilliantly with one class could fail spectacularly with another. All that said, at the end of the term, the course appeared to be a huge success.

This assessment is supported by the following anecdotal and statistical evidence:

- The students developed a great deal of camaraderie, and in their end-of-semester reflections, every student reported how much he or she enjoyed and benefited from the class. Most commented on the challenges of the class, but they felt more confident about writing than they did at the beginning of the class. A number of students reported that the cross-course links in assignments and instruction helped them become stronger readers and writers.
- The writing produced by the end of the semester was the finest I have seen in my five years of teaching English 099. This is not to say that all of the sentence and word-level errors magically disappeared, but several students were writing at a level way past English 101.
- Approximately 80% of the students, more than I have had in any previous class, attended the Writing Center on his or her own at least once for additional writing support. Several students attended on a weekly basis. In addition, nearly 70% of the class attended one or more extra-curricular ACT workshops offered by me and other English Departmental instructors. These figures indicate that the students took a great deal of personal responsibility in developing their writing abilities and recognized the importance of meeting the course performance objectives.
- Over 60% of the students who took the ACT exam at the end of the semester passed. That was over 100% the departmental average pass rate that semester, which was 29%.
- Nearly 70% of the students who took the Departmental Exit Exam passed. This is 30% higher than the typical English 099 pass rate of 40%.

Most gratifying, however, was that for more than a few of the students in the learning community, the experience represented the ultimate goal (and one might argue, the underlying purpose) of general education: student empowerment. Because most of the students were second-language learners, their progress as writers will, if recent studies are accurate, fluctuate. Sentence-boundary issues, word-form errors, and essay-structure concerns probably plagued them through English 101: College Composition. However, in that basic skills learning community, many of the students showed an impressive desire to enter into academic discourse and actively participated in it.

This engagement is powerfully reflected by an email I received from one of the students after he took the final exam, which included an essay prompt similar to the ones I created for the *Café* Sigmund Freud activity. In a letter with the subject heading, "The Essay Was Contradictive," the student took me to task for writing a misleading and seemingly impossible-to-answer writing problem. He wrote:

> Just wanted to let you know that the Essay Question on Interpretation of Dreams was not a good question. You made it tricky because in Freud theory when one dreams [about] a love one['s] death, it is cause by the suppressed memory the individual had during his childhood. On the other hand when one experience the embarrassing dreams of nakedness, this individual is going through a present situation where he/she feels powerless or scared. I hope you understand what I'm trying to say. I try not to change my argument but separated the two conditions on the same dreams. One couldn't put it together without contradicting Freud theory.

The student shows a solid understanding of the material, but more impressively, he demonstrates a willingness to enter into a dialogue about Freudian analysis with a perceived expert (which I am certainly not). He also reflected on his own choices in responding to the prompt and explained why he answered as he did.

In the same letter, the student showed his ability to focus on his own learning and simultaneously developed an awareness of the crucial concerns facing a democratic society.

> It's been a pleasure being your student, you help me not only with my English flaws but you open my eyes a little on the struggles that occur in this world.

Finally, the student concluded his email message to me by recognizing me as someone who, like him, is struggling with issues of writing, research, and sharing one's work with a public audience. Offering me a few pointers on my own book project, he wrote:

> Well good luck in your future success on your book. I have an advice don't make it [too] structure[d] let the pen roll, be yourself. Good luck and God Bless.

Aloi, Gardner, and Lusher outline the principal goals of a general education, and among these include, "higher-order applied problem-solving skills; enthusiasm for learning on a continuous basis; sense of responsibility for action, both personal and collective; and ability to bridge cultural and linguistic barriers" (2003, 241). My experience teaching in the Allied Health and Science learning community confirmed my belief that general education and basic skills do not have to be mutually exclusive. First-year students, especially those fulfilling basic skills requirements need more than just skill-and-drill activities and standardized tests. Meaningful experiences with disciplinary knowledge and inquiry-based problems can help incorporate them into the academy upon entrance to the college and go a long way to instill a respect, zeal, and love for learning from the outset.

EVER AFTER: WHAT'S NEXT?

We entered the "woods" of general education with a question: What creates the meaningful common experience in general education? LaGuardia's recent efforts have certainly been in the domain of "common aims" (core competencies) and "experiences" (learning communities, ePortfolio, Academies and first-year activities). In addition, we have developed a perhaps somewhat unorthodox definition of general education by including and integrating basic skills. We are striving to create common intellectual experiences for all students—acquiring basic skills and core competencies in the context of a discipline, engaging with a common reading, taking an urban studies and capstone writing intensive course, as well as becoming more self-reflective and taking ownership of the learning process through building an ePortfolio. Most of these initiatives are in various stages of implementation: attempting to bring ePortfolios or learning communities "up-to-scale" for the entire student body remains daunting. While all of the urban studies courses are now writing intensives—with all urban studies faculty having participated in our Writing-in-the-Disciplines faculty development seminars—we have only begun the process with capstone courses. Faculty development for the other competencies is just getting underway as well.

All that said, what about the "what" of general education? We have also questioned whether our approach was giving short shrift to knowledge and content—the actual courses students take. Certainly we continue to review and update our curricula—recently adding, for example, a more rigorous mathematics course to several programs—but should we be spending more time trying to create a common set of courses for all students? We want to consider the answer in light of a few points. First, Adelman's recent data show "nearly 60 percent of undergraduates attending more than one institution" (2006, xvi). Thus, even if a set of general education distribution requirements is agreed upon, how many students are actually completing the entire package? Second, while Adelman states that the best indicator of college degree attainment is the "academic intensity" of the individual student's high school curriculum, arguing that "the principal story line leading to degrees is that of content," he also acknowledges that "counting Carnegie units in English or science is not the same as describing and validating what students have learned" (xvii). Our contention is that "academic intensity" does not necessarily equate with specific content courses (even if one wants to grant that some subjects may be inherently more difficult than others), but that it has as much to do with the degree to which students are challenged and engaged in those courses. It is this kind of active learning and engagement with content that we have been most interested in stimulating through our general education efforts—agreeing with the principle that "the primary cause of genuine learning is the activity of the learner's own mind" (Paedeia Group 1991).

Finally, it is sobering to keep in mind that even the best constructed core curriculum or set of distribution requirements is subject to what Lee Shulman calls the "problem of amnesia," observing that "in liberal learning, one of the ubiquitous problems we face is the fragility of what is learned. . . . Students seldom remember much of what they've read or heard beyond their last high-stakes exam on the material" (557). The answer, he posits, is to promote active learning, writing, dialogue, reflection, integration, and opportunities for students to "go meta" about their learning and connect it to their goals—to have students "connect the dots" and create their own "La Grande Jatte," if you will. These are the aims of general education at LaGuardia, which in fact end up focusing us on content in the most important way: keeping us engaged in the hard work of empowering our students as learners, helping them understand more deeply whatever academic content they encounter and connect it more meaningfully to their lives.

NOTES

1.   The musical-theatre oriented reader will notice immediately that the essay and section titles derive from song lyrics by Stephen Sondheim. Not only is Sondheim the quintessential New York City composer, he is also known for his seamless integration of music, lyrics, and character. The songs originally appeared in the following shows: "Putting It Together" and "Move On," *Sunday in the Park with George* (1984); "Into the Woods" and "Ever After," *Into the Woods* (1988); "How Do I Know," *Phinney's Rainbow* (1948); "Show Me," *Hotspot* (1963); "All Aboard," *The Frogs* (2004); "Side by Side by Side," and "You Could Drive a Person Crazy," *Company* (1970); "Merrily We Roll Along," *Merrily We Roll Along* (1981); "Ah, But Underneath," *Follies* (London, 1987); "With So Little to Be Sure Of," *Anyone Can Whistle* (1964).

2.   The play was first presented in New York in the spring of 2000 and was subsequently published by Vintage Books in 2001.

3.   The sample student responses are used with permission from the writers. They have been edited only when a student's meaning may not have been clear. In general, spelling and grammatical errors have been retained to reflect the developmental elements in the writing.

4.   Written comment from the ACT Withdrawing/Nonreturning Survey, administered at LaGuardia in the spring, 2002 semester.

5.   Qtd. in Horner (1996, 209).

WORKS CITED

AAC&U. "What Is Liberal Education?" AAC&U Statement on Liberal Learning, 2006. http://aacu.org/issues/liberaleducation/index.cfm.

Adelman, C. *The Toolbox Revisited: Paths to Degree Completion from High School Through College*. Office of Vocational and Adult Education. Washington, DC: U.S. Department of Education, 2006.

Aloi, Susan, William S. Gardner, and Anna L. Lusher. "A Framework for Assessing General Education Outcomes within the Majors." *JGE: The Journal of General Education*, 52.4 (2003): 237–252.

Astin, A.W. *What Matters in College: Four Critical Years Revisited*. San Francisco: Jossey-Bass, 1993.

Boylan, H. R., and D. P. Saxon. *What Works in Remediation: Lessons from 30 Years of Research*. Report prepared for The League for Innovation in the Community College, 2002.

deWinstanley, Patricia Ann, and Robert A. Bjork. "Successful Lecturing: Presenting Information in Ways That Engage Effective Processing." *New Directions for Teaching and Learning*, 89 (Spring 2002): 19–31.

Ford, Marjorie, and Jon Ford. *Health Views*. Boston: Houghton Mifflin Company, 1998.

Gleason, Barbara. *College Composition and Communication*, 51.3 (February 2000): 488–491.

Grubb, W. N. *Basic Principles for Basic Skills: Criteria for Exemplary Approaches in Community Colleges*. Berkeley, CA: University of California, Community College Cooperative, 2001: 14.

Horner, Bruce. "Discoursing Basic Writing." *College Composition and Communication*, 47.2 (May 1996): 199–222.

Johnson, D. Kent, and James L. Ratcliff. "Creating Coherence: The Unfinished Agenda." *New Directions for Higher Education*, 125 (Spring 2004): 85–95.

Knefelkamp, L. Assessment as Transformation. Speech to the American Association for Higher Education Fourth National Conference on Assessment in Higher Education, 21–24 June 1989.

LaGuardia Community College, Office of Institutional Research. *2005 Institutional Profile*. 26 January 2006. http://www.lagcc.cuny.edu/facts/.

Shulman, Lee S. *The Wisdom of Practice: Essays on Teaching, Learning, and Learning to Teach*. San Francisco: Jossey-Bass, 2004: 559.

Somers, Nancy, and Laura Saltz. "The Novice as Expert: Writing the Freshman Year." *College Composition and Communication*, 56 (September 2004): 124–149.

The Paideia Group. *Paideia Principles*, 1991. http://www.Paideia.org.

Zeszotarski, P. "Dimensions of General Education Requirements." *New Directions for Community Colleges*, 108 (Winter 1999): 39–48.

Part V. Re-envisioning the Role
of the Disciplines and
Doctoral Education

CHAPTER TWELVE

Disciplinary Ways OF Knowing

The Value of Anthropological Thinking in General Education

ERIN MARTINEAU

The City University of New York

Education is what survives when what has been learned has been forgotten.
—B. F. SKINNER, "New Scientist," 21 MAY 1964

THE CONSTRUCTION OF DISCIPLINARY ORIENTATIONS

I came of age, disciplinarily, during a period of great debate about the nature and purpose of anthropology. It was a time, in fact, when many disciplines were examining the production of knowledge and the politics of representation, particularly in response to challenges arising from literary criticism and poststructural theory. Recognizing the impossibility of authorial intent to fix meaning, the production of canonical knowledge, and the elision of voices outside the conventions of the academy, I came to understand disciplinary knowledge as both historically constructed and fluid, rather than evident and immutable. My undergraduate years (1988–1992) were deeply shaped by this disciplinary questioning, epitomized in cultural anthropology[1] in the rejection of the possibility of an objective authorial voice in ethnography, and in the theoretical critiques of anthropology's role in essentializing difference, or "Othering."

In this "critical turn," my classmates and I read Napoleon Chagnon's study (1983) of the Yanomamö—not in order to simply learn about their beliefs and ways of living but to understand how ethnography can contribute to the exoticization of cultural groups. To learn to see gendered stereotypes in our own popular cultural artifacts, we studied Disney's *Snow White*, in which the evil, aging, frigid Queen hands the nubile, young, innocent girl a poisoned apple. The virtuous girl waits for her valiant rescuer, while the powerful woman is incapacitated by her jealousy and her desire to remain the fairest in the land. By studying this text, we came to understand that American culture is shaped by normative gendered narratives that are just as influential as the stories of other ethnic and national groups; we learned that "culture" is not something that belongs only to other people. Later, we were thrilled when we read Emily Martin's *The Woman in the Body* (1987), as it makes clear the ways in which "facts," even ones having to do with something as natural as the body, are powerfully shaped by human ideologies in time. For example, in the section, "Science as a Cultural System," Martin demonstrates how metaphor shapes our perception and understanding of the world around us by deconstructing the characterization of menstruation as "failed production" in medical textbooks. Similarly, my encounter with Peter L. Berger and Thomas Luckmann's book, *The Social Construction of Reality* (1967), blew open the framework through which I saw the world, allowing me to read the world in a fundamentally new way—as made and re-made by human action and belief, as interpreted through cultural frameworks, rather than as evident and naturally occurring.

"Reading," in fact, became the dominant metaphor through which I understood anthropological analysis. The influence of literary criticism on anthropology meant that as part of my anthropological education, I learned how to question the assumptions and ideologies present in a text, whether literary or cultural. Ethnographic writing was revealed as a creation of the writer, shaped by his or her context and interaction with others, rather than as an unproblematic representation of empirical reality. Not only did I come to see text as socially, dialogically, and situationally produced, but I began to understand that even one's physical experience of the world could be fundamentally shaped by expectation and convention. As I learned about fire-walking in rural Greece and birthing in Swedish and Mayan cultures, I came to understand that even pain—perhaps one of the most presumably natural of phenomena—was highly variable, dependent upon context, and socially constructed. I gained this new perspective by thinking deeply about the particular practices of a given society or group, rather than by simply memorizing content. With these influences, in that specific disciplinary moment, I came to understand the underlying question motivating anthropological investigations to be: "Which historically specific ideas, practices and institutions, and which workings of power, have brought about this present moment, this cultural pattern, this social form, this 'text'?" Practicing a scholarly gaze within that particular milieu, I developed little interest in categorizing the particular cultural attributes of a given society, such as whether it was matrilineal, nomadic, bartering, polytheistic, and so forth. I came to be less concerned with how societies "functioned" than with their contradictions and conflicts, and I grew to care more about the variety of voices represented in a text than the ethnographer's "objective" explanation of the social world. Anthropology for me became a way of asking, a way of reading, rather than a store of knowledge.

I have briefly traced this history here because it has deeply shaped how I define the discipline of cultural anthropology and its value as part of general education programs. My anthropological education—while full of uncertainties—was moored in its attention to power, the production of knowledge, the dangers of representation, and the ways knowledge can be used for purposes contrary to those for which it was intended. At the same time, I learned long-standing ways of thinking anthropologically: apprehending the importance of context, looking for connections between apparently discrete areas of the social world, and studying the social world through multiple perspectives and scales of analysis. My understanding of education is necessarily constructed out of this background, and thus affects what and how I teach.

I would like to emphasize that the debates that were occurring when I discovered anthropology have by no means been resolved. Many of the discipline's practitioners consider anthropology to be a science, while others see its possibilities better realized through interpretative and deconstructive methods, or even fictional representation. Departmental programs continue to diverge in emphasis. In one extreme example, Stanford's Department of Anthropology faced such internal divisions in the 1990s that it split into two, creating the Department of Anthropological Sciences and the Department of Cultural and Social Anthropology. My reflections here about the potential for anthropology in liberal education arise out of my particular, and politicized, orientation to the discipline, and would almost certainly be disputed by those who adopt a more scientific approach to anthropology.

DESIGNING INTRODUCTORY COURSES: WHAT DO WE THINK STUDENTS SHOULD LEARN?

Such divergence within anthropology begs the question of what constitutes disciplinary knowledge, and the ways in which we answer that question affect our practices as educators. If the value of anthropology is in the categorization of cultures based on a delimited number of attributes (such as economic, kin, and belief systems) that can be compared to identify patterns of causation and consequence, then that will have certain ramifications for course content and pedagogical methods. Conversely, if the value of anthropology is in the charting of the ways in which the social world comes—through power, belief, and practice—to be seen as natural or inevitable, then alternate approaches to teaching may ensue.

When I reflect on what I hope to accomplish as an anthropology teacher, I often remember witnessing—when I was about half-way through my doctoral studies—a professor complain that his introductory students could not recall the difference between "nomadism" and "transhumance." His frustration arose, I believe, out of a deeply felt sense that it was his duty, as a teacher of Introduction to Anthropology, to prepare students for advanced courses. This engendered in him a commitment to providing a thorough survey of the anthropological categories used to describe human practices and ideas. Even though the vast majority of students in his classes were fulfilling general education requirements and would not be enrolling in anthropology courses in the future, he appeared to feel that his obligation was to serve the few who would go on to be majors.

Listening to him, I realized that I had no idea what the difference in types of organization was. In fact, I was not sure I had ever heard the terms during my undergraduate years. Looking back, quite a bit of the material conventionally presented in introductory textbooks was never part of my early anthropological education. Perhaps I was only comforting myself, but I remember thinking: "Well, I may not know that much about the different types of nomadism, but I do know how to ask good questions." Given my disciplinary orientation, I believe that the central task of a teacher of anthropology is to teach students to think anthropologically, by which I mean guiding them to adopt a questioning stance toward the social world, rather than teaching them to categorize societies by sets of practices. Particularly in an age when we have become overwhelmed by the incessant increase in academic knowledge[2] and instantly accessible information, what becomes of great importance is the ability to form salient questions, to read "the literature" critically, to create thoughtful research questions with an awareness of the ethical challenges involved, and to analyze one's own role in the production of knowledge. The moment in which I "came of age" in anthropology showed me that "knowing" is a complex of activities, all shot through with power and privilege.[3] Coming to understand anthropology's nineteenth-century roots in theorizing cultural evolution and its contribution to colonialism meant realizing that our disciplinary knowledge has arisen out of deeply political projects, and that there has long been tension between anthropology's emergence within liberalism and its critique thereof.[4]

If one rejects the notion of anthropology as a storehouse of facts, of established and unquestioned knowledge, what then is the goal of an anthropological education, of "knowing anthropologically"? What does anthropology have to offer, particularly to those students whose only exposure to anthropology is through introductory courses that fulfill general education requirements? What is the content through which we can teach students to adopt a questioning stance about the world around them? These are important questions, particularly because so many students take an introductory anthropology course at some point in their undergraduate years, a development which is related, in part, to evolving notions of the purpose of liberal education. In the last few decades, the value of a liberal education has been articulated in terms of exposing students to a diversity of thought and ways of being, and of preparing students for citizenship in a globalized world. With these emphases, it is not surprising that introductory anthropology courses sometimes fulfill multiple general education requirements, and that large lecture halls are occupied every semester.

In designing my courses, I have asked myself numerous questions about my goals as a teacher and as an anthropologist: What do I want students to remember a year, five years, or twenty years after they have taken a course with me? Am I simply a gatekeeper to upper division courses or is there a more general value in an introduction to anthropology? If my goal is to provoke new ways of thinking, rather than transmit standardized knowledge, how does my teaching help to position students as producers of knowledge? My participation in CUNY's General Education Project has shown me that I also need to ask myself—and my peers—questions about the larger purpose of anthropology. In terms of general education, can we re-envision introductory courses as opportunities rather than obligations, as the chance to influence the way that thousands of students see the world and its potential, instead of something that keeps us from "real" intellectual work, like so much laundry? Could those of us who teach anthropology envision our introductory courses as influencing national conversations, for example, as impacting conventional wisdom about the incommensurability of ethnic difference and the inevitability of global conflicts? What would happen if we vigorously, as both scholars and professors, inquired into what is at stake in, and what is possible with, general education? Should not we, as scholars and professors, research various ways of teaching anthropological thinking, evaluate our practices and innovations, and require doctoral students to study the teaching as well as the content of our discipline?

"READING" THE CLASSROOM: CUNY STUDENTS AND THE CULTURE OF HIGHER EDUCATION

These are big questions, to be sure, and perhaps best engaged first through attention to the contexts in which we are working, both locally at CUNY, and more broadly in American higher education. With nearly a quarter of a million undergraduates, CUNY is the largest urban public university in the country, and each of the seventeen undergraduate colleges is shaped by its distinct history, sense of mission, and student population, making it difficult to draw a general picture of CUNY. There are some characteristics of the student body, however, that are important to recognize.[5] In the fall semester of 2005, among first-time freshmen, 40% were born outside the U.S. mainland. Approximately 46% of those students speak a native language other than English, and 117 additional languages are spoken.

CUNY students are immersed in astounding diversity, by virtue of attending CUNY and living in New York City, and by virtue of their own life experiences. CUNY students, furthermore, rarely have only their college courses to attend to: in the fall of 2005, among all undergraduates, 37% were attending college part-time; 48% were working more than 20 hours a week; and 59% reported household incomes of under $30,000. More than 80% of CUNY students belong to an ethnic or racial minority group, and nearly 33% are "non-traditional" students, over the age of 25.

What, then, does anthropology offer these students in terms of thinking about diversity, globalization, economic structures, and power? Most have personally experienced others' ethnocentrism against their ethnic or religious communities. Most are all too aware that a college degree can be a ticket upwards, but one without guarantees. For them, ethnic diversity, economic inequality, and global/transnational interconnections are already facts of life. The questions for those who teach anthropology at CUNY, then, may have a slightly different inflection than for those who teach more privileged students. How can we draw on the incredible student diversity within our classrooms in ways that engage with and expand upon students' personal experiences, in order to better explain the workings of structural inequality, the changing contours of the postindustrial economy, the myth of the "American Dream?" How can we make explicit the expectations and power structures of academia in ways that invite students into ongoing disciplinary conversations, and in ways that value the knowledge they already possess? How do we create connections between anthropology courses and the other aspects of our students' collegial and extracollegial lives? How do we prioritize the possible content of our courses, when our students' lives are so full of other obligations that it is simply unreasonable to assign hundreds of pages of reading each week? In short, how does our pedagogy reflect the context in which we teach?

Those of us at CUNY, as well, need to understand that the trends we are seeing in our University are happening across the country. In a recent report on retention and graduation at CUNY, it was noted that there exists a "curious preconception [that] CUNY's issues are uniquely its own" (Summerfield et al. 2006, 14). However, higher education trends across the country mirror those of CUNY. Nationally, the "time to degree completion" is lengthening, female students are now in the majority, and the number of students attending community colleges is increasing, as is the number of students who transfer between institutions. All of these trends, when combined with the development of online education, reduced federal financial aid, and the rising cost of tuition, paint a changing picture of higher education. In this particular climate of higher education, part-time and full-time employment is necessary for many, and students may well choose or be forced to pause their college careers for periods of time. In line with a late-modern, consumerist posture toward public services, it should come as no surprise that many students desire the quickest and most effective path to obtain their college diploma, and that many perceive general education requirements as obstacles to their professional success. Within this context, colleges need to take an active role in explaining the value of general education courses to their students' professional development and success. In addition, we as individual faculty and as members of professional organizations should also be able to clearly articulate the general value of our disciplinary ways of knowing. A cursory examination of the American Anthropological Association Web site reveals the high degree of specialization within anthropology, with its more than 50 sections and interest groups, but statements on the general value and utility of anthropological thinking are harder to find. Making clear the value of anthropological thinking is, or should be, of interest to all teachers of anthropology, in small programs or large. Studying the politics and the history of knowledge production is not enough: We must enact our intellectual principles by making visible the intended value of our courses, particularly within the larger politics and structures of higher education.

RETHINKING THE PURPOSE OF INTRODUCTORY COURSES

In writing this essay, I found myself time and time again wanting to name the "culture concept" as a specific contribution that anthropology can make to general education. In recent years, anthropologists have bemoaned the misapplication of the concept of culture, in some instances even calling for the rejection of the concept altogether. Particularly in the arena of ethnic and nationalist politics, anthropologists have drawn attention to the ways "culture" has been used to suggest that groups of people, or "cultures," are ultimately incompatible. This has been described as a kind of "cultural fundamentalism" (Stolcke 1999), where political conflicts are attributed to incommensurable ethnic difference a la Samuel Huntington's "clash of civilizations" thesis (1993). Clearly, a nuanced understanding of the internal variation within and changeability of "cultures" would seem an important way of knowing in a globalizing world. I struggled, however, in an attempt to characterize the value of this "intellectual property," as the concept is much contested. For example, prominent theorists and ethnographers such as Lila Abu-Lughod have pointed to serious, if not fatal, flaws in the concept that contribute to its being used in ways anthropologists never intended. In her seminal piece "Writing Against Culture,"[6] she writes:

> "Culture" operates . . . to enforce separations that inevitably carry a sense of hierarchy . . . Culture is an essential tool for making other. As a professional discourse that elaborates on the meaning of culture to account for, explain, and understand cultural difference, anthropology also helps construct, produce, and maintain it.

As but one example, I include this quote to demonstrate the deep questioning of the implications of the concept of culture, and the nature of the debate within the discipline.

Rather than compressing the debate by proffering simplistic descriptions of the value of the concept of culture and its potential in "thinking against" ethnocentrism, racism, and cultural fundamentalism, I would like to step back to more fully consider the purpose of the introductory course, and particularly in light of the debate on the concept of culture. What if the introductory course was imagined as an introduction to a constantly evolving way of thinking, rather than a body of knowledge? What if an "introduction to cultural anthropology" was structured as an introduction to the debates of the discipline, to the emergence of certain ideas and methods within particular political and socio-historical contexts, to the intellectual boundary making and boundary crossing that has made, and continues to make, the discipline what it is today? All too often, at least as suggested by most of the "introduction to cultural anthropology" textbooks on the market, the introductory course is seen as an overview of the "stuff" of the discipline—a chapter on kinship, on gender, on political organization, on ritual and belief, on globalization. In contrast, ethnographies of diverse cultural practices and ideologies could be presented not simply as anthropological knowledge, but as sites around which knowledge-making processes occur. Of course, such an approach would impact how we teach and what materials we use; imagine, for example, focusing on three key moments in the discipline's evolution, using ethnographic texts, newspaper articles, political speeches, and intra-disciplinary commentaries to make the historical context and the debates come alive.

What would be the value of such a course, so focused on the production of knowledge, in terms of general education? By making visible the way in which ways of knowing are shaped by their histories in specific times and places, we invite students into the long, ongoing conversations that are our disciplines. They see that knowledge making is a process that is both political and contested. Such an approach would make clear that disciplines are alive, organic, and, in so doing, also make clear that students can participate in changing them. In this book, Judith Summerfield writes about how, in opening the General Education Project, she asked each participant to recall (without defining what she meant) "a liberally educative moment." When she posed this question to me, I remembered the surprise and joy I felt when, after defending my undergraduate honors thesis, my outside reader suggested that I consider pursuing my research further in graduate school. The meaning of this moment for me was that I was seen as a potential knowledge producer, not simply a knowledge absorber. In inviting students into disciplinary conversations, we restructure the enterprise of education— we position ourselves as mentors rather than experts, by focusing on the debates and politics of knowledge making, we reveal the discipline to be multi-vocal and contested, rather than containable to a textbook. Envisioning introductory courses in this way has the potential to shape our students' perception of the purpose of education—rather than simply obtaining a diploma, students are also learning to be participants in multiple intellectual communities, no matter which major they choose.

THE VALUE OF ANTHROPOLOGICAL "HABITS OF THOUGHT"

Beyond the debates on the "culture concept" and the problem of opening up higher education, I do believe there are certain "habits of thought" that are valuable within the practice of anthropology, particularly within our quickly changing, heavily interdependent world. I make no assertion that these are singularly anthropological, and other disciplines might well claim the same habits of thought as their own. Anthropological analysis involves examining a problem from multiple angles, and at multiple scales, a practice that develops a flexibility of perspective. When examining the establishment of transnational communities, for example, students would learn about various political, historical, social, kinship, and economic factors that work to shape families, neighborhoods, cities, states, and international organizations. To take a different example, in studying the construction of gender, students could encounter the problem through looking at media messages, ideas about sex and procreation, family norms, consumption patterns around children's toys and automobiles, and workplace behavior and hiring practices. This flexibility of perspective is intricately bound up with another anthropological habit of thought: the practice of identifying connections across seemingly disparate areas. In anthropology, one learns that politics, economics, family, belief, work, sex, pain—all aspects of the social world—are intertwined. To understand a problem in one area necessitates that one finds the meaningful connections in other areas. Finally, anthropological thinking inculcates a certain level of uncertainty, challenging normative ideas about the way things should be. To study very different ways of being in the world makes it difficult to continue to perceive one's own world as given, as natural. More than simply developing empathy for others, the kinds of intellectual work that are required by anthropology are those that help students to shift perspective, see connections, and step out of certainties. Indeed, we all need these ways of thinking in the twenty-first century: These intellectual practices should assist students in apprehending the transformations of our late-industrial economy; the movements of people, ideas, and objects through globalization; the uneven impact of mass media and technology around the world; and the omnipresent but situation-specific workings of social divisions such as race, class, gender, and religion, all of which affect our lives today.

CONNECTING DISCIPLINARY KNOWLEDGE,
GENERAL EDUCATION, AND DOCTORAL EDUCATION

Just as I have tried in this chapter to think through the relationships between disciplinary knowledge and general education, I think it is important, in closing, to also explore the connections both of these have with doctoral education. Doctoral degrees are perhaps the ultimate expression of disciplinarity; in these programs, the future professoriate becomes immersed in the questions and challenges of their disciplines, acquires knowledge about specific topics within the discipline, and produces original research that is recognized as a contribution to the discipline. However, in many, if not most, programs, the question of pedagogy remains unexplored. The question of discipline-specific pedagogy, and the applicability of disciplinary knowledge to general education, should be approached as a serious intellectual problem. In anthropology, the entire social world is a potential object for study—why not the teaching of anthropology? Are some ways of teaching anthropology more effective than others, and how do we define what we mean by "effective"? How does one connect anthropology to the general education goals at a particular college?

CUNY doctoral students are fortunate to gain firsthand teaching experience within the University, as adjunct instructors and graduate teaching fellows. Imagine if doctoral coursework, comprehensive exams, and dissertations were complemented by sustained inquiry into teaching within the disciplines. Imagine if the departments at each of the undergraduate colleges developed discipline-specific statements on the applicability of their courses to general education, which would serve as guides to adjuncts and teaching fellows. At the Graduate Center, departments could institutionalize credit-bearing pedagogy seminars, connect junior students to experienced faculty on the campuses, arrange for students to observe classes at different colleges, and support research and publication on the teaching of that discipline. Individually acquired knowledge about teaching at CUNY should be shared in disciplinary and interdisciplinary forums, such as teaching colloquia and published journals. The University could establish a postdoctoral fellowship program, in which recent CUNY graduates would return to their former departments, facilitate inquiry into the scholarship of teaching and learning in the discipline, and collaborate with other postdoctoral fellows to publish their findings for the benefit of all CUNY faculty members.

Taking the problem and possibility of general education seriously means recognizing the intense intellectual work that must go into designing such courses. To see these as simply surveys, as stepping stones, as hurdles is to strip such courses of their larger social meaning and intellectual potential. In this society, which professes (and often only professes) to value education, and in which general education is thought to produce global citizens and flexible, creative thinkers, we as scholars and administrators need to critically approach the matter of what kinds of ways of knowing today's students need—not only as individuals working to further their careers and be successful in their chosen pursuits—but as members of the world we are all constructing, in which we are all participating, all the time.

NOTES

1. Cultural anthropology is, at some universities, a subdiscipline of anthropology, along with physical anthropology, archaeology and linguistic anthropology. At other universities, cultural anthropology has been separated into its own discipline. In this essay, when I use "anthropology," I am referring to the field of cultural anthropology.
2. Like many fields in the United States, anthropology has experienced an explosive growth in the number of its practitioners—and consequently in the sheer amount of disciplinary knowledge—since the opening of the academy as a result of the 1944 G.I. Bill, the expansion of the middle class, and the civil and women's rights movements.
3. The gerund form suggests that "knowing" is always active and situated, whereas the term "knowledge" implies stasis and universality.
4. Indeed, in recent years many scholars have been occupied with unpacking the workings and consequences of liberalism in late modernity. From a cultural perspective, liberalism is an ideology and set of practices that produces a certain level of political stability by creating "individuals" who conduct themselves in disciplined ways. This cultural project displaces attention to societal inequalities by focusing on the freedom of individuals. Anthropology, of course, arose out of liberal institutions and ways of thinking. For the purposes of this essay, I have put aside the larger questions regarding liberal education, governmentality, and the production of inequalities to discuss the immediate problems of teaching anthropological thinking. This does not mean that I fully subscribe to the ideology that underlies liberal education. As a teacher of anthropology, I attempt to demonstrate to students that there are and have been other ways of organizing the social world, and that liberal ideals are embedded within political projects.
5. The following statistics are taken from reports published by CUNY's Office of Institutional Research and Assessment, http://condor.cuny.edu:7778/pls/portal/docs/PAGE/OIRA/OIRA_HOME/PROFILE.F2005.PDF.
6. As quoted by Christoph Brumann (1999, S2). The original piece by Lila Abu-Lughod can be found in *Recapturing Anthropology*, edited by Richard G. Fox (Santa Fe: School for American Research), 1991, 137–162.

WORKS CITED

Berger, Peter L., and Thomas Luckmann. *The Social Construction of Reality: A Treatise in the Sociology of Knowledge*. New York: Doubleday/Anchor Press, 1967.

Brumann, Christoph. "Writing for Culture: Why a Successful Concept Should Not Be Discarded." *Current Anthropology*, 40 (1999): 1–27.

Chagnon, Napoleon. *Yanomamo: The Fierce People*, New York: CBS College Publishing, 1983.

Huntington, Samuel. "The Clash of Civilizations." *Foreign Affairs*, 72.3 (1993): 22–28.

Martin, Emily. *The Woman in the Body: A Cultural Analysis of Reproduction*. Boston: Beacon Press, 1987.

Stolcke, Verena. "New Rhetorics of Exclusion in Europe." *International Social Science Journal*, 51.159 (1999): 25–35.

Summerfield, Judith, Paul Arcario, Crystal Benedicks, David Crook, Phyllis Curtis-Tweed, Erin Martineau, and Timothy Stevens. *Creating the Conditions for Students to Succeed, A Report by the CUNY Task Force on Retention*. New York: CUNY Office of Academic Affairs, 2006.

CHAPTER THIRTEEN

Opening THE Invisible Gateway

Some "Common Things" About Student Writing

CHERYL C. SMITH

Baruch College

> It is, I believe, a good field to work in, but you have to be willing to pay attention to common things.
>
> —DAVID BARTHOLOMAE, *WHAT IS COMPOSITION* (1996, 29)

I open with the above quote to foreground some questions about how Bartholomae characterizes work in composition, what its "common things" suggest about teaching writing and its status in English departments. That is, how does composition engage in something common? In what sense? Moreover, how does its very commonness make it a good field to work in? As opposed to what? Exploring these questions and the perception of composition in the academy is as critical as ever. Attacks on the quality of student writing, from forces both within and without our institutions, seem to surface on a regular basis, pressuring English departments to provide remediation and enforce measurable objectives for teaching and assessment.[1] These kinds of imperatives on course design, learning goals, and testing are further intensified by increasingly complex undergraduate populations, including the students whom, thirty years ago at CUNY, Mina Shaughnessy called "strangers in academia" (1977, 3) to underscore their alienation from traditional academic discourses and standards. Combined, these forces—the charged climate around literacy issues and increasingly diverse undergraduate populations—can aggravate differences between colleagues and institutional units, deepening fissures where connections most need to be secured: in our classrooms and curricula, within our departments, between departments and administration, and between individual faculty and their peers, chairs, deans, and students.

In this chapter, I will discuss what we are doing at Baruch College in the face of such pressures on writing education. As my main example, I will offer what I am calling an invisible gateway to academic literacy and student success—the English immersion program—to illustrate some of the issues at stake in rethinking our approach to teaching composition. In 2003, as the new director of my school's immersion program, I quickly came to appreciate the significance of basic writing initiatives, even though they directly apply to a relatively small percentage of Baruch undergraduates. The limited immersion population is due largely to a 1999 decree to phase out remediation in CUNY's four-year schools and concentrate remedial courses (and students) in the system's community colleges. Despite the phase-out, traces of remediation survive in the senior colleges; they are just more marginal and invisible than ever. Immersion, for instance, offers only non-credit courses, designed primarily to help students pass proficiency tests in reading and writing, and the courses and tests are tenuously connected to departmental concerns and agendas. Compounding these challenges, immersion delivers the most basic (or "common") type of writing education in the college, making it a low-status program serving low-level students. Though English immersion may be marginalized by its status and low enrollment, its goals for student literacy inform the broader concerns we have at Baruch. Our students represent over a hundred countries and speak over a hundred different native languages; only about a quarter claim English as their native language. Many come from New York City public schools, where they get a range of education experiences, and many are from the City's ethnic enclaves, where they use a variety of languages other than standard English. How do we effectively respond to this extraordinary language diversity? How do we strike a balance between what we see as our students' knowledge, their actual experience and abilities, and what we identify as their needs, the abilities they should demonstrate upon graduation? How do we help them acquire the kinds of skills they hope to get out of a college education? Finally, how can we rearticulate our school's goals for literacy education within a liberal education mission that makes all our students feel less like strangers in academia and more at home?

In the process of looking at student experience through the lens of English immersion and its conflicts, I will unpack the idea of composition's common things. All of us, in English and beyond, can use an understanding of what is common to our work to build coalitions, shift priorities, and, perhaps most meaningfully, establish a working commons for teaching and learning across the academy. We have the potential to accomplish so much. We can improve the intellectual challenges and working conditions for many practitioners of English studies; help provide for an integrated general education curriculum emphasizing the teaching of the literacy skills our students need; and lend credence to the scholarship of teaching and learning (SoTL), a burgeoning area of academic study that prioritizes the activities of the classroom as worthy of and producing serious academic research. In refocusing attention on classroom inquiry, we at CUNY will be well poised to use the extraordinary laboratory of our unique, dynamic public urban setting to add to a growing community of pedagogical scholarship.

Thus, when Bartholomae calls attention to composition's common things, what is he getting at? Is it the labor of composition: the grading of papers or the teaching of nuts and bolts of grammar, from subject-verb agreement to correct comma placement? Alternatively, is he using "common" to mean basic, emphasizing the teaching of transferable skills and entry-level students? Facing stacks of papers and laboring with basic skills may partially account for what Bartholomae means by common things, but beyond merely emphasizing these activities, he is making a statement about how they are regarded in the academy: as secondary to other work. His contention that you "*have to be willing* to pay attention to common things" gestures toward the long-standing tension between writing and literature in English departments. While composition willingly takes on the teaching of rudimentary skills, literary study traditionally sees itself as providing the more elevated and refined aptitudes of textual interpretation and appreciation. In turn, composition commonly gets cast as a lower, service activity while literature enjoys a higher, humanistic status.[2] Evidence of this intellectual hierarchy elevating the teaching of literature above writing, and pitting the two fields against each other, has long existed in our institutions. As early as the beginning of the twentieth century, the work of teaching courses such as first-year composition fell to probationary faculty. It still remains largely in the hands of graduate students and adjuncts (Crowley 1998, 4). Judith Fetterly testifies to just such an experience of the place of composition when she was a graduate student in literature; she explains how she internalized a clear impression that she and writing had landed "together at the bottom" (1999, 703) when she was assigned to teach composition. Hers is a familiar tale about entrenched hierarchies in English that place TAs and other marginalized faculty in composition courses. Teaching writing is commonly the least desirable, least reputable work of an English department, often assigned to a provisional faculty least empowered to address the most pressing needs of our (often) most needy students. As a result, composition instructors have to be willing to be humble, to relinquish the lure of what some may regard as the loftier literary agenda along with the academic esteem (and power) that attends it.[3]

Importantly, Bartholomae does not merely gesture toward the tension created by the hierarchy of literature and composition; he subverts it. To equate the teaching of composition with common things evokes the idea of a common good, elevating its agenda and standing. Composition, Bartholomae suggests, is not denigrated by its commonness. Quite to the contrary, it has a higher purpose. It is about teaching first-year students and sharing responsibility for a general education curriculum. It resists the appeal of upper level students and courses. Read thus, Bartholomae's common things are a celebration (though, as we will shortly see, not an unproblematic one) of teaching; of close interactions with students, especially entry-level and remedial learners; and of faculty investment in larger college initiatives like the first-year experience, student retention, and graduation rates. These are "things" that many compositionists feel make their work more meaningful but routinely rank fairly low, and certainly lower than traditional, discipline-based scholarship, in securing faculty status.

Bartholomae's chair's address at the 1989 Conference on College Composition and Communication (CCCC) helps further unfold the meaning of composition's common things and their connection to faculty work and rank. He takes a moment to reflect on his candidate's statement when he ran for chair, in which he emphasized his personal debt to CCCC for attaching value to the vocation of composition and providing a community for sharing that sense of value: "I said that CCCC was the organization that made work in composition possible—and in saying that, I felt its truth in the context of my personal history" (1989, 38).[4] He elaborates:

> CCCC (and in particular the annual meeting) seemed to provide the terms and context that allowed people to get to work, and to work with energy and optimism, not cranking out just one more paper, not laddering their way up to the top, not searching for difficult texts and dull readers, not bowing and scraping before another famous book or another dull person, but doing work that one could believe in, where there was that rare combination of personal investment and social responsibility, where we felt like we could make things happen, not just in our own careers, but in the world. (1989, 38–39)

His words here take on the energy of a testimonial and highlight how one of composition's primary concerns, close work with students, transforms the priorities of the professionals in the field and sets them apart from other academics. Bartholomae seems to argue that because compositionists focus more on teaching, they enjoy renewed energy, greater optimism, and a deeper sense of social responsibility. These priorities represent the chance to throw off what gets framed, in stark opposition to the joys of teaching (and teaching-centered research), as the shackles of traditional academic life, characterized by the need to crank out "just one more" article, confront difficulty and dullness, and bow and scrape before academic stars. A traditional field such as literary studies—from which many compositionists, including Bartholomae, come—presumably belongs in the shackled category. Another compositionist with training in literature, Peter Elbow, corroborates this view of composition in opposition to literary studies. He confesses, "When I finally came to see myself as a composition person, I felt an enormous relief at finally feeling *useful*—as though I could make a difference for people" (2002, 536, original emphasis). Bartholomae puts it in only slightly different terms: "there are forms of professional life that are deadening; there are forms that make useful work possible" (1989, 50, note 1).

Again, it takes little reading between the lines to presume that literary studies might just be a prime location for all this useless, deadening work. Such a characterization of the comp/lit divide pits the social value of teaching against what is presented as a more self-serving, less meaningful commitment to research. Undoubtedly, many academics feel a sense of hopelessness at some point in their careers, maybe even to the extent of feeling caught in the shackles of the publish-or-perish world of higher education. Nevertheless, most still defend the significance of scholarship in maintaining the rigor, vibrancy, and legitimacy of the academy, where professors both generate and share specialized knowledge—not only through teaching but also through publishing in forums beyond the classroom. Both acts are crucial to the active intellectual exchange that, at its best, distinguishes higher education from other sites of work and learning. Effective teaching and scholarship, that is, contribute equally to the integrity of higher education.

So for my purposes here, the conflict comes down to this question: If composition is a field gladly and even selflessly invested in common things, what does that say about literary studies, a field generally identified as more elevated than common? Even more importantly, what does it say about the potential for partnership and shared intellectual mission between the two disciplines? Sharon Crowley claims that the marriage of literature and composition "entwine[s]" partners "in an uneasy embrace" (1998, 11); Elbow calls it a "vexed tangle of misunderstandings and hurt" (2002, 533). Entwined, uneasy, vexed, tangled, misunderstood, hurt. With this kind of language in the air, our relations get cast again and again as confrontational and hostile.[5] Significantly, it is not only literature scholars who denigrate composition and perpetuate the conflict; the prejudice runs both ways. As composition and rhetoric gains momentum as a field, with its own active and growing body of scholarship and its own research stars, its practitioners assume their own disdain for more traditional research paradigms, a kind of backlash against their literary colleagues.[6] In sustaining these tensions, we succeed in rehearsing and more deeply entrenching old hierarchies; we fail miserably in terms of imagination for the future. That is, we fail to come up with new, collaborative paradigms for faculty work that would bridge and even use our perceived differences to inscribe a more seamless narrative of literacy education into our departments and, just as importantly, beyond them, into our general education programs. What we need is reciprocal, open-minded respect for other disciplines if we hope to learn from one another and heal our historical differences that, quite simply, hinder good work and the advancement of both teaching and scholarship in our institutions. I will go on to explore some ways for us to discover our commonalities and transform the relationship between writing and literature from confrontational to collaborative. In the process, we can open up ways to expand our view of legitimate scholarship, increasing our understanding of each other's work and energizing all our research agendas.

I should pause here to make clear that I am offering the state of affairs in English as a model for the kinds of tensions and potential existing across the academy. In many ways, the hierarchy that has historically pitted writing against literature in English departments is derivative of a larger split in the academy that designates the teaching of general education courses as inferior to the teaching of advanced courses for majors and graduate students. In turn, this split derives, at least in part, from a larger academic value system that ranks teaching below research instead of seeing both activities in a sort of academic dance, the partners evenly balanced. Once we shift our view of teaching and scholarship to see them as dancing on common ground, I believe we can ease a lot of uneasy embraces in the academy.

One of the most important realities defining our common ground is our students' complicated and often vexed relationship to language—and our need to respond to it. Individually, we have to become more aware of our struggles with student literacy, our personal assumptions and doubts about student ability, and our solutions and failures. We will then be able to identify where we see our own struggles, assumptions, doubts, solutions, and failures reflected in one another's practices, gaining insight into directions for change. Recognizing our common experiences is critical, in part because it will help us see that disciplinary difference does not separate us as much as we may imagine, especially when it comes to teaching. Christopher Thaiss and Terry Myers Zawaki studied writing across the disciplines and found, in a variety of departments, a "community of values" represented by a "number of common terms in the [departmental assessment] rubrics" that point to a "detailed sharing of beliefs" (2006, 88) as to what makes for good writing. Again and again, for instance, faculty in the study stressed the value of compiling valid evidence, crafting a logical organizational structure for presenting ideas, and writing grammatically coherent prose. At the same time that faculty evoked common terms to discuss good writing, however, Thaiss and Zawaki discovered that they sometimes held very divergent notions of those terms. Further, they frequently reframed them, depending on their audience. For example, they would define what constitutes solid evidence differently from their colleagues in other departments, or they would explain style one way to freshmen and another way to more advanced students. What this tells us is that across our academic fields, we hold similar values about how to read, structure, and communicate knowledge. However, the terms we use to describe our values are slippery; they can mean different things in different contexts. As a result, we need to acknowledge that we share important criteria in how we conceptualize our teaching and our students' learning while reminding ourselves to check assumptions about what we mean when we articulate these criteria. We all have our idiosyncrasies: our own ways of carrying out and talking about research, our own agendas and relationships to the larger whole. Still, when it comes to how to capture and communicate our ideals, we are not as different as we may think. Across the disciplines, we grapple equally with how to put the concepts of our intellectual work into meaningful language that transfers the energy and enthusiasm of our fields. Moreover, we all desire to teach students how to access the ideas of our subjects through the same basic elements of effective discourse.

In an essay borrowing Shaughnessy's catchphrase, "strangers in academia," for its title, Vivian Zamel characterizes the importance of writing within different disciplinary contexts, especially for ESL students. According to her studies in the 1990s, teachers in various departments could identify commonalities in writing across the disciplines: They felt they shared important values about teaching and learning how to write. Nevertheless, like the faculty in Thaiss and Zawaki's study, they acknowledged concrete benefits in learning to write over time and within diverse, content-based courses. As a result, Zamel reports:

> faculty have begun to understand that it is unrealistic and ultimately counterproductive to expect writing and ESL programs to be responsible for providing students with the language, discourse, and multiple ways of seeing required across courses. They are recognizing that the process of acquisition is slow-paced and continues to evolve with exposure, immersion, and involvement, that learning is responsive to situations in which students are invited to participate in the construction of meaning and knowledge. They have come to realize that every discipline, indeed every classroom, may represent a distinct culture and thus needs to make it possible for those new to the context to practice and approximate its "ways with words." (1995, 517)

Over time, the traditional complaint that the English department "isn't doing its job" when students struggle to write in their more advanced courses will become a thing of the past. Change can be slow to occur, however, and for now, we are still working to fully realize the goal of writing education as a practice that depends on, and develops in tandem with, disciplinary knowledge making. In order to expedite this crucial change in our culture, we need to repeatedly rearticulate how our work and agendas coincide despite their important singularity.

We also need to continually question the integrity of our modes of assessing writing. If progress in student writing depends on situating it within defined disciplinary contexts, then many of our writing tests, which treat writing as a set of isolated skills, are based on flawed premises. In an article condemning the new SAT essay test as "revers[ing] decades of progress toward literacy" (2005, B14), Dennis Baron promotes the imperative of teaching and evaluating student writing within meaningful contexts. One reason the SAT essay test fails, Baron contends, is because it does not meet this imperative. Instead, it takes written English out of context and attaches it to a free-floating and therefore largely meaningless formula, such as the five-paragraph essay, which impacts the teaching of language and writing by forwarding the notion that it, too, can be accomplished out of (disciplinary) context. Baron explains:

> The fact that the new SAT's writing section values correct English more than competent writing will have a negative impact on the teaching of grammar and usage in our schools. Correctness in language is not learned through memorization. It evolves through complex choices conditioned by the social and rhetorical context of specific acts of communication. The SAT's idea that questions about language can be answered a, b, c, d, or "none of the above [the kinds of questions that account for more than two-thirds of the writing section score] promotes the mistaken notion that there is only one right answer when it comes to good English, and thus will force language instruction to revert to simplistic, one-size-fits-all grammar drills. As a result, the new SAT will widen the gap between high and low achievement for speakers of nonstandard English and for those who speak English as a second language. (2005, B15)

The complex choices that writers make, along with the social and rhetorical situations that condition them, evolve within and as disciplinary sites of learning. That is, students learn to read and write, say, a lab report for biology in terms that are distinct from how they learn to read and write a film critique. As Thaiss and Zawaki conclude, even though we share definitions of good writing, academics respond to and generate texts differently depending on their field of study, diverging, for instance, not only in their standards for sound evidence but in how they frame the very idea of evidence. We make a grievous mistake in our teaching, therefore, when we attempt to isolate one literacy skill from another, and all skills from the disciplines. In our own work, we read and write in tandem; similarly, our students will learn to write better if given concrete contexts within which to read, process, and apply language.

With this concept in mind, it becomes easier to see that composition and literature have more in common than their historical divisiveness may suggest. Our classes contribute to the same process of advancing student literacy, even though we may see ourselves as disciplinarily distinct. Indeed, Fetterly identifies the origins of our conflicts in English as owing to disciplinary differences that, I would argue, are perceived as incompatible. To illustrate, she explains how, as a graduate student, she felt "caught up in the massive contradictions of earning [her] right to read literature at an advanced level by teaching first-year students how to write expository prose. [She] did [her] job with minimal instruction and without any sense of how this 'job' related to [her] profession' " (1999, 702–703). This struggle to reconcile the right to read literature with the imperative to teach writing represents a deeply embedded sense of stratification in the mission and ways of thinking in literary studies versus composition. Training the future professoriate that teaching writing and doing one's intellectual craft are "massively" at odds with each other inculcates an attitude toward teaching and research that develops into a modus operandi for many

English faculty, helping to sustain a belief in an essential—but often unexamined—disparity in values that can evolve into unnecessary departmental conflict. Such conflict parallels the scholarship versus teaching divide. We come to see writing (or teaching) and literature (or the disciplines) as operating on very different intellectual spheres and therefore as antithetical. One field gets framed as grudge work, a service activity geared toward communicating generic, transferable skills to students, while the other is seen as more central to the intellectual life of the academy, one of the places where students can apply the skills learned in courses like composition. More specifically, one is seen as non-disciplinary and the other as disciplinary.

Even so, for generations of students and teachers of writing and literature, the link between the two fields simply makes sense. Both, after all, are deeply invested in the workings of language, in how authors frame ideas in order to communicate them more effectively and generate complex meanings. Further, more and more, we are thinking about the essential connections between reading and writing; we are realizing the inherent problems in trying to teach students how to write as if it exists in isolation from what they read, how often they read, and how well they understand it. These factors point to where faculty in composition and literature—indeed all faculty—share in an important mission: teaching students essential aptitudes in how to read and write with a close, critical eye, and how to engage in the dynamic relationship between writers (knowledge makers) and readers (consumers of knowledge). All of us, at all points in the process, are invested in how language functions in our fields: how students grasp concepts in and through words and how their ability to first distill and then communicate information helps ensure their success.

If we think about student learning as enacting the practice of connecting language fluency to disciplinary study, then first-year composition and even English immersion start to seem much less marginal to undergraduate education as a whole. In fact, the reading-writing connection that I am arguing is at the heart of so much of the work of the academy proves to be the most crucial aspect for students enrolled in English immersion classes. As director of Baruch's immersion program, I quickly discovered that students often fail the essay test before they even start writing because of the challenge of reading: They misunderstand the prompt. They do not grasp what the test is asking them to write about. They therefore start from a position of deficit, derailing their essays before they even begin composing them. I found that if students can do one simple thing—understand the prompt—they can establish a position of clarity from which to elaborate a response and assert their authority as writers. They then have a much better chance of passing the test, even if—and this is the important part—their standard written English does not improve much, which it rarely does in the three to four weeks of immersion instruction. Thus, passing the test does not hinge on grammar and surface error; rather, it has an awful lot to do with reading. Based on this finding, I have spoken with teachers about restructuring class sessions by limiting grammar drills and dedicating more time to reading and deconstructing test prompts and other texts. Students really benefit from this kind of work, both in the short term of retaking the entrance exam and in the long term of facing the demands of future coursework.

Thus, it turns out that my ability to read beyond surface error in student writing, to refuse the primacy of the wall of words and look past it for deeper meaning—a craft honed in years of advanced literary study—is central to my success as a writing program administrator. In other words, in applying my discipline's standards for reading, I find explanations for student error that lead to creative solutions for classroom practice. Further, I have the language to persuasively explain my findings to others, most notably the teachers with whom I work. In thinking like a literary scholar, I am able to generate effective plans for advancing a basic writing program.

However, while my disciplinary context of literature has enabled my work with basic writers, my work with basic writers has challenged my disciplinary identity. When I came to Baruch College in the fall of 2003—a literary scholar with over ten years of experience in the ESL and composition classrooms, including two intense years of full-time teaching in a deeply self-reflective writing program—I would immediately encounter the sometimes vexed and vexing gaps created by the assumption that we in different realms of English support divergent, mutually exclusive agendas. I have had to struggle to define a viable professional and research agenda within those gaps. My department houses nearly fifty full-time literature, writing, and journalism faculty and hires more than sixty adjuncts every semester to teach ESL and first-year composition, as well as the sophomore-level world literature course required of all Baruch undergraduates. Many, but not all, full-timers teach both writing and literature. I joined the department as a literature person with a writing focus, slated to teach both types of classes, and hence I immediately occupied a potentially complicated, crossover position. To complicate matters even more, I was hired into both faculty and administrative roles—not an uncommon kind of appointment for people with skills in writing instruction and program administration. As director of Baruch's English immersion program, I would be designing a program for students who, while admitted to the college, do not meet minimum score requirements on the SAT or New York State Regents tests in English. They then have to take CUNY-specific tests in reading and writing. If they fail one or both of those, they may enroll in a free summer and/or January immersion program; if they decline and are designated ESL, they are required to take a non-credit ESL course during the academic year.[7] These students with compromised literacy skills thus represent a provisional population at Baruch, admitted to the college with a crucial caveat: If they do not pass the basic skills test, they stall out, barred from introductory classes, like first-year composition, that serve as the gateway to all upper level courses. In her landmark book, *Errors and Expectations*, Shaughnessy explores the serious failings of this educational reality that often forces teachers to concentrate on getting students to pass a standardized test to the exclusion of helping them transition more authentically to college-level work. She argues, "the remedial model, which isolates the student and the skill from real college contexts, imposes a 'fix-it station' tempo and mentality upon both teachers and students" (1977, 293). The word *isolate* strikes me as especially crucial here; when I came to Baruch, the specter of isolation quickly became something I wanted to exorcise from the immersion experience for both students and myself. I wanted to see how we could transform the "fix-it station" of basic writing into a core, integrated part of a student's general education. How, in effect, we could turn the isolation of remediation into a commons for learning.

Similarly, I wanted to find a way to shift the reality for writing teachers. Administering to and teaching students in programs like immersion traditionally represent the lowest level of intellectual and professional activity in an English department. Basic writers, those deemed not adequately prepared for even the most preliminary English course, are frequently objects of wonder and resistance: Why should *I* have to teach them what they should have learned in high school? Do they even belong in college at all? Shaughnessy captures the conflict that basic writers provoke in the academy: "[T]he teacher who wishes to give his best energies to the instruction of ill-prepared freshmen must be ready to forego many of the rewards and privileges of his profession" (1980, 95). If teaching freshman comp is already a low-level, service-oriented activity, teaching basic or remedial learners barely registers as a worthwhile college-level endeavor. Faculty members at CUNY and across the country continue to wrestle with the conflicting demands on their careers, time, and identities that Shaughnessy documents, weighing students' needs against their own professional status. Noting these conflicts, Zamel calls sites like immersion "marginalized position[s]" (1995, 515). Indeed, they may be marginalized at best: Bruce Horner labels them "peculiar position[s]" (1996, 199), suggesting their lack of any place at all in the world of higher education. As peculiar, they are indefinable, un-namable, outside the very lexicon of the academy. Horner elaborates on the peculiarity by pointing out the dual identity of basic writing as both "the specialty of some of the leading figures in composition studies," making it a place of esteemed scholarship in some circles, and "the province of teachers and students placed at the bottom of the academic institutional hierarchy" (1996, 199), denying it any status in practice. If composition was Fetterly's bottom, immersion is the bottom of the bottom, assumed to function outside the world of disciplinary rigor, to have, as Zamel puts it, "no authentic content" (1995, 515)—a particularly damning assumption in an environment that prioritizes discipline-specific learning.

The assumption damns faculty by denigrating the value of their work with the mistaken view that it is non-disciplinary. However, as I have already argued, the teaching of writing does not happen in one place or course but is carried out across the academy, shaped by different, and rigorous, disciplinary standards and ways of knowing. We do not have to create this reality; it already exists. We just have to find more concrete ways of recognizing it and understanding the complex disciplinarity of writing. I will explore such ways later in this chapter.

It damns students by marginalizing their experience, making their very entrée into college an invisible encounter with college life. They are doing what is seen as the non-intellectual work of catching up, a process deemed unworthy of higher education and therefore ignored. It is as if we are saying: "We'll let you do that, but it's a little humiliating, so we'll look the other way." We do a grievous disservice to our students by perpetuating this attitude. At Baruch, it may be true that only a small percentage of entering students go through immersion, but many, many more are not traditionally prepared for college-level reading and writing. Decades after open admissions radically altered the undergraduate population, many of our students could still be accurately identified by Shaughnessy's remarkably resilient phrase, strangers in academia: They remain largely "unacquainted with the rules and rituals of college life, unprepared for the sorts of tasks their teachers [are] about to assign them" (Shaughnessy 1977, 3). The solution is not to marginalize them in a program or with an attitude that drills formulas and skills, but rather to welcome them into the challenges of undergraduate study through an integrated curriculum focusing on how college-level inquiry and skills development authentically intersect. We can no longer afford to separate the learning of language from the learning of disciplinary content, a common separation that Zamel argues is "shaped by an essentialist view of language, in which language is understood to be a decontextualized skill that can be taught in isolation from the production of meaning and that must be in place in order to undertake intellectual work" (1995, 510). This is precisely the view we succumb to in imagining immersion and composition as quick fixes that will, once and for all, teach literacy skills so students can move on, able to read anything and write about it with confident fluency, able to encounter the content of a discipline with fully honed skills. We all recognize the appeal of such mythical students. They make the jobs of communicating our course content and reading student papers easier because, quite simply, they get it. The ease, however, also "releases faculty from the ongoing struggle and questioning that the teaching-learning process inevitably involves" (Zamel 1995, 510). We may desire such a release from what sometimes seem like intractable student problems, yet it is the ongoing struggle and questioning about student learning that leads to our most important advances in the classroom and will help us define a common ground, revealing ways that our teaching and research, as intellectual endeavors, can meaningfully coincide across disciplines.

At CUNY, we have recently made sweeping changes to immersion as a university-wide initiative, determining that it must resist being mere test prep and instead establish itself as part of a continuum of the struggles and successes of literacy development: begun in immersion programs and first-year composition, fostered through the language expertise of the English department, supported by locations for supplemental instruction, and continued throughout students' careers in all majors. To do this effectively, each college has been empowered by the Office of Undergraduate Education to design its own individualized immersion curriculum, built around its particular students and the courses of study they most often pursue.[8] For instance, at Baruch, where about 85% of our undergraduates major in business, our immersion classes teach students writing but also introduce the oral presentation skills practiced in the business school. Furthermore, because we are especially concerned that many of our entering students have a particularly hard time making the adjustment from high school to college academic standards, I hired a New York City public high school teacher to work full time with immersion. Her job is to counsel students on their new challenges, help design the reading and writing curriculum, plan faculty development sessions with an eye to giving teachers insight into where students are coming from, and lead a conversation workshop that provides students with the opportunity to talk about their learning experiences thus far and express concerns and hopes about the next stage of their education.

Along with this teacher, I coordinated an immersion instructor, the college ESL director, two journalism faculty members, who serve as advisors for student publications, and two undergraduates to put together an original English immersion workbook that articulates the program's evolving mission. The book welcomes students to their new institution; incorporates materials from immersion, ESL, and first-year composition classrooms as well as the CUNY WriteSite and other national Web sites on college writing; and features Baruch undergraduate essays from a cross-section of freshman classes and student publications, including *Dollars and Sense: Baruch College Review of Business and Society*. The articles from *Dollars and Sense* are particularly useful in grounding students in the business discourses that many of them will encounter in their majors. Through these kinds of student essays, as well as literary texts, the book makes reading central to writing. Students struggle to comprehend, and they see how other undergraduates have interpreted difficult texts like Emily Dickinson's poetry. In the act of working to understand what one has read, notions and functions of expression—of how words make meaning—begin to unfold. In reading, that is, students learn to write more effectively, especially for academic contexts.

Thus, the book aims to make immersion a place of movement, of entry into college communities and language, instead of a place to be stalled in a test-prep limbo that narrowly focuses on skills acquisition. The success that comes with merging insight and materials from a number of people, representing a range of educational levels from high school and basic writing to first-year composition and upper level writing, testifies to the fact that literacy transcends borders. When we openly acknowledge that the teaching of college writing does not only occur in first-year composition, we come closer to fully realizing the variety of places it does occur, and how it happens. Further, by blending perspectives, we more effectively foster an environment for immersion that resists invisibility and reinforces the program's potential as a place, not outside of or prior to undergraduate learning, but of beginning: a place to pick up on the past and initiate a new, ongoing process.

To focus on how the immersion program connects to the undergraduate curriculum as a whole does more than forward the significance of student writing. It encapsulates the liberal education ideal itself, which reinforces learning as a process in which students are always moving out of and into different courses and stages of their intellectual lives. Each class, along with a student's personal experience, combines into an individualized process of intellectual, social, and ethical growth. Each class is part of a dynamic encounter with learning that taps into what is not fully visible to us as teachers—our students' prior and future education—but is nonetheless essential to our classroom realities and our role as educators. In his sometimes scathing indictment of being *Clueless in Academe*, Gerald Graff insists we have to move "beyond the privacy of 'the classroom' to organizing the curriculum in just such a connected and coherent way. Curricular mixed messages are the result of a system in which teachers know little about what their colleagues do in their classes. Students' cluelessness about academia is rooted in teachers' cluelessness about each other" (2003, 30). Clearly, gaining insight into what happens beyond our own classes and specialties and valuing that insight are crucial to inscribing a seamless narrative into undergraduate learning, not only of writing education but also of liberal education more comprehensively. We in English, like all teachers across the disciplines, can learn from one another. In fact, we can reciprocate insights without flattening out what should be our generative differences—in teaching and learning styles, in academic and personal research priorities—into a debilitating coherence. Some unity of purpose and effect does not have to equal utter uniformity and consistent agreement. All our work, our teaching and our research, our program building and curricular development, has to do with knowledge building. Thus, regardless of our disciplinary affiliation, we share a common role in the academy. We are parts of the whole (sometimes messy) process of basic and advanced studies that combine into what we hope will be a comprehensive student experience.

Early on, Fetterly internalized the troubling impression that she and writing were "together at the bottom," but she also gained an awareness of something that powers English in the academy: What we do is especially central to this messy whole, to the broader liberal education agenda. She recalls how, "No one explained why the work we now call general education was the English department's responsibility, but . . . I imbibed a sense that we in English were somehow nobler, more disinterested, more deeply devoted to the general good than those in other disciplines. And certainly more central to the operation of the university" (1999, 703). The nobility and centrality of English may be questioned by some and, like the landscape of higher learning in general, the role of English studies in the academy may well be changing, a possibility I will consider momentarily. For now, the point I wish to underscore is Fetterly's implication that the priorities common to all English faculty, along with a shared importance to institutional goals, should bond us as professionals and intellectuals.

Kathleen Blake Yancey might argue that forging such bonds is not only justified by the significance of our efforts to the whole. It is absolutely crucial to the future of English. In letting rifts between our professional activities and priorities widen, we create gaps into which the integrity of our departments, and their ability to move forward, can too easily fall. In her 2004 CCCC Chair's address, Yancey focuses on how to move forward, insisting that we need to find some common ground upon which to reconfigure English studies so we can keep pace with the changing times and students' developing interests. Communication has radically changed through the introduction of new technologies, such as blogs, prompting Yancey to ask if our writing programs and English departments are losing pace with the times and may even become obsolete. "Some disturbing data suggests that traditional English departments already are," she says. "According to the list of departmental administrators published in the PMLA, over the last twenty years, we have seen a decline in the number of departments called English of about 30%" (2004, 302). Yancey speculates on the causes for this dramatic decline:

> They may have simply stopped being represented for a number of reasons: a shortage of funds, a transfer of the listing elsewhere. Naturally, this statistic doesn't mean that English is disappearing as an institutional unit. Most obviously, it means that fewer units calling themselves English are listed in the PMLA. And when plotted against another trend line—the *increase* of units called something other than English, like departments of communication and divisions of humanities—it seems more plausible that *something* reductionist in nature is happening to English departments generally. They are being consolidated into other units or disappearing. (2004, 302–303, original emphasis)

For Yancey, the statistics clearly carry a meaning that she is not yet willing to name, other than to say that "*something* reductionist . . . is happening." It is wise, of course, not to jump to alarmist conclusions about the future of English, but it is also interesting to take a look at our histories to observe what changes and what stays the same. How students develop as writers, as Yancey points out, has dramatically changed over the last two decades with advances in technology and the growth of the Internet. What students choose to study as a result of cultural transformations due to technology, among other forces, is also always changing. However, the need for basic literacy and communication skills—the social currency of reading, critical thinking, and writing—remains constant. It is in this very constancy that we can fortify our departments' integrity, fostering a sense of shared mission as we seek better ways to impart these social currencies to our students, keeping in mind who they are, where they come from, and where they are aspiring to go. How can we bring our diverse students into the same classroom, create ways for them to learn from one another, bridge their differences and work effectively with them all, and pass on sustainable knowledge that they can carry with them to the next class, the next challenge?

We cannot accomplish as much as we like if we allow what divides us to close down conversations about what we share, and one of our common goals is to help students use the interpretive facilities of reading and writing to translate their understanding of disciplinary knowledge into their own purposeful language. We have remarkably similar ways of defining this work: We want our students to employ sound evidence, craft logical organizational structures, and use correct, audience-appropriate grammar and terminology. In fact, we do this very work ourselves when we write up lesson plans, assignments, syllabi—even our own scholarship. Unfortunately, our work that does not fall into the last category, scholarship, does not get talked about very much. President of the Carnegie Foundation for the Advancement of Teaching, Lee S. Shulman, describes our silence around teaching as a "pedagogical solitude," a state he contrasts to our attitudes about research, which he calls "community property." Research gets public forums, such as conferences and funding in the form of grants, to foster its expansion. Conversely, teaching is seen as personal and idiosyncratic, a private affair. "We close the classroom door and experience pedagogical solitude," Shulman asserts, "whereas in our life as scholars, we are members of active communities: communities of conversation, communities of evaluation, communities in which we gather with others in our invisible colleges to exchange our findings, our methods, and our excuses" (2004, 140). That last word may be especially significant when it comes to opening up candid conversations about teaching. Perhaps we are afraid of having to offer those excuses, of being held accountable for students not grasping concepts that they "should" have gotten, and we close our classroom doors even more firmly to shield ourselves: from unrealistic or undesirable expectations that might highjack our courses, from having to explain the inevitable unresponsive or disengaged student, from public exposure of classroom experimentation that does not work out the way we had planned. Teaching, unlike our scholarship, is not entirely under our control. We can be—or feel—at the mercy of students who have not always freely chosen to be sitting in our classes and may not be driven by goodwill or understanding for our pedagogical efforts. This interaction, of course, is part of what energizes teaching and makes it matter. We break though differences and barriers and enact growth and change. However, it also can make it harder to talk about, which blocks our efforts at advancing the scholarship of teaching and learning into the kind of community property that would help qualify it as significant in our institutions.

By the twenty-first century, we have evolved enough of a discourse and community around teaching and learning to begin to transform our academic environments—including our individual classes, departments, and college-wide interactions—into a functional commons with the core goals of improving teaching and learning and fostering an appreciation for the significance of SoTL in advancing undergraduate education. Huber and Hutchings delineate this ideal in *The Advancement of Learning: Building the Teaching Commons*. A main reason to build a teaching commons, they argue, is that "teaching has, traditionally, had so few ways to improve itself" (2005, 18). They elaborate:

> *Individual* faculty work hard at their classroom craft, but the larger, collective enterprise of teaching does not move forward because the work of improvement is so often done in isolation, in the school of hard knocks, one might say, and by the seat of the pants. In contrast, the scholarship of teaching and learning offers the prospect of work in which teachers—to use Sir Isaac Newton's famous image—"stand on the shoulders of giants." (2005, 18, original emphasis)

Our exclusively individualized approach to teaching leaves us stranded in a sea of students where we can sink or swim—where, too often, managing to tread water is enough. According to Huber and Hutchings, however, there is potential for change. If we create the teaching commons, a space where the practice and scholarship of our classroom experiences are prioritized, "conversations about teaching and learning—informed by evidence and grounded in practice—can become the norm rather than the exception. Disciplines can engage in active trading of ideas about pedagogy. Ways of sharing and citing one another's work will emerge and become commonplace. And faculty will stand on the shoulders of others who have gone before" (2005, 32).

The image they paint may sound overly optimistic to our ears, trained as they are to the tensions and debates that have long vexed some of our best efforts. Nevertheless, hailing our differences and seeking to appreciate our common ground—hoisting one another up, as it were, to succeed—can be more than a feel-good activity. It can be an intellectual endeavor, "informed by evidence and grounded in practice." It can help move us away from potentially divisive dichotomies that, for instance, prioritize a limited research agenda or celebrate only one part of what we do as representing a willingness to pay attention to common things. It can edge us toward discovery about our commonalities and their potential to help us find solutions to our shared challenges. My experience at Baruch in fostering a more integrated learning environment in English immersion supports the notion that if we embrace a new paradigm for legitimate work in literacy education (for both students and faculty)—remaking marginalized or peculiar spaces into valuable parts of the whole—we will be able to see more clearly how our activities intersect: in and out of the classroom, and within and beyond our departments.

All of this activity can shift the terms of our discourse around liberal education in foundational ways, freeing us from the limited notion of common things, from distinctions between teaching and research, basic and elevated, and even teaching and learning. SoTL requires us to look at classroom practices seriously, as a text that produces evidence worthy of reflection.[9] To thus approach teaching as generative of literature, a literature that could be culled for meaningful academic scholarship, is to expand the identity of the engaged and esteemed professor from someone who primarily bestows knowledge to someone who receives, absorbs, and processes it, becoming part of the ongoing narrative of the classroom. This identity shift requires agreement about the value of teaching and the shared nature of our intellectual endeavors that would go far in helping us resist what Bartholomae characterizes as the deadening of our work, a deadening that is misleading to equate with the study of literature or any discipline commonly perceived as more theoretical than practical. It does not derive from the content or focus of any particular subject area but rather from the reduction of teaching's consequence across all fields of study, from a failure to appreciate the deeply disciplinary nature of both teaching and learning. One thing composition and its struggles for disciplinary legitimacy can teach us is how writing connects to content. Students learn to write through struggling to read and comprehend a subject. Then, and only then, are they able to begin to write successfully within and about it. Scholars learn to teach through much the same process: through struggling with the language of a discipline and working out ways to communicate its resonances.

In his introduction to Shulman's 2004 collection of addresses and essays, *Teaching as Community Property*, Russell Edgerton, former president of the American Association for Higher Education, characterizes Shulman's early research into teaching expertise as the work of an "explorer . . . map[ping] a land that no one knew was there" (quoted in Shulman 2005, 1). Edgerton goes on to more specifically define this unknown terrain:

> The new land was a domain of knowledge, a "missing paradigm," in the prevailing view of what expert teachers know and can do. Yes, Lee argued, expert teachers understand the subject matter they are teaching, and, yes, they have a grasp of general teaching techniques. But they also possess something more—a knowledge of how to transform the particular subject they are teaching into terms that their students can understand. In addition to *chemistry* (the subject) and *teaching* (generic methods) there is, Lee argued, a third domain of knowledge: the *teaching of chemistry*. (quoted in Shulman 2005, 2, original emphasis)

As Edgerton unpacks it here, the scholarship of teaching and learning is intimate with the disciplines, showing us from inside a subject area how individuals think about and come to understand its parameters. For it to function as legitimate scholarship, it has to be seen as adding to the intellectual knowledge and discourse of a field. This is a foundation of Shulman's argument for SoTL.

In the 1970s, Shaughnessy framed basic writing in a way similar to Edgerton's depiction of SoTL: as an unmapped frontier territory. She called the field she is now credited with launching a "pedagogical West" (1977, 4), uncharted land being explored by a few brave pioneers: those teachers willing to see and advocate for what had been an invisible, or marginalized, facet of academic life. Horner argues that this portrayal worked to legitimize the field in part by invoking a "utopian . . . purely intellectual rather than political space" (1996, 210). That is, it drew attention away from the heady social reality fueling open admissions at CUNY and the basic writing situation that Shaughnessy brought to light. I would agree that *Errors and Expectations* does represent, as its primary concern, how and why to teach basic writing better. It emphasizes the need to rethink how we promote literacy in a substantially changed academic environment that is, indeed, so new as to be unmapped territory. However, it is certainly not blind to the political and social forces fueling the changes: the links between class, race, ethnicity, and language. For instance, when Shaughnessy flatly states that the new students coming to CUNY as a result of open admissions, "were in college now for one reason: that their lives might be better than their parents" (1977, 3), she confronts head-on the powerful social forces that impact quests to redefine higher education. She even openly acknowledges that her exploration of error in student writing aims to "mov[e] [higher education] deeper into the realizations of a democracy" (1977, 294). For Horner, though, her characterization of the frontier nature of the emerging work pulled the focus off the entrenched race and class divisions, off issues of social responsibility and the struggles against resistance to change, to make it more about "teachers ventur[ing] into uninhabited territory as so many pedagogical Adams and Eves" (1996, 210). As the territory was uninhabited and new, they could appear to be "poach[ing] on no one's turf" (1996, 210), deemphasizing the political ramifications of the work that needed to be done.

Of course, frontier explorers always poach on *somebody's* turf, which is largely Horner's point in examining what the early imagery of basic writing as an unmapped West elided in order to make something else come across more strongly—in this case, the quest for the legitimacy of the new field. Horner argues that we need to think seriously about the "blindspots consequent on conceptualizing basic writing, or indeed any work on the teaching of writing, as new, 'frontier' territory" (1996, 211). I would like to interrogate our emerging view of SoTL along similar lines, looking for our blindspots in our figurations of SoTL as a new frontier.

Our view of the disciplines as isolated from skills acquisition, and of teaching as generic, are two of our big blindspots. They make a lot invisible to us: all the elements of learning that we may not want to acknowledge as being part of the intellectual development of our students, like remediation, and all the ways that faculty endeavors intersect. These kinds of blindness must be cured to effect the collaborative attitudes I am advocating. Current research into SoTL stresses how the work of teaching in every field is, in fact, profoundly disciplinary. We have to continually examine how we define our disciplines and open them up to redefinition and expansion in order to evolve new visions for our work and see how our agendas coincide.

Teaching, like writing, happens within a context. There are common features of good teaching, just as there are of good writing, that apply across the board. Still, how differently trained faculty define excellence in teaching, and what makes it work in various contexts, can (and should) vary. To define teaching as a generalizable activity is to minimize its intellectual and institutional value. As Shulman asserts: "Like it or not, the forms of scholarship that are seen as intellectual work in the disciplines are going to be valued more than forms of scholarship that are seen as non-disciplinary" (2004, 141). To illustrate how teaching is regarded largely as non-disciplinary, he points out how the advancement of teaching occurs in most schools:

> Institutional support for teaching and its improvement tends to reside in a university-wide center for teaching and learning where many of the TAs are trained, and where faculty—regardless of department—can go for assistance in improving their practice. That's a perfectly reasonable idea. But notice the message it conveys—that teaching is generic, technical, and a matter of performance; that it's not part of the community that means so much to most faculty, the disciplinary, inter-disciplinary, or professional community. It's something general you lay on top of what you really do as a scholar. (Shulman 2004, 141)

To the university-wide center for teaching and learning, Shulman adds the example of student evaluation forms that are identical across disciplines, suggesting that "teaching civil engineering and teaching Chaucer [are] the same" (2004, 141). All of these "norms," so established in our colleges that we do not even give them a second thought, silently forward the notion that teaching is secondary to the real work of the academy. In a way, our ingrained attitudes toward teaching as generic have constructed another invisible gateway—closing off strategies for improvements in undergraduate education—that we should endeavor to open in the twenty-first century. Shulman puts it plainly: We need to "recognize that the communities that matter most are strongly identified with the disciplines of our scholarship" (2004, 141). In treating any aspect of our academic work as non-disciplinary, we cordon it off; we refuse it admission. Therefore, just as we need to align student writing within the singular contexts of disciplinary processes and standards in order to elevate it into a meaningful process of literacy education, we need to think about teaching within our discrete disciplines. This may mean changing our departmental priorities to include more discussion of what happens in the classroom, what works and why. It may mean more inter-departmental collaborations, more coherent and integrated offerings of faculty development, and more co-teaching. It may mean accepting teaching into the research club. However, it has the potential to enliven our work in so many ways, helping us turn divided notions of common things into a teaching commons. By thinking about all the forms of professional life that make useful work possible and reframing faculty research agendas to include teaching as something worthy of vigorous investigation, we can begin to close the gaps that reduce the impact of our endeavors, within departments and across the curriculum, and for faculty and students alike.

NOTES

1. See, for instance, Karen W. Arenson's (2006) article, "Federal Panel Explores Standard Tests for Colleges."
2. In *What Is English?* Peter Elbow articulates the slightly different notion that all of English studies, not just literature, enjoys an elevated status: "As grammar and literature are taught in schools and colleges, they are characteristically experienced as agents of gentility and good taste or as mechanisms for discriminating—discriminating among linguistic forms, among texts and elements in a text, and also among people: who has taste and sound judgment and who is crude" (1990, 111). By the time students reach college, however, they are assumed to have learned the grammar necessary to speak and write well and are themselves judged as "crude," or not ready for the challenges of post-secondary English, if they have not yet absorbed the "basics."
3. A book like Gary A. Olsen's *Rhetoric and Composition as Intellectual Work* (2002), bringing together many voices in defense of the ongoing scholarly research within the field, proposes that comprhet is already an intellectually rigorous discipline and argues for institutional recognition of its status. To a degree, the very need to advance such an argument stands as a testament to the tensions I explore here.
4. I read his reference to his personal history to be a nod to his scholarly background in literature and his professional pursuits in composition, a variance in training and vocation that many share and, as a result, has impacted the shape and direction of English studies in recent decades.
5. This is not to say that Bartholomae, Elbow, Crowley, and others do not promote ways to heal the rifts; they do. Still, terms like "vexed" and "uneasy" have embedded themselves in our parlance. In fact, they have such resonance that more and more compositionists and writing program directors promote the separation of writing and literature programs when the ill will just seems to run too deep. For instance, in a recent *CCC* "Re-Visions" forum revisiting Maxine Hairston's 1985 Chair's address to CCCC and examining the current state of the field of composition and rhetoric, Susan H. McLeod maintains, "We are now a mature discipline, or at least one old enough to strike out on our own if home [the English department] is not a happy place" (2006, 529). Similarly, Joseph Harris argues that "the teaching of writing does not depend on the lukewarm support of English . . . we have other and more influential allies across the university" (2006, 539). Even so, Harris also insists that the more essential question "is not where we belong but what we can do now—in English, or in writing, or outside of both—to offer more students the sort of writing courses they deserve" (2006, 536). He maintains that the trouble with undergraduate writing programs is not a problem of disciplinarity but one of programming and practice, an argument that I find both compelling and important as we look to the future of composition programs and requirements. Considering the tenor of our discourse and these kinds of debates, what can we do

to create a more vigorous and inspiring atmosphere for students and faculty alike, whether our writing programs exist inside or outside English departments?

6. While McLeod argues (see note 5) that "we are now . . . old enough to strike out on our own" (2006, 529), she also maintains that we must not burn bridges, that we must not succumb to continued "bickering," and that "we must not only respect but can learn from the research traditions and resulting discourses of other disciplines. The scorn for other research traditions is in fact a form of prejudice and we need to get over it" (2006, 531).

7. Students' options are also determined by their status with math. For instance, they generally are designated "ESL" only if they have passed the quantitative skills test but not the language tests, and if their errors on the writing test are read, by a certified CUNY ACT reader, as indicative of writing by a second language learner. In addition, the situation and options can be even murkier for students with compromised reading and writing skills who are not ESL. They might, for example, be advised to enroll in a community college and later transfer into a baccalaureate program.

8. In the spring semester of 2006, Judith Summerfield, University Dean of Undergraduate Education, officially ended the old model of immersion and invited all CUNY schools to design new summer and winter intersession programs suited to their students, programs that would provide a meaningful gateway to their particular colleges.

9. Shari Stenberg and Amy Lee argue for this kind of scholarship, promoting a "process of pedagogical inquiry" (2002, 327) and urging us to open up "ways of studying our teaching, of reading our pedagogical interactions and our pedagogical development (exploration, critique, revision) as texts" (2002, 328).

WORKS CITED

Arenson, Karen W. "Federal Panel Explores Standard Tests for Colleges." *New York Times*. 9 February 2006, A1+.

Baron, Dennis. "The College Board's New Essay Reverses Decades of Progress Toward Literacy." *Chronicle of Higher Education*, 6 May 2005, B14–15.

Bartholomae, David. "Freshman English, Composition, and CCCC." *CCC*, 40.1 (February 1989): 38–50.

Bartholomae, David. "Postscript: The Profession." *Writing on the Margins: Essays on Composition and Teaching*. Boston: Bedford Press, 2005.

Bartholomae, David. "What Is Composition and (If You Know What That Is) Why Do We Teach It?" *Composition in the 21st Century*. Eds. Lynn Bloom, Donald Daiker, and Edward White. Carbondale: Southern Illinois University Press, 1996.

Crowley, Sharon. *Composition in the University: Historical and Polemical Essays*. Pittsburgh: University of Pittsburgh Press, 1998.

Elbow, Peter. "Opinion: The Cultures of Literature and Composition: What Could Each Learn from the Other?" *College English*, 64.5 (May 2002): 533–546.

Elbow, Peter. *What Is English?* New York: MLA, 1990.

Fetterley, Judith. "Symposium: English 1999: Dreaming the Future of English." *College English*, 61.6 (July 1999): 702–711.

Gorzelsky, Gwen. "Ghosts: Liberal Education and Negotiated Authority." *College English*, 64.3 (Jan. 2002): 302–325.

Graff, Gerald. *Clueless in Academe: How Schooling Obscures the Life of the Mind*. New Haven: Yale University Press, 2003.

Harris, Jospeph. "Déjà Vu All Over Again." *CCC*, 57.3 (February 2006): 535–542.

Horner, Bruce. "Discoursing Basic Writing." *CCC*, 47.2 (May 1996): 199–222.

Huber, Mary Taylor, and Pat Hutchings. *The Advancement of Learning: Building the Teaching Commons*. San Francisco: Jossey-Bass, 2005.

McLeod, Susan H. "'Breaking our Bonds and Reaffirming Our Connections,' Twenty Years Later." *CCC*, 57.3 (February 2006): 525–534.

Olsen, Gary A, ed. *Rhetoric and Composition as Intellectual Work*. Carbondale: Southern Illinois University Press, 2002.

Shaugnessy, Mina P. *Errors and Expectations*. New York: Oxford University Press, 1977.

Shaugnessy, Mina P. "The English Professor's Malady." *Journal of Basic Writing*, 3.1 (Fall 1980): 109–114.

Shulman, Lee S. *Teaching as Community Property: Essays on Higher Education*. San Francisco: Jossey-Bass, 2004.

Stenberg, Shari, and Amy Lee. "Developing Pedagogies: Learning the Teaching of English." *College English*, 64.3 (January 2002): 326–347.

Thaiss, Christoper J., and Terry Meyers Zawacki. *Engaged Writers and Dynamic Disciplines: Research on the Academic Writing Life*. Portsmouth, NH: Boynton/Cook, 2006.

Yancey, Kathleen Blake. "Made Not Only in Words: Composition in a New Key." *CCC*, 56.2 (December 2004): 297–328.

Zamel, Vivian. "Strangers in Academia: The Experiences of Faculty and ESL Students Across the Curriculum." *CCC*, 46.4 (December 1995): 506–521.

Part VI.   Afterword

Afterword

On Metaphors and Genres

CRYSTAL BENEDICKS

Queensborough Community College

When we put out our call for papers, we asked contributors to this book to "tell the story of the General Education Project at CUNY from their varied institutional and scholarly perspectives." The goal was to "get to the assumptions, beliefs, discourses, practices and structures" that shape the ways we think about general education at the nation's largest urban public university.

The call for papers read:

> The rhetorical form of the book is the essay, in the classical sense: the first-person singular commenting upon, questioning, debating, arguing about—a subject. The essays should center on those rhetorical explorations that engage readers in the debate, and leave them with that to mull over. Positionality—where the essayist stands—is fundamental, so that we can hear from those in the distinctive contexts of the community college, the four-year college, and the comprehensive college, as well as from different disciplinary perspectives, from the lived and multiple relationships to the academy, and to CUNY's students.

In calling for essays—rather than reports or narratives or position pieces—we were doing two things: harkening back to a privileged and deeply humanistic genre within the liberal education tradition this book seeks to interrogate, and also implying that the enterprise of rethinking liberal education for the urban university is one that finds more use in posing and exploring questions than in asserting answers: "rhetorical exploration" over argument or conclusion. We were looking for writing that imagines the writer as one who is also seeking and questioning, one who lives and works in the blurred space between teacher, student, writer, and reader.

Essays, by their very nature, entail a blending of genres: non-fiction and fiction, journalism and history, case study, ethnography, argument, literary analysis, scientific report, legal brief. We expected a mingling of genres, but, even so, we were surprised by the ways we all found ourselves struggling with our writing in the spaces opened up to us. Writing from the intersections between the personal and the public, the individual and the institutional, all of the essayists in this volume grappled with ways of representing the liminal spaces we had entered. We struggled with finding ways to describe the complexity of our inquiry without foreclosing its possibilities. Most especially, we struggled to break the back of the "what-I-did-in-class-that-worked" classroom narratives or the conclusion-driven administrative reports that often characterize publications in higher education. One essayist, reflecting on her writing process, wrote that her essay was "both more difficult and more exciting" than she expected. She floundered until she stopped and examined her rhetoric: "The shift happened when I began to write reflectively about my writing of the essay, when I noticed my tendency to slide into prescriptive declarations about what should be and how it should be done. I began to pose questions, which helped me to adopt an imaginative stance to the problem, rather than trying to be a problem solver or expert." At their best, the essays collected here are experiments in rhetoric, self-conscious attempts to write the history of a large-scale general education initiative in a form that respects the inquiry-driven spirit of the project.

There is not an essay in this book (including the present one) that did not go through several drafts, several experiments with how to represent students, institutional and curricular structures, our work as teachers and scholars within a discipline. Some essayists dropped out of the volume in frustration, and others, at the time of press, are still trying to work out the complicated implications of their writing choices. One pair of essayists, for example, used the figure of *Alice in Wonderland* in their first draft to describe the experience of students arriving at their college. While the comparison admirably captured the disorientation and confusion of immigrant and working-class students transitioning into a foreign space where new cultural assumptions are made and new expectations are set, it also unfortunately characterizes the college as a mad, violent dream world. After grappling with the idea through a few more drafts, the essayists dropped the Alice image to seek out other modes of representing the disorientation that necessarily comes with entering a new learning terrain. Their experience speaks to the paucity of positive images and tropes available for describing generative and enabling confusion. Meanwhile, another set of essayists was working with a jazz metaphor to describe general education reform, and ended up doing a significant amount of research into jazz in order to see the unusual comparison through. In the end, they learned about their own process as a committee by exploring the metaphor. When a new member of the college community was appointed recently, the committee, with whom she was expected to work, gave her a copy of the essay to help her understand both the goals of general education reform at that college, and also the nature of the collaborative work prized in that college's culture.

The crucial question I take up in this concluding essay is: What kinds of assumptions are embedded in the linguistic choices we make in these struggles to represent our work? What follows is a metadiscursive reading of the language of this volume, of CUNY's project on liberal education.

WRITING STUDENTS

In publications about higher education, from mission statements to course catalogues to teaching reports, students are commonly represented as learners to whom we have a responsibility to impart knowledge and a passion for learning. Students become the "them" to a professorial "us," the deficient ones in the face of a curriculum that categorizes according to embedded assumptions about which forms of knowledge "count." Other times, students are simply absent from writing about higher education. There is a good reason for that: A lot of the work of higher education reform happens at the administrative or institutional level, and significant change takes a while to get to the students at all.

Before accepting my current position as assistant professor of English at Queensborough Community College, I served for two years as Judith Summerfield's deputy director for undergraduate education at the CUNY Central Office. One of my first tasks was to contribute to an internal study on the admissions process by critically reading the letters each college sends to newly admitted students. As the first communication to students, the letters contain critical information about the ways the colleges imagine students. Some letters were exemplary—they welcomed students into the college as scholars, congratulating them, and describing the quality of the faculty and peers the student would encounter. Others were more problematic. They perfunctorily informed students that they had been admitted and then listed the placement exams, paperwork, and possible remediation work the student faced. Reading these letters, I understood that the assumptions the university makes about the abilities and motivations of its students are apparent in its official language, and that efforts at reimagining educational structures must start with close attention to language.

A sustained analysis of assumptions made about students in these pages reveals just that: the effort to reform curriculum must start with an effort to reform the ways we think about students. In the following paragraphs, I will turn my attention to four essays that construct students in very different ways. Each of these essays sets out to examine what happens when we attempt to practice liberal education—in this case, at four very different colleges (two senior colleges and two outer-borough community colleges) and a host of perspectives (one dean, one associate provost, four full-time faculty, and one adjunct instructor). Because these four essays are intended to take us into the classroom, they engage most thoroughly with students and ways of representing student voices.

Paul Arcario and James Wilson use the metaphor of pointillism in "Putting It Together: General Education at LaGuardia Community College" to describe their efforts to create a coherent general education experience at the community college level, where most students are enrolled in basic skills courses. For these essayists, the important thing is to connect the dots, to see the complete painting, without losing pointillism's innovative recognition that the mind derives pleasure from fitting pieces together, the act of envisioning a whole from disparate but related parts. This central metaphor informs the way they write about students as those who exist in an uneasy relationship to the college experience.

> "As a way of *connecting students to the larger college community and their own academic pursuits,* I . . ."

> "It is no wonder that retention is at its most precarious [during the basic skills segment of a student's education]—*at the moment they should be most strongly connecting to their college life,* they are made to feel not quite a part of it."

> "First-year basic skills students often complain . . . *they do not feel connected.*"

> "General or liberal education . . . may be defined not only by the mastery of a set of discrete skills or knowledge sets, but by *the student's ability to make connections* between courses, disciplines, and college experiences."

In these excerpts, integration of college and student is the goal; and the implication is that colleges fail to welcome students, especially at the crucial remedial level. A failed education is a fragmented one, and the responsibility of both the individual professor and the college curriculum is to make the connections visible and accessible. Students are not imagined as essentially deficient; instead of essentializing them at all, Arcario and Wilson understand student experience in terms of students' relationships to the curricular structures that either succeed or fail at welcoming them. Thus, "being a student" means "being a citizen of the college."

For Robert F. Cohen and Kim Sanabria, on the other hand, students are yearners. In "Our Mission at Hostos: Charting a Course to Self-Empowerment," they write about the challenges of reconfiguring basic skills education at a bilingual community college in the South Bronx, a college that teaches some of CUNY's least advantaged students. Students in this essay are described as those who long for a better future once they graduate college, yet they often find themselves lost in "remedial" education:

> ". . . Hostos Community College embodies the vision of success that all *students carry in their hearts*"

> "The *special desires of each individual,* multiplied by a population of over four thousand students, *create a pulsating current,* wherein each traveler sees the college as a kind of buoy guiding them towards the *realization of their hopes.*"

Students "*urgently seek* . . . the rewards of economic security and a higher degree of comfort in life."

"*Laden with hope*, many of them are entering an unfamiliar educational terrain . . ."

While both this essay and the one discussed above similarly critique inhospitable college structures at the basic skills level and call for a more inclusive curriculum, student identity is construed very differently. Here, students are physically realized: They have hearts pulsing with "desire," they are almost painfully "laden" with hope. Cohen and Sanabria's definition of students as "urgent seekers" of "comfort in life" points to the high stakes involved in educating the urban working class while refusing to blame students (as is so often done) for seeing the economic and social (rather than moral or humanistic) benefits of a college education. "Few among us," they write, "can compete with our students in naming a novel written in Chad, . . . in listing government leaders in Ecuador, Columbia, or Puerto Rico, in speaking four African dialects. . . ." By understanding basic skills students as possessors of undervalued knowledge (African literature, South American government) rather than as essentially "underprepared," Cohen and Sanabria are able to launch an alternate curriculum that envisions all students as scholars. Further, in respecting students' economic and social motivations for success, Cohen and Sanabria bypass the common assumption that the professional and the liberal arts tradition are inherently oppositional. As a result, they are able to envision innovations such as a Saturday Academy, an enormously popular optional weekend program, not for credit, that explores interdisciplinary topics while improving writing skills. Embedded in this approach is the assumption that students are willing to commit to "extra" work if it is the kind of work that allows them to participate as scholars and the explicit result is an increased chance at graduation. In describing students as impassioned yearners, Cohen and Sanabria respect both the amount of work that these students, most of whom face several semesters of "basic skills" courses, will have to do, while also recognizing their ability and desire to do it, especially when the curriculum is conceived in such a way that "basic skills" work is not seen as remedial or prior to the real work of the academy.

Turning now to the senior colleges, David Potash, associate provost at Hunter College, titles his piece "A Shared Classroom" in reference to an upper level history course that he designed to involve students as participants in the generation of knowledge. Potash devotes the first half of his essay to an overview of efforts at Baruch College (where he also served as associate provost before his current post) to envision a general education experience that respects the liberal arts as well as the professional orientation inherent in a business college. The college decided to focus on oral communication "skills" as similarly central to the liberal arts ideal of the well-spoken individual and the business executive who must excel at sales pitches and boardroom presentations. In this section of his essay, Potash describes students consistently as learners: "I was deeply involved in issues of student learning" and "[we evaluated] what we really thought students should learn." In the second half of his essay, after deciding that "I wanted to share the responsibility of teaching and learning with the students," Potash uses verbs such as "engaged," "grappled," and "challenged" to describe student participation. Students found the course "surprisingly hard" and "were not sure how to deal" with some of the elements of the class. Here, students, like the administrators Potash describes at the beginning of the essay, are "grappling" with complicated sets of knowledge and pressing issues about how to set priorities. Students are taking on the work of the academy, rather than receiving knowledge as static. In enacting administrative innovations in the shared classroom, Potash's essay also switches from the passive voice to the active voice of verbs to describe student participation.

Finally, Ann Davison and Sue Lantz Goldhaber, writing out of Queens College, a four-year, liberal arts school, approach students novelistically, threading their essay with creative mini-scenes of their students immersed in "Reacting to the Past" games. The students are described at the moment of their performative engagement. For example, "In [the student's] hand, which trembles a bit, is a written copy of the memorial . . . she is anxious, but she is determined not to read her text verbatim." Later, another student "stands nervously at the podium, looking at her notes. Around the conference table, 18 of her classmates watch her intently, expectantly. . . . It is the summer of 1776, and . . . everyone knows that a victory for the loyalist or patriot factions hangs on [her] vote." In writing about these students, Lantz Goldhaber and Davison capture the anxiety students often face in the classroom, although the nervousness they describe is not the disabling kind experienced by a student who feels disconnected from the literacies and practices privileged in the classroom, but the generative kind that accompanies real, sustained participation in classroom activities. In casting students as initially nervous performers, Davison and Lantz Goldhaber hint at the theatricality of all classrooms, and the knowledge that "being a student" is one type of performance in the academy, alongside "being a teacher."

Taken together, these four essays attempt to represent students as fully realized participants in the academy, as people with discrete pasts and plans. In doing so, they expose some of the linguistic difficulty inherent in "writing students." It is easy to fall into deficiency models that focus on what students lack or need, or sentimental models that see all educational institutions as nurturers of infantilized students. However, experimenting with classroom practices in the ways these essayists have done also means envisioning students as those who arrive in the classroom with significant prior knowledge. For these essayists, students need to be "nurtured" less than they need to be invited—into the power structures that characterize higher education, into the process of creating meaning in the classroom, and into the ongoing challenge of connecting the dots of their own education. We need new metaphors for thinking about students and their relationship to college culture: This is the message we get from the essayists who claim that curricular structures do not reflect students' realities.

WRITING CHANGE

Another significant struggle essayists faced had to do with representing the process of institutional change. More than any others in the volume, the essays that take up this project are stories, in the grand tradition of conflict-driven narratives. They each chronologically narrate the various efforts of committees and task forces to bring about new policies for general education at their college. The impulse to general education reform serves as the protagonist, adrift in a sea of institutional obstacles. Nevertheless these essayists ultimately reject the comforts of linear narrative in favor of a more open-ended approach. Taken together, they represent an effort to carefully examine how entrenched institutional structures determine what we believe is possible. In the course of telling their stories, each essayist, coming from a different college and thus a different set of structures, employs a different metaphor to imagine what is at stake in institutional change.

Donald Scott, history professor and founder of Queens College's incipient Center for Teaching and Learning, for example, envisions general education reform as a journey over uneven ground: "the general education reform effort moved . . . onto new, tricky terrain," finding itself "in a tricky and somewhat unprecedented position." The "formidable obstacles" to a culture of interdisciplinary cooperation and shared responsibility for articulating a general education framework figure large on the landscape: "silo-like" departments and isolating disciplinary specialties. They are "not insurmountable," but they would require a "culture change." Scott is here imagining institutional change as an issue of landscape, orientation in space. This concept is reflected in Queens College's recent decision to construct a new feature: the inter-disciplinary Center for Teaching and Learning. The statement is striking: a new "center" from which to negotiate the rocky terrain. Colleges across the country are similarly reconfiguring the landscape.

For Robert Whittaker, a scholar of Russian literature and language, two metaphors for institutional change co-exist: evolution ("survival of the fittest discipline," he writes, "is the law of the curriculum"), and warfare ("battles" over "dividing the turf" lead departments to feel "under heavy attack"). These metaphors meet in the brute struggle for survival they articulate but also pull in different directions. Change comes about organically over time, but it is also a process composed of violent acts. Both are apt descriptions for what change means at Lehman, Whittaker's home college, where the curriculum has had to scramble to keep up with shifting student populations (in the 1970s, Whittaker was chair of the Russian division of the Germanic and Slavic Languages Department; he is now a member of the Spanish-dominated Language and Literatures Department that subsumed his original department as student populations and interests changed). The idea here that change is both gradual and violent, organic and war-like, suggests the charged relationships between the impulse to renewal and the appeal of stasis that any attempt to spark institutional change must bridge.

At Queensborough Community College, the metaphor is music. Linda Stanley, professor of English, has drawn together a group of faculty from across the curriculum: Anita Ferdenzi from the Education Department, Paul Marchese from the Physics Department, and Margaret Reilly from the Nursing Department. Together, they describe the process of general education reform as "A Jazz Performance." The metaphor of the musical performance allows them to investigate the ways members of an interdisciplinary committee can come together to create a new "sound." Their emphasis is on compromise and improvisation, the musician's readiness to "riff" with the instruments and sounds they have mastered. At a community college that has committed itself to exploring the relationship between the professions and the liberal arts (this was the theme of a general education conference held at Queensborough Community College in 2006), the collaboration between faculty from the humanities and the professions makes sense. This essay takes into account the need for faculty from various disciplines to play off one another, to "improvise" together toward a common sound.

Each of these essays plays with common genres: the quest narrative (Scott), the war story and the narrative of gradual evolution (Whittaker), the jazz set (Stanley et al.). Even so, they trouble these narratives by not bringing them to a conclusion: the Holy Grail is never found, the war is not over, evolution is still going about its business, no completely satisfying compromise has been reached, and the song is not over. All of these stories about institutional change are without conclusion. They challenge the narrative genre by refusing to end it because the end has yet to be written, because it won't ever be. These are epic and episodic, ongoing stories that encode shifts in governance, policy, and theoretical frames—shifts that these essays envision as happening again and again, for as long as the college stands.

WRITING INSTITUTIONAL STRUCTURES

For the essayists described in the last section, institutional structures are not inevitable or natural, as we also sometimes think narrative structures are; rather, they are created and embedded in cultural and historical and economic realities. The authors of these essays have made an effort to recognize the artificial and malleable nature of institutional structures and to make visible the assumptions embedded within them, to understand curricular practices as expressions of a particular historical rootedness. Thus, they speak to one of the key principles of the General Education Project at CUNY: that change is possible only if we understand the nature and history of the institution we want to change.

This metacritical stance has characterized the work of the General Education Project from the beginning, as we began to read course catalogues and admissions letters as scholars, trying to see what assumptions they make about students and about general education. Some of the essayists in this volume turn a metacritical gaze on their own disciplines, asking questions about how various disciplinary conventions shape general education. Cheryl Smith and Erin Martineau write from their very different perspectives as an English professor and a new Ph.D. in anthropology, respectively. Although they have different aims, they both write their disciplines in the fullest sense of the word: structures that shape one's thinking (that "discipline" thought) and frame one's experience. Both Martineau and Smith write about their disciplines as living fields of knowledge that do more than house the work of individual scholars. In their writing, these structures exist to be probed, questioned, unpacked, and bent. A similar conviction underwrites Philip Anderson's essay, which examines the history of curricular structures in American higher education, and Sean Egan, who turns to nineteenth-century culture wars over education and the working class to understand CUNY's institutional legacy. For these essayists, the bodies of knowledge, pools of funding, and historical power relationships that compose disciplinary ways of knowing are as available for scholarly inquiry as the cultures, genres, and conventions those disciplines take as their objects.

WRITING THIS BOOK

The questions raised by this book are as much about general education as they are about rhetoric. How do we talk about students? What words and tropes do we use to construe liberal education? How should language be used to imagine different structures? How can we escape the rhythm of standard academic writing: conclusion-driven, assertive, or seductive? We say in the title of this volume that we are "re-claiming" the public university. This is what we mean: re-claiming—and in the act, re-affirming—its complications and confusions in the name of our best efforts to bridge them without losing the richness of the productive tensions. This book is studded with moments of recognition and insight, as essayists record the realizations that come with sustained scholarly attention to the university and what it teaches. Robert Whittaker tells of spending hours and hours probing with his peers the question of how to shape the curriculum to allow for the fact that most CUNY students are transfer students, only to come to the sudden understanding that he in fact was a transfer student—dentistry to chemistry, two different majors at different institutions—and had never quite seen his experience in the context of his students'. Sean Egan reflects on studying recent thinking about general education as part of a CUNY fellowship, while also researching nineteenth-century debates over education for his dissertation. "It only took me half the year to connect the dots," he writes in his essay.

All of these moments are about coming together on what Judith Summerfield has described as the "common ground" of inquiry into higher education. Here, in the attempt to work out our mutual mission of educating nearly a quarter of a million students, we meet one another, and ourselves, in unpredictable ways. This volume is an effort for us to stake out common ground—common ways of understanding students, disciplines, institutions, and our work within them—made uncommon by our close critical examination of the things we do every day in the course of running the university.

In "Blurred Genres," social scientist Clifford Geertz writes that "something is happening to the way we think about the way we think" (1980, 166). He describes an epistemological shift in the ways social scientists explain social phenomena: Where scholars used to rely on analogies to the physical or mechanical to understand the ways institutions and societies behave, they now rely on cultural performance as the privileged interpretive lens. For Geertz, the resulting scholarship blurs the boundaries between the humanities, the sciences, and the social sciences, creating something "at once fluid, plural, uncentered, and ineradicably untidy." This book exemplifies such hermeneutic untidiness, the fecundity that results when twenty different scholars, administrators, and doctoral candidates from ten different fields struggle to represent their most pressing thoughts about general education. If performance is the metaphor social scientists now use to describe the world, this book is about CUNY as cultural performance, as a loose federation of scholars performing what it means to be a liberally educated liberal educator every day, in offices, classrooms, and libraries. To that end, these essays are the attempt—sometimes labored, always blurred—to experiment with the representation of our project in all the genres and languages available to us.

WORK CITED

Geertz, Clifford. "Blurred Genres: The Refiguration of Social Thought." *American Scholar*, 49 (1980): 165–179.

Contributors

Philip M. Anderson is Professor of Secondary Education at Queens College, CUNY, and Professor of Urban Education at the CUNY Graduate Center, where he currently serves as the Executive Officer of the Ph.D. Program in Urban Education. He received his Ph.D. in curriculum and instruction from the University of Wisconsin-Madison. He has written extensively on curriculum theory and development, aesthetic education, and pedagogy in the humanities. His most recent publications include the joint editorship of the *The Praeger Handbook of Urban Education* (2 vols.) and various essays on curriculum, pedagogy, and assessment.

Paul Arcario is Dean for Academic Affairs at LaGuardia Community College, CUNY. He holds an Ed.D. in TESOL from Teachers College, Columbia University. In addition to authoring language textbooks and articles on LaGuardia's ePortfolio, First Year Experience, and online advising programs, he is the co-producer of the first American-language ESL videotape series broadcast in The People's Republic of China.

Robert F. Cohen serves as Chair of the Department of Language and Cognition and Director of the Hostos Success Academy at Hostos Community College, CUNY. He holds a Ph.D. in French from Harvard University. He is co-author of *North Star: Focus on Reading and Writing, Advanced* (Pearson Education) and *Reason to Write: Strategies for Success in Academic Writing* (Oxford University Press), which is a multi-level series. In addition, he has co-edited two ESL series for universities in Turkey and the United Arab Emirates.

Ann Davison is visiting Assistant Professor of the Department of English at Queens College, CUNY, where she also serves as the Associate Director of the Freshman Year Initiative. She holds a Ph.D. in English literature from New York University. In 2003, she received the President's Award for Excellence in Teaching from Queens College.

Sean Egan is a Ph.D. Candidate in the English Program at the CUNY Graduate Center. He is currently writing his dissertation, which is titled *Gardens and Grasses: The Question of Literature and Democracy for New York City's Public Intellectuals in the Era of Greeley and Whitman*. He has taught literature and writing in the CUNY system at Queens College and Lehman College.

Anita Ferdenzi is Associate Professor for the dual/joint AA/BA liberal arts and sciences and education degree at Queensborough Community College in association with Queens College, CUNY. She holds an Ed.D. in curriculum as well as a professional diploma in instructional leadership from St. John's University. She has published as a learning styles specialist with research interest and experience in effective strategies in math and science instruction for community college education majors, authentic assessment using multiple intelligences framework, and student-conducted action research. She is now working with other faculty at Queensborough Community College to design an education academy at the college.

Sue Lantz Goldhaber is Lecturer in the Department of English at Queens College, CUNY, with a specialization in College English as a Second Language. She also serves as the College Now ESL Coordinator/Professional Development Facilitator at Queensborough Community College, CUNY. She holds an M.A. in TESOL from Teachers College, Columbia University. Sue is the co-author of *Discovering American English: Writing* and *Discovering American English: Reading* (Macmillan Publishing Company).

Paul Marchese is Associate Professor of Physics at Queensborough Community College, CUNY, where he is also working to develop the technology academy. He received his Ph.D. in physical oceanography from Columbia University Graduate School of Arts and Sciences. Paul is the recipient of a National Science Foundation grant to support his teaching of lasers and fiber optics technology to high school science teachers. His publications include "Hubble ultra deep field object surface brightness variation," published in *Nuclear Physics* and "The Laser Academy: An After-School Program to Promote Interest in Technology Careers," published in the *Journal of Science and Technology Education*.

Jane Marcus-Delgado is Associate Professor of Spanish and International Studies at The College of Staten Island, CUNY. She received a Ph.D. in international relations from the Nitze School of Advanced International Studies of Johns Hopkins University, with concentrations in Latin American studies and international economics. Her interdisciplinary research primarily focuses on political corruption, trust, and leadership. Additionally, in the area of pedagogy, Professor

Marcus-Delgado has written on innovative approaches to teaching international studies and foreign languages.

Erin Martineau is Associate for Teaching, Learning, and Research in the CUNY Office of Undergraduate Education. She received her Ph.D. in anthropology from the CUNY Graduate Center. She has taught anthropology at Queens College, Brooklyn College and Hunter College, and served as a Writing Fellow at New York City College of Technology, CUNY. Her research focuses on public engagement, tolerance, and individualization in the Netherlands, and has been supported by a Fulbright grant from the Institute for International Education and the CUNY David Spitz Dissertation Fellowship in the Social Sciences.

David Podell is Senior Vice President for Academic Affairs and Provost at The College of Staten Island, CUNY, where he also chairs the General Education Committee for the College. He received his Ph.D. in educational psychology from New York University. His research in special education focusing on mental retardation has been published widely in such journals as *The Journal of Special Education, Teacher Education and Special Education*, and others.

David Potash is Associate Provost and Vice President for Academic Affairs at Hunter College, CUNY. He also served as Associate Provost for the Teaching and Learning Environment at Baruch College, CUNY, where he oversaw a number of college-wide projects aimed at integrating liberal education and the business major, increasing student engagement and retention. He holds a Ph.D. in history from the University of Cambridge and is currently working on a book about early 20th century American conservatives.

Margaret J. Reilly is Associate Professor of Nursing at Queensborough Community College, CUNY. She earned an MSN in community health nursing and an ANP as a Nurse Practitioner in adult health & pediatrics at Hunter College, CUNY. She has published a chapter on management of respiratory problems in the *Core Curriculum for Home Health Nurses*. Margaret has also published articles, served as a consultant and presented at several national conferences on the topic of integrating community nursing into associate degree nursing programs. Currently, she is working in partnership with the Visiting Nurse Service of New York on a $300,000 grant from the Jonas Center for Excellence in Nursing to develop an internship program in home health care nursing for associate degree nurse graduates.

Kim Sanabria is Professor of Spanish at Hostos Community College, CUNY, where she serves as the Title V Activity Director. She holds a Ph.D. in Spanish from Columbia University. She is the author of *Academic Listening Encounters: Life in Society* (Cambridge University Press) and co-author of *North Star: Focus on Listening and Speaking, High Intermediate* (Pearson Education) and *The Compact Reader, Seventh Edition* (St. Martin's Press). In addition, she has co-edited two ESL series for universities in Turkey and the United Arab Emirates.

Jonathan D. Sassi is Associate Professor of History at The College of Staten Island, CUNY, and the CUNY Graduate Center. He holds a Ph.D. in history from the University of California, Los Angeles. He is the author of *A Republic of Righteousness: The Public Christianity of the Post-Revolutionary New England Clergy* (Oxford University Press) and his articles have appeared in *Journal of Early Modern History* and the *Journal of the Early Republic*.

Donald M. Scott is Professor of History at Queens College, CUNY, and the CUNY Graduate Center. He has been a contributing member of CUNY's General Education Project since its inception. His scholarship and research on American intellectual history has led to a number of publications, including the joint editorship of *The Myth-Making Frame of Mind: Essays in American Culture* (Wadsworth).

Cheryl C. Smith is Assistant Professor of English at Baruch College, CUNY, where she is also the WAC/WID Coordinator. She holds a Ph.D. in English from Tufts University. She has received teaching awards from Harvard, Tufts, and Baruch College. Her articles on teaching American environmental literature and Early American literature have been published in the *Journal of American Culture*, *Academic Exchange Quarterly*, and *Teaching North American Environmental Literature*.

Linda Stanley is Professor of English at Queensborough Community College, CUNY, where she serves as the co-coordinator of the Writing Across the Curriculum program and as the writing program director. She holds a Ph. D. in comparative literature from New York University. She has been cited in *Change Magazine* for her work in Writing Across the Curriculum at the college and in the high schools of Queens, New York, and has received several Outstanding Teacher Awards. Linda has also received several Outstanding Teacher Awards. Most recently, she received an Excellence in Faculty Scholarship Award from Queensborough Community College for her two volumes on F. Scott Fitzgerald's foreign critical reputation, and for articles and a collection of essays on Writing Across the Curriculum at the community college published by Jossey Bass.

Robert Whittaker is Professor of Russian at Lehman College, CUNY, where he also serves as the Coordinator of General Education. He received his Ph.D. in Slavic languages and literatures from Indiana University. He is the author of a biography of the Russian critic and poet Apollon Grigor'ev: *Russia's Last Romantic: Apollon Grigor'ev (1822–1864)*, and a compiler and editor of the collected letters of Grigor'ev and of the correspondence of Leo Tolstoy with Americans.

James Wilson is Associate Professor of English at LaGuardia Community College, CUNY, where he teaches basic writing, composition, drama, and African American literature. He received his Ph.D. in theatre history and criticism from the CUNY Graduate Center. His articles have appeared in *Urban Education*, *Teaching English in the Two-Year College*, and *Theatre History Studies*. He is currently working on a book about lesbian and gay theatre and performance in the Harlem Renaissance.

Index

Questions about the
Purpose(s) of Colleges
and Universities

Norm Denzin,
Joe L. Kincheloe,
Shirley R. Steinberg
General Editors

What are the purposes of higher education? When undergraduates "declare their majors," they agree to enter into a world defined by the parameters of a particular academic discourse—a discipline. But who decides those parameters? How do they come about? What are the discussions and proposed outcomes of disciplined inquiry? What should an undergraduate know to be considered educated in a discipline? How does the disciplinary knowledge base inform its pedagogy? Why are there different disciplines? When has a discipline "run its course"? Where do new disciplines come from? Where do old ones go? How does a discipline produce its knowledge? What are the meanings and purposes of disciplinary research and teaching? What are the key questions of disciplined inquiry? What questions are taboo within a discipline? What can the disciplines learn from one another? What might they not want to learn and why?

Once we begin asking these kinds of questions, positionality becomes a key issue. One reason why there aren't many books on the meaning and purpose of higher education is that once such questions are opened for discussion, one's subjectivity becomes an issue with respect to the presumed objective stances of Western higher education. Academics don't have positions because positions are "biased," "subjective," "slanted," and therefore somehow invalid. So the first thing to do is to provide a sense—however broad and general—of what kinds of positionalities will inform the books and chapters on the above questions. Certainly the questions themselves, and any others we might ask, are already suggesting a particular "bent," but as the series takes shape, the authors we engage will no doubt have positions on these questions.

From the stance of interdisciplinary, multidisciplinary, or transdisciplinary practitioners, will the chapters and books we solicit solidify disciplinary discourses, or liquefy them? Depending on who is asked, interdisciplinary inquiry is either a polite collaboration among scholars firmly situated in their own particular discourses, or it is a blurring of the restrictive parameters that define the very notion of disciplinary discourse. So will the series have a stance on the meaning and purpose of interdisciplinary inquiry and teaching? This can possibly be finessed by attracting thinkers from disciplines that are already multidisciplinary, for example, the various kinds of "studies" programs (women's, Islamic, American, cultural, etc.), or the hybrid disciplines like ethnomusicology (musicology, folklore, anthropology). But by including people from these fields (areas? disciplines?) in our series, we are already taking a stand on disciplined inquiry. A question on the comprehensive exam for the Columbia University Ethnomusicology Program was to defend ethnomusicology as a "field" or a "discipline." One's answer determined one's future, at least to the extent that the gatekeepers had a say in such matters. So, in the end, what we are proposing will no doubt involve political struggles.

For additional information about this series or for the submission of manuscripts, please contact Joe L. Kincheloe, joe.kincheloe@mcgill.ca. To order other books in this series, please contact our Customer Service Department at: (800) 770-LANG (within the U.S.), (212) 647-7706 (outside the U.S.), (212) 647-7707 FAX, or browse online by series at: www.peterlang.com.